HOW TO BUILD
PERIOD CORRECT
HOT RODS

Gerry Burger

CarTech®

CarTech®

CarTech®, Inc.
838 Lake Street South
Forest Lake MN 55025
Phone: 651-277-1200 or 800-551-4754
Fax: 651-277-1203
www.cartechbooks.com

© 2011 by Gerry Burger

All rights reserved. No part of this publication may be reproduced or utilized in any form or by any means, electronic or mechanical, including photocopying, recording, or by any information storage and retrieval system, without prior permission from the Author. All text, photographs, and artwork are the property of the Author unless otherwise noted or credited.

The information in this work is true and complete to the best of our knowledge. However, all information is presented without any guarantee on the part of the Author or Publisher, who also disclaim any liability incurred in connection with the use of the information.

All trademarks, trade names, model names and numbers, and other product designations referred to herein are the property of their respective owners and are used solely for identification purposes. This work is a publication of CarTech, Inc., and has not been licensed, approved, sponsored, or endorsed by any other person or entity.

Edit by Paul Johnson
Layout by Monica Seiberlich

ISBN 978-1-934709-32-0
Item No. SA192

Library of Congress Cataloging-in-Publication Data

Burger, Gerry
  How to build period correct hot rods / Gerry Burger.
    p. cm.
  ISBN 978-1-934709-32-0
  1. Hot rods–Design and construction. I. Title.
  TL236.3.B877 2011
  629.28'786–dc22

2010050673

Printed in U.S.A.
10 9 8 7 6 5 4 3 2 1

Front Cover:
Ronnie Staples has been at this hot rod game for a long time, and there seems to be an endless stream of great cars that come out of his Colonial Heights, Virginia, garage. His tastes range from contemporary to nostalgic, but he always seems to "get it right." When Ronnie decided to build a traditional hot rod he once again "got it right," using the perfect blend of vintage pieces and new parts to come up with a vintage-flavored hot rod that looks like it was driven in 1962.

Title Page:
Lewis McMillan originally purchased this 1932 Ford as a body only at the L.A. Roadster show. Thirty years later, he mated the body to an original frame and in the process discovered the car has a real hot rod heritage. The car was originally hot rodded in the 1940s by Arvel Youngblood.

Back Cover Photos

Top Left:
The small-block Chevrolet is the quintessential hot rod motor, and you can dress one up in any vintage you like. This vintage-flavor motor is stunning in gold and chrome. Six deuces top the small-block while very short zoomie-style headers must make quite a racket. The ground-smooth block, billet clamps on the fuel line, and modern-style coolant recovery are all permissible liberties taken on a vintage-flavor hot rod.

Top Right:
The great looks of 1935 Ford wire wheels come from the fact that they are 16-inch wheels. However, all Ford wire wheels were designed for cars with mechanical brakes. When using 1928–1935 Ford wire wheels on a car with hydraulic drum brakes, a support plate must be run inside the wheel.

Middle Left:
The ultimate rear gear for any period correct hot rod is the quick-change rear. While quick-change rears are available new today, there are still many vintage units to be found at swap meets or online.

Middle Right:
Ford produced banjo wheels in the mid 1930s, as did other automakers. Their intrinsic good looks are as elegant today as they were 80 years ago. An aftermarket horn button carries the famous V-8 logo to complete the picture.

Bottom Left:
These NOS tie rod ends are for early Fords. Why is that important? Simple: They have a Ford script stamped in the face, which immediately dates the car.

Bottom Right:
Lewis McMillan's Deuce roadster is a study in period perfect engine building. All finishes are period correct, and those speed parts are all vintage pieces, no reproduction parts.

CONTENTS

Acknowledgments 4
Introduction 4

Chapter 1: The Perfect Plan: The Recipe for Building a Period Correct Hot Rod 7
- Finding the Right Rod 9
- Tracing the History 12
- Barn Find 1937 Ford 12
- Old Car Hunter Gary Moore 15

Chapter 2: Period Power 19
- Ford Flathead V-8 23
- Cadillac Motors 26
- 1949–1964 Oldsmobile V-8 27
- Ford Y-Block 29
- 1957–1966 Buick Nailhead 29
- Chrysler Hemi 31
- Pontiac Motors 32
- Small-Block Chevrolet 34
- W-Head Chevrolet 35
- Oddball Stuff 36
- In Summary 36

Chapter 3: Rolling Stock: Choosing Wheels, Tires and Accessories 37
- Wire Wheels 38
- Steel Wheels 39
- Birth of the Mag Wheel 40
- Mag Wheel Manufacturers 43
- Hubcaps 48
- Evolution of the Whitewall 50
- Selecting The Right Vintage Tires 53
- Other Visual Options 54
- In Summary 56

Chapter 4: Building a Vintage Chassis 57
- Boxing Plates 58
- Motor Mounts and Brackets 58
- Suspension Choices 60
- Rear End Choices 62
- Brake Choices 64
- Steering Choices 67
- A 1933 Plymouth Reconstruction Project 69
- In Summary 70

Chapter 5: Interior: Real Hot Rods Have Upholstery .. 72
- It's the Last Step 72
- Fitting the Driver to the Car 74
- Mounting Gauges and Switches 77
- Carpeting 78
- Seats 79
- Upholstery 80
- Dashboard 82
- In Summary 83

Chapter 6: Body and Mods: Selecting the Right Sheet Metal for an Era 84
- Body-Style Choices 84
- Body Modifications 88
- Fender Choices 91
- Reproduction Bodies 93

Chapter 7: Choosing the Right Paint, Pattern, Texture and Finish 94
- Choosing the Proper Finish 96
- Lacquer Paints 97
- Enamel Paints 100
- Urethane Paints 102
- Special Effects 104
- Picking the Final Finish 107

Chapter 8: The Vintage Car Gallery 109
- Reviving the Youngblood Roadster 110
- The Class of '59 113
- A+ for Flavor 117
- Dream 1940 119
- T-Time 121
- The Shoaf Roadster 124
- '40 Found 126

Chapter 9: Cool Old Parts 129

Source Guide 142

ACKNOWLEDGMENTS

A project, such as this book, cannot be done without help, and so thanks go out to all who contributed to the project. I'll list them in no particular order as each contribution was as important as any other. Thanks go to companies, such as Honest Charley's Speed Shop, Speedway Motors, Pete & Jake's, Coker Tire, Rodcrafters, Stainless Specialties, Bob Drake Reproduction Parts, and the Early Ford V8 Club for their excellent reference manuals. Without hot rod builders and owners, this book could not exist, so thanks go out to every owner and builder whose car appears in this book. I tried to include names whenever possible, but many of the photographs come from my archives with no owner names attached. Builders and owners include Mike Goodman, Larry Shoaf, Lewis McMillan, Gary Moore, Wayne Pugh, Derrell Dudley, Paul Duval, Frank Brown, and Bob Van Horn, who all made their great hot rods available for photo shoots. Mike Goodman and Lewis McMillan were especially helpful. Mike gave me full access to the parts at Honest Charley's, and Lewis helped with his vast knowledge of vintage hot rodding. And finally, thanks to my wife, Jill.

INTRODUCTION

Few things stir the soul of a car enthusiast like a traditional hot rod. It seems every hot rodder has a clear vision of his perfect hot rod. Is it a Deuce roadster streaming across the dry lake just ahead of a huge plume of dust, or is it the memory of a covey of carbs topping off a 409 neatly nestled in front of a white 1940 Ford firewall? Maybe your tastes run a bit later and the thought of a big-block motor in a chopped-and-dropped 1939 Chevrolet quickens your pulse. If you're conservative by nature and love the lines of vintage automobiles, you may be dreaming of wire wheels, black fenders, and woodgrain dashboards. The beauty of hot rodding lies in its diversity.

Hot rodding has a rich history dating back to before World War II, some might say dating back to the very invention of the automobile. Hot rods are amazing in many ways, and the fact they still exist and are still being built today is amazing in itself. Looking back at all the changes of the past 75 years, it is a tribute to breed and the American spirit that good hot rods continue to draw crowds of all ages today. Hot rods and rock 'n roll are both defined by multiple time periods, and both continue their evolutionary journey today.

In the beginning, hot rods were built by young men on a quest for

INTRODUCTION

speed. The goal was to build a car that was faster than factory offerings, and most hot rods entered speed contests at dry lakes, salt flats, and drag strips to get official timed results. This was long before the luxury of owning two cars, so most early hot rodders drove their cars during the week and raced and showed them on weekends.

Some hot rodders were more serious than others, some being focused on record-breaking speed, while others drove hot rods out and ran them "to see what she'll do." It's interesting to note that hot rodding seems to be an affliction of the young. I believe it is fair to say hot rodding is highly contagious in the formative years, as most people I know were smitten between the ages of ten and twenty. Of course not all of those who caught hot rod fever kept it for life; like so many adolescent afflictions many people had it, took the cure, and got over it—no different than chicken pox or acne. For others the fever would go dormant for years, only to resurface stronger than ever.

But for many, this early attraction to the hot rod created an incurable itch that continues non-stop for a lifetime. Happily and hopefully, there are still young people being stopped in their tracks by a good hot rod, we also now have the largest surviving population of elder hot rodders ever. Yes, the graybeard with his hot rod is a reality. But regardless of age, the hot rod is still based on the youthful exuberance, the freedom of spirit, and the flashback of days gone by. For all of us "experienced" hot rodders, building the latest hot rod is directly connected to building that first hot rod and the memories acquired in the process. Flashbacks are one of the symptoms of this life-

long affliction, and a certain exhaust note, a profile, a glimmer of chrome, or feel of a vintage steering wheel has the ability to transport me back in time. Possibly that is the attraction of both hot rods and rock 'n roll: the magic ability of time travel. Ask a hot rodder about something in the past and the thought process will go something like this, "Hmmm, let's see. When I bought that house I had just finished my 1939 pickup; that was 1975." Yes, hot rodders tell time with cars.

All this serves to illustrate the diversity of hot rodding and the inevitable attachment of the car to a certain time period, even if that time period is today, as you construct a contemporary interpretation of the American hot rod. For most of us, the definition of a real hot rod was indelibly etched in our mind by a certain car, at a certain time. For me that time was somewhere around 13 years of age, 1960 or so, when my only contact with hot rods was through the magazines I bought at the local candy store. I can remember it like it was yesterday, a moment frozen in time.

I was standing on the corner of Landing Avenue and Main Street in Lynn's Shell gas station when it appeared. Actually I heard it before I saw it roll up to the traffic light. There it was, a black Deuce coupe, chopped and channeled with full Moon discs and whitewall tires. The driver was barely visible through the small windshield. I was beyond smitten; I was possessed and remember one very clear thought at that moment. Someday I will have a hot rod coupe. Frozen in time, that encounter made my perfect hot rod an early 1960s-style car.

I went on to build a Model A coupe in 1969 and fulfilled that dream of rolling up to the very stoplight where I had seen my first real hot rod. A typical East Coast hot rod in an atypical time. The muscle car wars were raging and here I was building a channeled coupe; for traditional hot rodders there was no other cure. *Rod & Custom* had become the sole remaining connection to this part of the hobby, and thanks to the likes of Tom Medley, hot rodders could learn more about building a car, but more

INTRODUCTION

importantly, Medley and his great staff of folks like Bud Bryan, Tex Smith, Jake Jacobs, Tom Senter, and others managed to fan the flames of traditional hot rodding and keep the movement alive. They fostered the concept of a national rod run, and the National Street Rod Association. As they say, the rest is history.

And so for many hot rodders, building or finding the perfect hot rod is a matter of time. Finding or building a car can capture that moment when you realized you were hooked on hot rods. For others it is about building, finding, and restoring cars that came before them, cars that capture an era perfectly, either through actual documented history, or constructing a car that captures the feel of the time. And that's what this book is all about, time periods and how to capture them accurately—time in a bottle, if you will.

Of course there were no clear cut-off dates, no "the day the flathead died" or a particular day the small-block Chevy became King. Bits and pieces of different periods can often be found on vintage hot rods, and so they can be blended on vintage-looking rods too. There will be no hard, fast rules to live by from this book, rather things to look for that will make your car authentic enough to capture the mood. You might find yourself headed to the garage to take a piece off your car or add something that would authenticate the car.

Maybe you're reading this simply because you admire vintage American hot rods, or perhaps you're considering constructing just such a car. So why would you build a vintage-style hot rod over a more contemporary interpretation of a hot rod? Quite simply, it seems that hot rods hit their styling pinnacle early on, and evolved from there. Since hot rodding is closely identified with the 1940s, 1950s, and 1960s, these cars seem to be forever in vogue. It's been said that fashions change, but style endures, and nothing could be more accurate in the world of hot rods. You need only look at a tweed interior to understand the process.

Combined with the lasting style and timeless look of a vintage hot rod comes the utter simplicity of the car. Hot rods were originally designed to be a no-frills, go-fast car, and to that end they become elegant through their simplicity and pureness of purpose. A good rule to follow is this: If it doesn't make it go, stop, or turn you might not need it on a real hot rod. This simplicity also translates into a car that is basic to build, easy to repair, and provides a raw visceral drive like few cars can.

My focus in this book is on early body styles, but bear in mind that all through the 1950s and 1960s cars were purchased brand new and quickly hot rodded, so many of the pieces, tips, and styles presented here apply to your 1956 F-100, '55 Chevy, or shoebox Ford. It was part of the times, all sharing the same scene with speed equipment of the period finding its way onto a large variety of cars. The time period is 1940 through 1972, a period that clearly defines the traditional hot rod.

As I researched this book I took into consideration the geographical differences of early hot rodding. The lack of roadsters in the eastern and northern climes and some basic style differences ensure you recognize an East Coast rod from a West Coast rod. And I have long enjoyed showing some of the great non-California hot rods, because although the West Coast was the hot bed of early hot rodding, the fact is hot rods were found all across the country, but not in the concentrations found in California. This makes finding a New York, Minnesota, or Texas hot rod of the 1950s all the more fun; although few of them had the hot rod heritage of dry lakes and such, they are nonetheless bonafide period hot rods.

I also show hot rods that are good examples of the day, but maybe not the iconic examples of the time. Other books, such as *Hot Rod Milestones* by Ken Gross and Robert Genat, have done a great job of covering these cars, and much can be learned from such books. Regardless of the location, vintage hot rods are hotter than ever, and the timeless looks and spirit of the American hot rod endure.

I once said, "There are no rules in hot rodding until you break one," and I stand by that statement. Often great things are difficult to define, but you know it when you see it. Likewise, we've seen many very nice cars that are nearly period perfect only to be distracted by a few out-of-place items. It doesn't make the car wrong, but it is a distraction for the complete package, something most hot rodders strive to avoid. This book helps to illustrate correct-period style, but it's not intended to be an end-all for everything vintage. That would take volumes, so for those parts, pieces, and people left out, I apologize. The reality is that space is always at a premium in any book.

And finally, I hope this book will stir some memories, inspire more great hot rods to be built and provide a reasonable reference to different time periods in the colorful history of hot rodding. If it does that, it will have been a success.

CHAPTER 1

THE PERFECT PLAN: THE RECIPE FOR BUILDING A PERIOD CORRECT HOT ROD

Regardless of what you are building, success relies on a good plan. One of the very first decisions is to choose one of three approaches. The first is to build a car from scratch using only parts from a certain dateline. Here, you pick a date, say 1963, and then set about building a car using only parts produced prior to that date. It makes for a very authentic car and the search for parts, pieces, and information is another part of the fun. Date codes, casting numbers, and stampings are all part of the game. If you're lucky, unearthing these pieces bit by bit can actually provide some history to your final product if you learn of their prior use. Tales of prior use, such as: Gauges were purchased from a guy in California, his dad built a Deuce Tudor 1953, he sold

Hot rods with history are everywhere, and this one has a great story. Claude and Sara Kern have owned this car since 1960, but Claude grew up with a guy named Karl Kinsler; yes, that Karl Kinsler, the World of Outlaws king. In 1957 they found an old hot rod body in an Indiana barn and set about building a hot rod, complete with a nearly new 1956 265-ci Chevy motor. Kinsler sold the roadster to Claude in 1960, and he's had it ever since. The car was street driven and drag raced through the 1960s with a best time of 13.35 at 105 mph—one quick little roadster. Today, the car is on the street, and Claude and Sara share wonderful stories with fellow hot rodders.

HOW TO BUILD PERIOD CORRECT HOT RODS

the car but kept the gauge cluster, it's been in his garage since 1956. Suddenly your "new old car" has a bit of composite history.

The second approach is to build a car with period flavor. This approach tends to mix reproduction frames, suspension, and new pieces, such as gauges and suspension, but it visually gives you all the styling of a vintage hot rod. This is no doubt the most popular approach to building a period car, as you are now free to get new parts from your favorite businesses, rather than scouring flea markets and the Internet for years. It also provides a degree of reliability and improved performance over many of the true vintage cars and parts. If you'd prefer 12-volts to six, an alternator to a generator and happen to think that a new Vega-style steering box is superior to a 1940 Ford box, this is the way to go. The focus of these cars is flavor, and the trick is to get it right.

Adding every 1950s or 1960s iconic piece to one car can make it a bit overwhelming and not a realistic representation of the period. So restraint is a big part of building a flavor car (or a chosen date car). Possibly the best way to accomplish a good flavor car is to mentally transform yourself back into that young hot rodder in 1963 and chose items for your car in the same fashion, which means selected items suited for your car by personal tastes and budget. It's been said, "Happiness is liking everything you have, not having everything you like." A good hot rod can be summed up the same way, in the end you should like all the parts on the car, but not have every part you like on one car.

The over-the-top flavor problem is most common in 1950s-style cars, as a result they have about as much appeal as a theme restaurant filled with reproduction automobilia. Laden with vinyl decals, fuzzy dice, checkerboard firewall, a foxtail, ten skulls, a Coke cooler, dice valve stem caps, eight ball shifter, and a fuzzy mirror surround the car is easily overpowered by accent pieces. Remember, none of the over-the-counter accents available during that time period were ever designed to go on one car simultaneously. Think of accents as the spices of the particular flavor you are going for and use them accordingly.

The third approach—and I believe this is the one every hot rodder dreams of—is finding an old hot rod with history and bringing it back to life. This is generally the most difficult course to take but often the most rewarding. Every hot rodder's dream is to get a lead on an old car, track it down, locate the owner, and then finally see the car. Oh, to drive up to that old barn, warehouse, or garage and have the door swing open to expose the unmistakable silhouette of an old hot rod . . . As your eyes adjust to the dim light and the dank air spills out of the garage your mind races. Is it a three-window or a five-window? Is it a hot rod or original? And, of course, the biggest question of all: Is it for sale?

Yes, this is the stuff of dreams and while we all know lucky people, for the most part they make their own luck by tracking down leads and spending time looking at old cars of little interest before finally finding that one special car. As one old-car hunter told me, "You gotta kiss a lotta frogs." And that too is part of the game.

So, if you want to find that ghost from the past, my suggestion is to keep searching, look for that glimmer of chrome through the woods, and peer in any open garage possible. Talk to local hot rodders who have been around a while, talk about cars that roamed the streets of your home town years ago, and wonder aloud at where that car might be today. Talk to your UPS driver, meter reader or mail carrier, you might be surprised at what they know. Much like a detective, one tip could send you in the right direction.

Not all barn finds are still in the barn; many are hauled to swap meets looking for a new home. This great 1940 coupe was found in a swap meet. This standard coupe was tucked away in a garage for 49 years. It hasn't been driven since 1960, and with an asking price of $12,500, I'd be surprised if someone didn't take it home. Check out the cool front nerf bar. Once you buy a barn car like this the detective work begins to find out the rest of the story.

Finding the Right Rod

It also pays to know vintage car parts and common traits of cars. Many old hot rods have been updated over the years, and recognizing one vintage piece might tip you off to what lies beneath. It could be a trace of metal-flake paint on the bottom side of the car, an early fuel block, or a set of unique taillights that provide the clue that this car has been a hot rod for a long time. We've all heard the story of finding a vintage hot rod or race car, and the new owner will tell the story, "You know, I was looking at it and somehow I felt like I knew the car, then I saw that dashboard and realized this was Bill's old car." So looking at old photos, magazines, and Web sites can prove to be invaluable when looking at vintage hot rods.

Many hot rodders insist all the good stuff has been found, and to that I simply say bunk. Hot rodding has been around long enough that many treasures are out there to be found from various eras. You don't have to find a roadster that held the record at Bonneville in 1954–1957 to be lucky. How about finding a very nice 1940 Ford coupe that was built in the early 1970s and stored for 35 years? Yes, cars of the 1970s are now almost 40 years old, and that's plenty of history for most hot rodders. How about all those T-buckets of the 1970s? While they might not be everyone's idea of the perfect hot rod, there is no denying the impact these cars had street rodding, and there must be hundreds of them tucked away in garages. Then there is always the chance some unknowing owner will refer to that Model A Highboy roadster as a T-bucket—it always pays to look.

Of course, good hot rod material also comes in the form of original cars, and there seems to be a bumper crop of amateur restorations coming on the market today. Finding a restored Model A sedan for less than $10,000 is a pretty easy job, and even the more desirable coupes and Victorias can be found at reasonable prices. Often these cars have been inherited by a family member who knows little about cars and simply wants to sell it, or it sits in the garage for 20 years before you discover it. Either way, restored cars are fertile hunting grounds.

These cars, often referred to as barn finds, can be invaluable as a time capsule. Once you have established how long the car has been in hiding, you know exactly what the newest part on the car could be. If you're lucky enough to buy a barn car, try not to be so overcome with enthusiasm that you forget to talk to the seller. Take time after the sale to engage the previous owner with questions, lots of questions. Ask about anything that might provide a clue to the past before leaving with the car.

Not all history is good for the car. Although this 1934 Ford five-window coupe no doubt had a colorful past, and may have won some Saturday night heats, the racing past has taken its toll. Crude construction and welding were all part of the 1950s and 1960s stock car racing scene. This car could be saved, and it looks as if two good doors come with it, but do you restore it as an old race car or build a vintage hot rod? Either way it makes for an interesting story.

This Model A coupe obviously had an amateur restoration from the past, and a darn nice car for an asking price of $13,500. Any good horse trader should be able to get 10 percent off an asking price, so that would bring it in around $12,000. If you sold off the original pieces you won't be using, you would have one heck of a start for $11,000.

CHAPTER 1

For example:
- Do you have any old photos of the car? This may help to illustrate the changes this owner has made to the car.
- Do you know who the previous owners were?
- Are there any interesting stories about the car? If the previous owner says, "Oh, it was at the First Street Rod Nationals," that's interesting, and also adds pedigree to the car.
- Who built the engine?
- Is there is a photo of the car at the first Nats?
- How about the dash plaque?
- Do you have timing slips from even a local drag strip? Whether 1977 or 1957, these are all part of the car's past, and well worth gathering whenever possible.

And remember to keep the seller's phone number and email address so you can correspond with him while you rebuild the car. Leave your personal information along with a note, "I'd be interested in a buying that dual-quad intake if you find it."

Dubbed the Golden Rod, Frank Mundrick's Deuce coupe was found with shoe polish from its last race still in the windows. Sadly, the car had been left outside for many, many years, causing extensive damage and rust, but it was still salvageable. The Deuce ran B/coupe at the local drags and was a class winner many times with "kill stickers" to prove it. The Hemi-powered Deuce roams the streets of New Jersey today, resplendent in gold and red.

While the interior was pretty much destroyed by the elements, the basic theme was maintained in the rebuild. Today, red and white rolls-and-pleats again fill the cockpit, but the original wood dash was replaced by a steel '32 Ford dashboard filled with vintage Stewart Warner gauges.

This is what the car looked like when it was dragged out of the mud and brought home. Check out those massive push bars. In typical East Coast fashion, this hot rod was channeled but not chopped.

The same Hemi motor that brought this car class wins remains in the car today, but now street duty is all the coupe sees.

THE PERFECT PLAN: THE RECIPE FOR BUILDING A PERIOD CORRECT HOT ROD

Swap meets are a great place to find old treasures, but get there early and be prepared walk and walk some more, for that special car could be just around the corner. The Internet seems to be the new approach, and while this is a good method of locating vintage hot rods, the bad news is there are a couple million other eyeballs on the same car if it is for sale. Don't overlook unorthodox methods of finding a vintage hot rod or parts.

A story I enjoy telling happened to a fellow club member in the 1970s. He was driving down a street in his neighborhood and passed a typical garage sale. On the lawn was a pair of 1935 Ford wire wheels. Being a true hot rodder he stopped to look and casually asked the owner if he had any other old Ford parts for sale. As unbelievable as this may sound, that simple question lead to the purchase of a set of Ardun heads, *still in the crate!* Yes, a set of NOS Ardun heads pushed in the corner of a neighborhood garage, it was quite the find and quite the purchase. The moral of the story is simple, if you're going to find something you must first look for it, and then stop, look, listen, and ask questions. You'll be amazed at what you might find.

If you are fortunate enough to find a vintage hot rod, try to respect the history of the car. I realize these are old cars, but if your dream is to build a 1940 coupe with hidden hinges, Mercedes headlights, a digital dashboard and LED taillights, that's fine. But you should, if possible, start with a clean slate, a car that needs everything, and save that vintage hot rod with history for another enthusiast.

Of course, finding an old hot rod with history brings with it a whole new set of choices. Since most hot rods are a constant work in progress, after finding an old hot rod with history your work has just begun. Do you restore the old hot rod? And if

Things often are not as they appear. While this Deuce roadster has all the trappings of a vintage hot rod, the truth is this car was built by James Wolk within the past 10 years. The floors appear to be "patched" with old license plates and power comes from a vintage Caddy motor, but the body is actually fiberglass—proof positive that artificial flavor can taste good.

It took a few years, but finally the coupe was returned to full hot rod status. The coupe underwent extensive rust repair, including a new floor, and now rides atop a completely refurbished '32 chassis. The big Hemi valve covers are now plated.

Bob VanHorn owns this 1940 coupe with a colorful past. Gene Winfield did this bodywork in the 1960s. The coupe was yellow then, and was stolen in California but subsequently recovered and then stored for many years before Van Horn brought the coupe back to the street.

so, to what form? Do you go back to the first build when it was flathead powered? Do you use the existing equipment and keep the dual-quad, solid-lifter 283 under the hood? The choice is yours, and both are vintage hot rods, pure and simple, but which era is right for you and the car?

If the car in question has big history, speed records, magazine covers, and such, many owners tend to go with the time period that first made the car famous, and frankly that's not a bad choice. However, if the hot rod changed hands over the years, honoring the original build is often a sound choice, but bear in mind, even original builders would change their car every few years—new paint, new upholstery, and engine swaps were common.

Then it is up to you to choose the most appealing version of the car you are lucky enough to own. Photos are great because even previous owners may get it wrong, mistaking different elements of the car. Remembering how much you chopped the top on a 1936 coupe 56 years ago might not be as easy as you think. Photos don't lie, so they tend to be invaluable when restoring a vintage car with history.

And while we're talking about restoring old hot rods, there is one more question: Do you truly restore the car to its original glory (my personal choice), or do you over-restore the car with a fit and finish that rivals a modern BMW? The choice is yours.

Tracing the History

Even the term history is relative, with different meanings to different people. It need not be a magazine cover car to qualify, rather it could be a local hero car, one that you remember seeing on the street or strip. I personally would love to find Bob Zorn's old Deuce coupe, the car that got me started on this path of lifelong hot rodding. It had been featured in some of the small, pocket-size magazines, but in Smithtown, New York, it was simply known as Zorn's coupe. Everyone who cared about cars in the area knew this hot rod. Where it went is hard to say. Did some later hot rodder put the body back on top of the frame and add fenders? Anything is possible. Even finding an anonymous hot rod is exciting, wondering who built the car and attempting to trace the past is an on-going part of hot rod stewardship. It is amazing how many hot rods can eventually be traced back to the builder. The world of old cars is a small, tight-knit community that tends to remember cars and owners for many years.

Lest you think all the good stuff is gone, let's take a look at a couple vintage cars that were recently unearthed and brought back to life. They both have a great story to tell; one story is just beginning, while the other one has gone full circle.

Barn Find 1937 Ford

Larry Shoaf and Paul Talmon are hardcore hot rodders. Both were afflicted with hot rod fever at an early age and never even attempted a cure. Larry makes his living building hot rods, while Paul is retired. As it turns out, this is a good combination because Paul has time to go looking, and Larry has the space to store the occasional find. In June 2009 they learned of a 1937 Ford coupe that had recently been pulled out of a barn after resting quietly since 1981. Okay, not the longest history in the world, and no, not all barn cars are '32 Fords, but we'll take it, plus it gets better. It seems the car was originally built in 1965 in a style that would be considered very conservative for the 1960s. This serves to illustrate why it pays to ask questions. While finding an old car that has been inside since the early 1980s is pretty interesting,

Fresh from a North Carolina barn, this 1937 Ford coupe had been sitting since 1981, but the car was originally built as a hot rod in 1965. The car proved to be a well-built 1960s-style hot rod.

the fact that the car was originally built in the mid 1960s makes it all the more intriguing. It was definitely worth a look.

Upon arrival the duo was greeted by what appeared to be one very nice, very solid 1937 Ford coupe. Under the heavy layer of red North Carolina dust was black paint. The running boards were worn and cracked, but the fenders were perfect—nary a crack to be found in any of the four fenders. Further examination showed stock gauges in an original woodgrain dashboard and the stock steering column carried a vintage Signal-Stat turn signal conversion top with a red metal-flake steering wheel.

The seat was covered in what can only be described as 1962 couch material. Because the car was found in the furniture capital of the country, it is entirely possible that someone who worked with upholstery in one of the many North Carolina furniture factories actually did the seat. The workmanship was good, the material not worth saving, but it should be noted it too was in keeping with the conservative approach.

The access panel to the transmission was lying on the passenger-side floorboard, exposing an early Ford Toploader transmission and an engine adapter plate bolted between the transmission and the small-block Chevy motor. The floors had been repaired, and while the work was acceptable, the car came with two reproduction floor panels; evidently the owner had planned on replacing them.

A twist of the hood ornament released the hood. As it was raised, early-Corvette valve covers topping a small-block Chevy engine with a single Holley carburetor under a typical 10-inch chrome air breather came into view. A front cradle-style mount, possibly an actual Hurst mount, located the motor on the stock motor mount biscuits. Stock exhaust manifolds exited the spent gases, with the driver-side manifold being the desirable Chevrolet truck manifold that dumps forward, providing important clearance for the steering box.

Sure it was dusty, dirty, and neglected, but it was apparent that this was a very sanitary build by 1965 standards. Furthermore, the original builder stayed with the understated theme for the car from front to rear, building what would have been considered a sleeper of sorts, stock on the outside with plenty of power under the hood.

The car was resting on the stock Ford rear axle, with the spring removed and in the trunk. A set of 1939 Ford hydraulic brakes had been substituted for the old mechanical brakes, and tube shocks had been added, while little else had been changed. Front suspension was also the stock configuration with tube shocks and 1939 Ford brakes.

The body was nothing less than excellent, with no visible rust, rips, or tears anywhere on it, with the exception of a small crack or two around the mounting point of the hood strut, which is a common

Under the hood is a vintage small-block Chevrolet with a single 4-barrel mounted to an Edelbrock intake. Ramshorn exhaust manifolds are used, and the driver-side manifold is either a truck or early 265 manifold. It dumps forward, solving the problem of steering box clearance. Vintage Corvette valve covers complete the powerplant. By 1965 standards, these were all the right pieces for a sanitary V-8 conversion.

A generator was standard fare on 1960s hot rods, but by the late 1960s the alternator was introduced, and talk at many rod runs centered around the mystery of how to mount and wire a car for an alternator. Today, there are generator housings available with alternators inside, but this is one of those tests—if you're building an early- to mid-1960s hot rod, a 12-volt generator is period correct. End of story, nothing else is correct.

malady caused by people trying to close the hood without first giving a slight lift to release the hood strut. Even the glass in the car appeared to be original, and two vintage Offenhauser decals in the quarter windows were the only hint that this might be a hot rod.

The wheels and tires were the final touch of conservative building techniques. At first glance the wheels appeared to be stock, but upon closer examination the outer bands were 15-inch wheels with the large bolt pattern and associated 1937 Ford hubcaps. New for the period, narrow whitewalls wrapped the wheels, and once again just a hint that something may have been changed on this car.

It took several trips, but finally Larry and Paul Talmon merged some funds and purchased the car; it was just too good to pass up. And so the car was loaded on a trailer and taken to Larry's shop, where I got involved in the project. The rear wheels refused to turn, but the tires held air and this barn car was about to be reborn.

Getting a Great Find Running

The great fun of finding an old car is digging around to see what works what doesn't, and what other treasures might be found. Things like two new running boards, an NOS 1937 Ford taillight still in the box, and the fact that the engine turned over easily were all exciting discoveries. A little Marvel Mystery Oil was poured in all the cylinders and allowed to sit for a few days before the engine was spun over by hand, but it turned freely. Next up was a fresh battery. And yet another miracle, the engine turned over with the key.

A cleaning of the plugs, points, rotor, and cap was performed to help ignition. Then we gave it a splash of gas in the carburetor, a push of a remote starter button, and voilà— it came to life! The old small-block sputtered to life. The gas in the tank had turned to jelly, so a small gas can with a temporary line was used for fuel. The electric fuel pump seemed to work and a couple of quick pulls on the carburetor linkage established the fact that fuel was present. Once again, the starter button brought the long-dormant motor to life. After several attempts and some

This was a very conservative hot rod by 1965 standards, a true sleeper. Stock gauges are in very nice condition, and that red metal-flake steering wheel certainly dates the car.

Other than the modern-by-1979 standard tires and dual exhaust, the only external clue that this coupe was no stocker was this single Offenhauser decal in the quarter window. While there is no visible use of Offy parts on the motor, I suspect the decal may have come with the engine-to-transmission adapter.

Small pieces add up to a period perfect hot rod. The firewall-mounted, glass-bowl fuel filter is well worth retaining and is a good deal better looking than the cheap plastic filters available today.

Here's some of the fun of finding a time capsule car. The "late-model" ignition switch is hardly new, it appears to be off a 1960s GM product—once again, period perfect for this car so why not leave it in place? Note the nice condition of the stock gauges too.

THE PERFECT PLAN: THE RECIPE FOR BUILDING A PERIOD CORRECT HOT ROD

pumping of the carburetor, the old small-block just idled. It didn't miss, skip, sputter, or shake. It just idled as we all looked on in disbelief. This was a good motor that had not run in more than 20 years.

Next, we raised the rear of the car on jack stands and restarted the engine. Holding the motor at about 1,500 rpm, we eased out the clutch and slowly the rear wheels began to turn. Finally, the brake shoes freed themselves from the drums and the rear wheels rotated under power for the first time in more than 20 years.

So here it was, one day of tinkering and the driveline seemed to be in working order. The clutch and master cylinder had to be rebuilt, as well as all wheel cylinders, but the fact that this car moved under its own power made it a great investment. One more amazing thing: The brakes still worked on the car. The pedal was stiff and the car came to a smooth halt during a very careful drive around the industrial complex. Now the only question is, what to do with the car?

The jury is still out on this one, but if it were my car, it would be put back to its 1965 configuration. While the temptation is great to install an open driveline, an automatic transmission, and disc brakes, in my mind the car just seems to want to be a 1965 hot rod. One concession might be a 350 turbo transmission and 9-inch Ford rear with drum brakes, but that would absolutely be as far as I'd go with the car. Inside I'd opt for a 1960s-style rolled-and-pleated interior, and a fresh coat of black paint would finish the exterior. Under the hood would remain untouched other than cleaning and detailing. Time will tell what happens to this cool old hot rod.

Old Car Hunter Gary Moore

In the world of old car hunting, Gary Moore of Melbourne, Florida, would be considered a world-class big game hunter. Like any good hunter, he can only bag a trophy if he's on the hunt, so he hunts a lot . . . he hunts constantly.

There may be no better example of a guy making his own luck than Gary finding this car. It all began one day while visiting a local hot rodder's body shop. It was not unusual to see hot rods parked outside the shop, and maybe that's why this fellow stopped by on that fateful morning. The man walked in, mentioned he had an old T-bucket he wanted to sell, and would anyone be interested in such a vehicle. Well, three out of four of the hot rodders standing in that circle gave the easy answer of, "A T-bucket huh? Well, I don't think so, but thanks anyway." Gary Moore on the other hand, asked a simple question, "Where is the car?" The owner responded, "Oh, a couple miles from here." Gary replied, "Heck, let's go take a look at it."

When they arrived at the house and the garage door opened, Gary wasn't looking at a T-bucket at all. Oh sure, it was a Model T alright, but a more desirable 1927 model. And here's the good part: It was obvious from first glance that this was an old hot rod. From the early Oldsmobile motor to the upholstery, this was a late-1950s or early-1960s hot rod. Two intriguing decals from the 1965

By the time we arrived at Gary Moore's home shop, he had the roadster partially disassembled. The car was painted black after Don Nichols purchased the roadster in the 1990s. That paint job had long faded but the body was still very solid and all the good parts were still there.

This was a very well constructed hot rod, and the 1927 T body was mounted to a highly modified 1937 Ford frame. The front axle is not dropped, but mounted in front of the crossmember suicide style. Nicely built radius rods locate the axle, and tube shocks smooth out the road.

CHAPTER 1

and 1966 Dallas Autorama indoor car show were a major clue, and what about that rear nerf bar with the letter "C" in the center? The old car hunter had just gotten lucky, again proving that if you're going to find a vintage hot rod, you have to take the time to look.

One of the things I find so interesting about vintage hot rods is that it seems somehow the good ones survive, often with little or no changes over many years and several owners. The owner in this instance had purchased the car in the early 1980s in Mississippi and then moved to Florida with the car. The car was taken off the road in 1990s and had been sitting in his garage ever since.

Gary gave me a call one day to tell me of his latest find and to see if I was interested in helping track down the history on the car. I was editor of *Rodder's Digest* magazine at the time, and after a trip to his shop, we ran an article on the car. Interestingly enough, response was quick and from multiple sources. We had calls from Mississippi and New Mexico, saying

At some point, these bucket seats were added to the car, and while they look good in their period perfect white pleats, Gary opted to return to the original bench-style seat during the restoration. The 1950 Ford speedometer in the dash was a real identifying characteristic to the car.

Clues to the car's past were posted right on the windshield. The Dallas Autorama, put on by the Quartermilers Car Club in 1964–1965, proved the car had been in Texas during that time. The Mississippi 1982 inspection sticker indicates the last year the car was driven on the streets in Mississippi.

The single-stage master cylinder was state of the art for the period and lacks the safety of the dual master cylinder that was introduced on new cars in 1967. This means the single master cylinder is proper for the car, so locate a new unit. With regular fluid changes and limited miles, these master cylinders work just fine.

After several years of work, the Conley roadster is once again on the road, glowing in Titian Red paint, wide white-wall tires, and a potent 303 Olds motor. Like all great vintage hot rods, this roadster is a study in simplicity, and hats off to Gary for an accurate restoration.

THE PERFECT PLAN: THE RECIPE FOR BUILDING A PERIOD CORRECT HOT ROD

they recognized the car, and one of the callers was the nephew of the second owner. But wait; it gets better.

These conversations led to an ad in the back of the August 1964 *Hot Rod* magazine where we learned that Don Conley of Farmington, New Mexico, had sold his roadster for $900 to a gentleman from Mississippi named Malcolm "Two-Hair" Ellis. The car and Ellis spent several years in the Dallas area before returning to Mississippi, hence the Dallas show decals. Also, the roadster won back-to-back People's Choice Awards at the Dallas show with Ellis and his nephew Roly Scott showing the car. After the car returned to Mississippi, Malcolm Ellis turned the roadster over to his daughter Mona who drove it for a couple years before losing interest in the roadster. The car was then covered under a tarp next to the Ellis garage where it sat for almost 20 years.

Like so many of these cars, any number of offers were turned down for the old hot rod, and then one day in the mid 1980s a local fellow by the name of Dick Nichols was able to persuade Ellis to sell the car. As the story goes, Nichols actually drove the car home, which would be quite a feat for a car that hadn't been driven in almost 20 years. Nichols moved to Florida in 1999, and soon after, the Oldsmobile motor quit running. Once again the car sat until 2003 when he walked into that body shop where he always saw hot rodders hanging around.

Gary knew this would be a long shot, but some searching found a Don Conley in Farmington, New Mexico. Could this be the same Don Conley that built the roadster more than 50 years earlier? A phone call was made, and after some brief introductions a very surprised and pleased Don Conley went into a detailed description of his old roadster, mentioning the car had been featured in a 1961 *Hot Rod* issue. The car was originally built with a flathead, but Conley and friends swapped in the Olds motor shortly before the *Hot Rod* feature was shot in 1961. A friendship was forged among those three men, all around the bond of owning the same hot rod in different decades over a 50-year period.

From the rear this roadster defines 1960s hot rodding. The homemade nerf bar is well designed, and the addition of an owner's initial was common for both race cars and hot rods of the era. The bed was entirely handmade from sheet metal, proving there were some fine craftsman involved in the initial build.

The original Farmington, New Mexico, Road Runners plaque was left in the original patina; restoring this plaque would have been a mistake.

Gary added some period correct dress-up goodies to the firewall, like the aluminum coil covers. Note the magneto distributor, red fuel lines, and appropriate clamps on the fuel lines. They are all important details that make this vintage hot rod period correct.

Gary set about restoring the old roadster to its former glory utilizing as many original parts as possible. A different 303 Oldsmobile engine was swapped in place of the original hot rod motor, but from the front axle to the nerf bar and interior, the car was brought back to 1961 again. Conley even went so far as to donate his club plaque and several other parts he had saved for all those years, which added even more authenticity to this great hot rod.

There were some concessions made along the way. Early Ford drum brakes were replaced with early Lincoln drum brakes, favored for their self-energizing brakes. Likewise, the Olds motor is now topped with a two-deuce intake, rather than a single 4-barrel—simple personal taste that does nothing to detract from the original build.

The original Titian Red color was reapplied and the interior was stitched in the same pattern as Conley used in 1958. The original headers were too rough to repair, so new headers were built for the car. The chrome wheels and whitewalls are proper for the era, but when Moore bought the car it was rolling on some very rare, albeit rusty, Morbec wheels. Conley had simple cone-style hubcaps on the car, so the decision to go with chrome wheels and early Ford caps is entirely in keeping with the spirit of the car.

And so, with due diligence an old hot rod is returned to glory, new friendships are formed and all the owners of this roadster (past and present) are smiling again, which is the true reward of rescuing old hot rods. With the heritage clearly spelled out on the Don Conley roadster the history of this roadster will continue.

If you're building a vintage roadster, study this profile. Note how the headers pick up the line of the chassis, the drag link, and the chrome-plated radius rods. Nothing is hanging below the frame rails, and all these things contribute to a clean profile. Also worthy of note is the rather high steering wheel and seating, which is typical of the period. This hot rod was built long before the lowered seat trend.

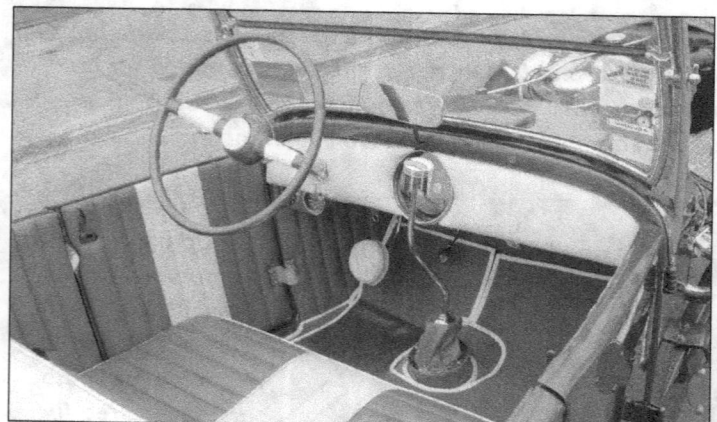

The white piping on the floormats would be considered busy by today's standards, but is perfect for vintage style. A 1940 Ford steering wheel mounts atop a simple steering mast while the single round gauge is mounted in a padded dash. The white cover on the brake pedal simulates typical covers that would have been used at indoor shows, not for actual driving.

Early hot rods and Moto-Meters go hand in hand, particularly Model Ts and Model As. The winged meter dresses up the original steel 1927 radiator shell. The Boyce Moto-Meter Company was located in Long Island City, New York.

CHAPTER 2

PERIOD POWER

One of the most important choices in defining the era of your hot rod is picking the proper engine. It is fair to say the earliest days of hot rodding revolved around the engine. The need for speed brought on this quest for power. For the most part, early hot rodders were working men with skill and ingenuity that often surpassed their earning power. For that reason, most of the cars that felt the hot rodder's touch were common, affordable cars and engines.

If you're building a prewar hot rod, your choices are limited to Ford inline four cylinders and flathead V-8s, while Chevrolet lovers will be working on the venerable stovebolt six-cylinder. The Dodge flathead was around, but did not enjoy the popularity of the Ford and Chevy. Early four-cylinder motors can be built to produce reasonable horsepower for lightweight rods like the Model T and Model A. There are few sounds more invigorating than the snarl of an OHV-converted inline-four. After 1932, one of the more popular combinations was the A-V-8, the blending of the flathead V-8 engine with the Model A chassis.

Building a car of this era takes a dedicated enthusiast, as you are limited to very old equipment and the driving experience is for the hardcore enthusiast only. But the rewards are great as you see very few prewar-style hot rods today, and the sight of a hopped up four-cylinder in an early body is the very essence of simplicity and a direct connection to the very roots of hot rodding.

The Model T engine produced a mere 22 hp, later lowered to 20 hp, so making big power from these engines was a tall order. The Model A four-cylinder cranked out 40 hp at 2,200 rpm, while the evolutionary Model B motor introduced in 1932

Six, stack-fed carbs and finned everything dress up this Buick Nailhead engine. Bob Sargis built one of the most beautiful Buicks ever to slip between a set of frame rails. When it comes to pure hot rod attitude, this motor has it all.

HOW TO BUILD PERIOD CORRECT HOT RODS

CHAPTER 2

Lest you think hot rodding was a bolt-on affair in prewar America, think again. People like Robert Roof were building exotic engines based on the Ford flathead. This Roof Blue Streak V-8 features dual plugs in aluminum heads. (Photo Courtesy Smith Collection Museum of American Speed)

This Riley multi-lift race engine is a fine example of an exotic race engine, once again dual plugs and even dual distributors are used on the motor. Such equipment is extremely rare today and probably not suitable for street use. (Photo Courtesy Smith Collection Museum of American Speed)

Frontenac was a major producer of speed equipment for four-cylinder Ford motors. Converting the engine to overhead valves made them good performers and great-looking motors in the process. (Photo Courtesy Smith Collection Museum of American Speed)

Hopped-up four-cylinder motors, such as this 1932 Model B motor, powered many hot rods built before World War II. Assembling such a motor today makes for a unique hot rod, and parts are still available.

managed 50 hp but at a substantially higher 2,800 rpm. So raw power was not built into the engines, rather it had to be squeezed out of them. Items, such as 16-valve Model T engines with single- and dual-overhead cams, were being built, and the Chevrolet brothers (Louis, Gaston, and Arthur) were busy making speed equipment for Fords when they weren't building Chevrolet cars. The speed equipment and race cars came from their Frontenac Company and proved to be very competitive in races ranging from hillclimbs to the Indianapolis. Other speed equipment pioneers, such as Robert Roof, built speed equipment for the Model T, Dodge four-cylinder motors, and Chevrolet six-cylinder engines. He would continue to build speed equipment well into the 1940s, changing his line of equipment to fit the latest offerings, such as the flathead Ford V-8.

Frontenac, Rajo, Craig-Hunt, Offenhauser, Miller, Riley, Ardun, Winfield, and others were fierce competitors on the track and in business. As you can guess, there was no shortage of speed equipment for these early hot rods and race cars. The Rajo heads were manufactured in Racine, Wisconsin, by Joseph Jagersberger; hence the RaJo name. Before World War II, the early speed industry was blossoming everywhere; after World War II, California became the focal point of the hot rod industry.

Hot four-cylinder motors were king for a while. When the Ford flathead V-8 arrived in 1932, the writing was on the wall, and the four-cylinder motors began to fade quite quickly. The new V-8 produced 85 hp at 3,800 rpm and the smooth V-8 responded well to all the usual hot rod tricks. It was an instant favorite among hot rodders and remained king of the hot rod motors for many years, eventually relinquishing the crown to the small-block Chevrolet in 1955.

The flathead Ford dominated the hot rod and racing scene before and after World War II. After the war the higher price models, such as Oldsmobile, Cadillac, Chrysler, and Buick, came out with new overhead-valve (OHV) motors that produced a lot of power and torque and quickly captured the eyes of the returning hot rodders.

Shortly after the war, auto manufacturers were frantically developing new bodies and engines. Like so many mechanical concepts, Ford stubbornly stuck with the flathead design until 1953, but it was an improved version of hot rodding's most popular motor. Chevrolet was also slow to change, clinging to the tried-and-true inline six-cylinder motors. Due to the availability of engines, speed equipment, and hot rod know-how, the flathead remained king for many years following World War II.

Fenton made speed equipment from exhaust and intake manifolds to finned-aluminum heads for flatheads. This fuel block for a dual-carb setup is a rare and proper 1950 piece.

Oil filters were not part of early engines, so remote oil filters are a must. To build an accurate vintage hot rod, all plumbing must be vintage too, such as this steel tubing with brass fitting and vintage-style hose clamps, all important details.

The simplicity of an early hot rod has a huge attraction and is a direct connection to the roots of our current-day hobby. This is a great example of a brand-new vintage hot rod.

One item often overlooked when building a vintage hot rod is the radiator cap. The Lev-R-Vent cap by Stant was first introduced in 1962, so it is not correct for hot rods before then; the new caps have a plastic lever, while the original design employed a metal lever.

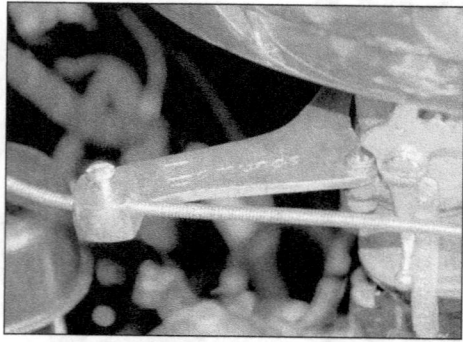

The McMillan roadster has all kinds of vintage details, such as this original Edmunds choke cable bracket. Reproductions are available from Vintage Speed in Vero Beach, Florida, but this is an original item.

Lewis McMillan's Deuce roadster is a study in period perfect engine building. All finishes are period correct, and those speed parts are all vintage pieces; no reproduction parts on this motor.

When building a period flavor car, transgressions, such as a chrome alternator and braided throttle cables, are excused. This gorgeous flathead has all the right stuff, and it should be noted that Powermaster makes an alternator that looks like a generator and Lokar makes throttle cables with black plastic shielding for people concerned with period correct appearances.

Now here's a vintage roadster worth studying. Period perfect in every way, the roadster has a presence about it that captures the lure of vintage hot rodding. The deep, deep purple roadster is powered by a full-house flathead sporting rare speed equipment and such nice details as thumb-screw hose clamps on the fuel lines. Mark Chapman's Toronto-based roadster is a true time capsule.

In 1949, Cadillac and Oldsmobile introduced all-new OHV V-8 engines. Hot rodders were quick to grab these new powerplants, but cost and availability meant there were still more flatheads in hot rods than overheads. Likewise, speed equipment manufacturers were quick to invent performance products for these new GM engines. Chrysler followed suit in 1951 with its new OHV V-8, the 331-ci Hemi engine, and thus, a legend was born. The popularity of the flathead remained, due in part to the sheer number of motors and speed equipment available. Slipping a hopped-up flathead into virtually any Ford was a bolt-in affair with modest fabricating skills required. The same could not be said of a true engine swap where transplanting a big Caddy motor into a Deuce required adapting many systems and fabricating motor mounts, modifying firewalls, and other such major jobs.

The choice of engine is a major decision for any vintage hot rod. Once the decision is made, the key to a successful period correct engine bay lies in the details. Building a great 303 Olds motor for your Model A is one thing, but ultimately it is the careful selection of external engine parts that will define the quality of your build. Vintage speed equipment is a must, but the real difference is in the small things such as vintage-style hose clamps, radiator hoses, fuel lines, motor mounts, and brackets. All must be from the same period. Building a great flathead and plumbing it with AN fittings provides a confusing statement. The key is to stay in the time period that your car represents. For a true, authentic 1950 build this is essential. For those hot rodders going for vintage flavor, there is a bit more latitude, but even then, mixing time periods can quickly change the attitude of your hot rod.

The good news about vintage engines in street-driven cars is you can perform all the modern tricks to the internals to make them run better, leak less, and stay cool, but dress them out with vintage speed equipment. If you're building a vintage flavor, rather than period correct hot rod, the options expand to modern electronic fuel injection hidden in carburetor bodies or the new offerings from companies (such as Hilborn) that offer the best of both worlds—vintage looks and electronically controlled fuel injection.

Ford Flathead V-8

If you are building an old hot rod with the venerable Ford flathead V-8, there are several things to consider. On the plus side, the flathead V-8 is a great-looking motor and even people who don't know much about hot rods seem to be able to identify a flathead V-8. The looks and sounds of the flathead are reason enough to want one, and the good news is most of the problems that plagued this motor have been sorted out.

Ford produced the flathead from 1932 through 1953 in the United

A closer look at the Chas. Caproff Power & Speed heads includes the unique three-outlet cooling tube on top of the heads. The tapered tube casting is a thing of beauty.

Check out the super-rare set of Fenton exhaust manifolds on this Olds motor. They are hard to find and expensive, and most of them were made for the early round-port 303 motors, so be certain they will fit your motor before you buy. Note the use of copper plumbing fixtures in the cooling system, a practice that did occur on some early hot rods.

States, and through 1954 in Canada. The engine continued to be produced and improved upon in France until the late 1980s. There are three basic subgroups of the Ford flathead. The first design was the 21-stud motor produced from 1932 to midyear 1938. The name refers to the number of head retention studs on each head, and the 221-ci engine produced 65 hp. Speed equipment for these early motors is scarce, and like almost any evolutionary motor, the flathead improved over time. I suggest avoiding these early motors.

The "baby flathead" (the 60-hp 136-ci V-8 engine) was introduced in 1937. This economy engine was in production from 1937 to 1940, and unless you're building an early-style sprint car or track-T there is little need to consider this motor. Plenty of speed equipment is available for the motors as they were popular with oval track racers and midget racers.

Beginning midyear in 1938, the new 24-stud motor was introduced and while it still displaced 221 ci, the horsepower was now up to 85. Commonly referred to as 59A casting, these engines feature a front-mounted distributor and new insert-style main bearings. The bellhousing was still cast with the engine as one piece,

Most hot rod builders today are opting to use a ceramic coating on headers and exhaust manifolds because the material holds up so well, and it blends well with alloy and chrome parts. Of course, this stuff was non-existent in the 1950s, so white or black header paint was the finish of the day. The bad news is the paint doesn't hold up well, requiring repaints often, but the good news is white ceramic coating is available from Swain Coatings and others.

Of all the speed equipment ever made for the Ford flathead V-8, the Ardun OHV conversion reigns supreme. These legendary heads were originally designed to provide more power for trucks, but hot rodders had other plans for the power-enhancing heads. (Photo Courtesy Smith Collection Museum of American Speed)

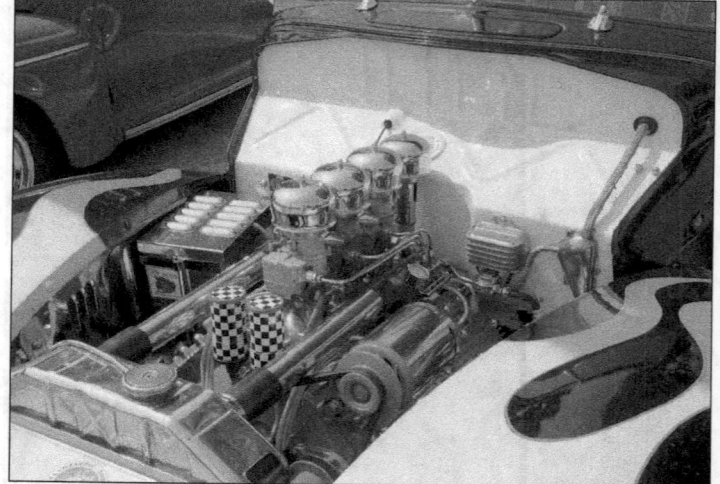

This flathead Ford V-8 looks good with the three carburetors and the oil filler all wearing the same breathers. At a glance, it appears to be four carbs. Dual coils are shrouded in a checkerboard pattern. Note the vintage-style radiator cap, an important detail.

PERIOD POWER

This deeply channeled Model A roadster captures the 1960s in style. Mag wheels wrapped with cheater slicks set the mood, and the rear nerf bar completes the look. Through the windshield six stacks are in clear view on Nick Giacalone's roadster.

The beehive oil filter was another very popular remote oil filter. One look at the gorgeous design should tell you why they are offered in reproduction form today. Speedway Motors has a reproduction unit of the Offenhauser beehive.

and hot rodders quickly produced many varied speed-equipment pieces for this engine. Since flathead motors are cooled with two water pumps, twin upper hoses flow to the radiator as well. On the 59A engines, the hose outlet is located in the top center of each head. If you find a good 59A block, it is easy to hot rod, and adapters are available to mate later transmissions and clutches to these motors. If you are building an early-vintage hot rod, the popular 1937 to 1950 Ford Toploader transmissions will bolt up directly to this engine, or an adapter will enable you to use the stronger Caddy-LaSalle transmission.

The final iteration of the flathead is the 8BA series introduced in 1949 with production ending in 1953, bringing the flathead's 21-year reign to an end. This newer engine is the best for hot rods, as it has a bolt-on bellhousing, full insert bearings on rods, and main bearings. The distributor is now located on the top front of the motor making access easier. The radiator hoses have been moved forward to the front corner of the head and 24 head bolts hold the head in place rather than studs and nuts.

The 8BA motors were good for 100 hp in the Ford and up to 125 hp in the Mercury. With good hot rod building techniques, these motors can reliably pump out 200 hp and more. The mystery of overheating problems has been solved with new water pumps available from companies, such as Speedway Motors, Dennis Carpenter Reproductions, and Bob Drake Reproductions. Using these pumps in conjunction with a modern 16-pound pressure radiator and modern fan all but eliminate flathead cooling problems, assuming the block and heads were thoroughly cleaned internally before the motor was built. The key to that high-pressure radiator cap is to find one that is simple in design, such as those sold in the 1950s.

In 1949, Mercury flatheads came with the famous 4-inch-stroke forged

Cadillac introduced its OHV V-8 in 1949 and hot rodders instantly recognized the power potential. Three deuces, chrome valve covers, and a generator give the engine a great look, while red transparent fuel lines and ignition wires date the motor nicely.

HOW TO BUILD PERIOD CORRECT HOT RODS

crankshaft that bumped the displacement from 239 for the Fords up to 255 ci for the Mercury. This was a natural performance upgrade for hot rodders and the 4-inch-stroker motor was a common starting point for many hot rod flatheads. Finding a Mercury crankshaft today is still very cool, but don't spend too much time searching as there are several different companies making stroker crankshafts for the flathead that range from 4 inches up to 4.5 inches.

There are any number of flathead specialty builders and suppliers and parts are plentiful. Remember, there is an ample supply of buildable engines around, so shop carefully. If possible find an 8BA or Mercury 8CM motor and use modern-day building techniques to assemble it. In the end, you'll have a great motor that will prove to be reliable, reasonably powerful, and guaranteed to provide the ultimate 1950s hot rod experience. While the flathead Ford motor could be considered correct for hot rods into the early 1960s, it is best left to hot rods built in 1959 or earlier.

Cadillac Motors

Cadillac's offering for 1949 was a 331-ci motor with a bore and stroke of 3 13/16 x 3 5/8 inches. The same basic engine was found under all Caddy hoods through 1955. The compression ratio was 7.5:1, and the engine was offered with only a Carter 2-barrel carburetor. At 3,800 rpm the engine produced 160 hp. In 1952, with the addition of a 4-barrel carburetor the horsepower rating jumped to 190. While many people attribute the Detroit horsepower wars to the muscle car era, make no mistake, the horsepower wars were in full swing by the early 1950s. Horsepower increased each year for the 331, culminating in 1955 with the dual-quad-fed Eldorado 331 pumping out 270 hp.

In 1956 the new 365-ci engine with the single 4-barrel was rated at 285 hp and the 305-hp option used dual 4-barrel carbs. These were big horsepower numbers, and hot rodders took note, but with the proper speed equipment a small-block Chevy could produce similar numbers for less money and with less weight. The days of Caddy motors in hot rodding were numbered. Cadillac motors through 1964 could still be found in some hot rods, but parts were much more expensive, and the speed equipment selection was small compared with that of the new Chevrolet motor.

In 1955, Cadillac offered a new block with a more modern flat-back design and the starter mounted to the bellhousing. This basic design would remain in effect with the 365-ci engine produced from 1956 to 1958, the 390-ci engine produced 1959 to 1963, and the 1964 429-ci engine. While you could buy a Cadillac with a stick-shift, three-speed transmission, the vast majority came equipped with the heavy—and not

Maybe it was availability or affordability or a combination of the two, but the Oldsmobile motor that was introduced in 1949 seemed to be the most popular OHV motor swap of the early 1950s. For that reason, there is still ample speed equipment around, but oddly enough we don't see a lot of these motors in hot rods today.

Typical engine-to-transmission adapters can be purchased new or found used at swap meets. The advantage of having new parts is the tech support from people, such as Wilcap, Honest Charley, and others. Swap meet parts are a good deal if they are complete. Check for cracks or worn and missing parts before buying used adapters. This unit mates a Ford flathead to the stronger Cad-LaSalle transmission.

exactly crisp-shifting—Hydramatic-drive transmission. Often referred to as slush-boxes, existing Ford transmissions or more modern transmissions replaced these early automatic transmissions using adapters to mate to the modern motors.

There were any number of engine adapter companies around at the time. One such company, WilCap, is still serving the hot rod community producing quality engine-to-transmission adapters. They've been doing it for more than 60 years and have a vast knowledge of mating transmissions and engines.

If you are building a true period piece, the adapters may be limited to transmissions for the 1950s or 1960s. Popular adapters of the day hooked the Caddy motor directly to the early Ford transmission and fed back either through a torque-tube or open drive-shaft unit from an early Ford truck.

If you are building a period piece from the ground up, I recommend looking for a 1955–1964 engine. They are available in 331, 365, and 390-ci configurations, and the modern-style block brings with it many more transmission adapter options. Virtually anything from an automatic overdrive to a 4-, 5-, or 6-speed manual transmission can be adapted to these blocks.

If you have an early block with the integral cast bellhousing, your transmission choices are a bit more limited with the GM Turbo-350 or adapting to early Ford transmissions, which are the most common adapters. It should be noted that these OHV engines provide enough torque and horsepower to destroy an early Ford Toploader transmission at will. Therefore, if you're working on a Cadillac mated to a 1939 Ford Toploader, I advise against side-stepping that clutch or speed shifting.

The Cadillac motor can also be considered correct for hot rods well into the 1960s, but for the most part Cadillac power was a brief period of new overhead powerplants found in hot rods of the early 1950s. You can use a motor up through 1963 in these early cars, as they tend to look the same, and you can benefit from the additional power and improvements of the later motors. One downside to consider when looking for Cadillac power, parts, and speed equipment is that they tend to be limited and pricey.

1949–1964 Oldsmobile V-8

Oldsmobile introduced a modern, OHV motor in 1949. The 1949 to 1953 motors displaced 303 ci. These engines are easy to recognize because the bellhousing is an integral casting with the block, and the heads have round exhaust ports. For 1949 to 1951 the 303-ci Rocket V-8 produced 135 hp at 3,600 rpm. In 1952, the output of the 303 Olds with the 4-barrel carburetor jumped to 160 hp, and by 1953 the 303 was up to 170 hp.

In 1954, Oldsmobile introduced the 324-ci motor offering 185 hp, so you can see, when choosing a motor for your vintage hot rod the newer motors are always an improvement over the older versions of the same family. By 1954 Oldsmobile went to

This early Olds sports an Edmunds dual-carb intake and homebrewed headers using a tapered torque tube for the collector. Note the welding of the Siamese exhaust ports, typical of the day. Edmunds speed equipment is readily available from Vintage Speed in Vero Beach, Florida.

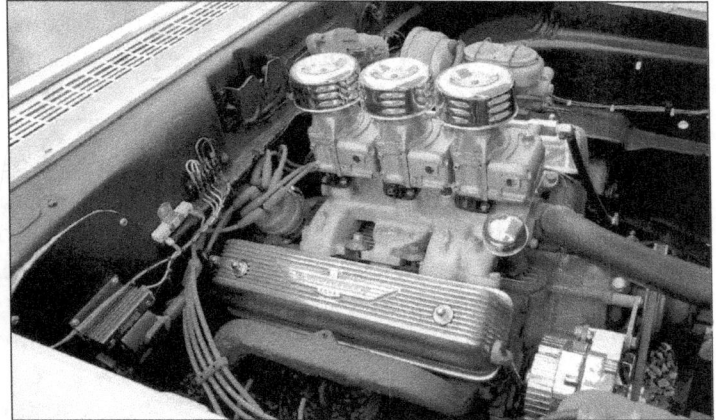

Here is a typical vintage-flavor motor found in my 1957 Ranch wagon. Reproduction T-Bird valve covers and an Edelbrock intake are period correct, but the chrome alternator, Demon carbs, dual master cylinder, modern ignition, and abundant use of tie-wraps are all modern appointments.

This early intake is an Edelbrock OL 396 for the 1949–1956 Oldsmobile. It appears to be in very good condition and the asking price was $575. Carburetor choices were either the Stromberg 97 or Holley 94 for these three-bolt intake manifolds. Later four-bolt manifolds accept the more modern Rochester 2-barrel carbs.

Race-application Hilborn injection can be found, and with some serious machine work they can be converted to modern electronic fuel-injection. This unit was for sale at $675, but Hilborn now offers an EFI version for street applications.

The famous Ford Y-block E-code motor ran dual 4-barrel carburetors from the factory, and the stock air breather looks great on a hot rod, too. Rare factory performance items date a car perfectly.

a bolt-on bellhousing with the starter attached to the bellhousing, and this affords more transmission options to adapt to the later motors. By 1955 Oldsmobile had cracked the 200-hp level with 202, and in the final year of production the 1956 324-ci motor produced 240, again indicating that newer is better.

For 1957 Oldsmobile introduced the 371-ci motor that produced 277 hp with a single 4-barrel carburetor. But 1957 was also the year of the famed J-2 option that included three 2-barrel carbs, 10:1 compression ratio, and internal changes that pumped up the horsepower rating to 300. The J-2 option was offered for a mere $83 and immediately became popular with hot rodders. This is the ultimate vintage Olds motor for many hot rodders.

A second J-2 option, reserved mostly for NASCAR racers and drag racers, incorporated solid lifters and forged pistons. These motors came with dimpled valve covers to clear the adjustable rockers. Since the valve covers were also sold in a chrome-plated version by speed shops, there are many more valve covers than race motors in existence. This race version of the J-2 cost $395 and "was not recommended for the street."

The J-2 option continued in 1958 with a rise in horsepower to 312. In 1959 the 371-ci motor was still produced, but it was in the shadow of the bigger 394-ci/300-hp motor. Horsepower climbed to 345 by 1963. When searching for these engines, note that the 394 powered the Olds 98, Super 88, and Starfire models, while the less-expensive 88 used the 371.

The good news about the Olds engine is that modern design gives good service, gobs of torque, and plenty of horsepower. Speed equipment and dress-up items are easy to find, and a limited number of transmission adapters are available too.

The Oldsmobile motors are period perfect for hot rods from 1949 into the 1960s. The performance of the Olds Rocket V-8 lasted longer than the Cadillac's performance, as Oldsmobile embraced performance while Cadillac opted for the luxury market. The Olds motor seemed to be the OHV engine of choice for most hot rodders replacing a flathead. Myriad aluminum adapters were available to mate the Olds motor to the Ford transmission.

The Olds motor is a great choice for your vintage hot rod, but it is best to find a complete motor as interchange between the different iterations is difficult. The motor also has a left-side starter, which provides clearance challenges around the steering

This adapter for a Y-block Ford to an early Ford transmission appeared to be in good condition. Be sure to check all the tapped holes to be certain they are not stripped. Stripped bolt holes can be repaired with helicoil inserts but such damage should reduce the price.

box. Motor mounts can be fabricated for a front-style system using the side-mount bellhousing, or side mounts can be fabricated. Oddly enough, as popular as the Olds was, it is seldom seen today. They're great looking engines, and while adapting Rocket valve covers to small-block Chevy may be popular today, it is no substitute for putting a real Rocket between the rails. Dropping a 371-ci J-2 Olds under the hood of a 1940 Ford will forever be a legendary combination.

Ford Y-Block

You might think when Ford made the leap to overhead valves in 1954 it would have captured the hot rod world with this new motor. Unfortunately for Ford, that was not the case. The new OHV motor did find its way into hot rods, but not nearly in the number of the Oldsmobile, Buick, and Chevrolet motors.

The Y-block began life in a Lincoln in 1952 with 317 ci on tap, but Ford wouldn't get overhead valves until 1954 when the 239-ci Y-block motor made its debut. The following year the motor expanded to 272 ci and 162-hp with an optional 292-ci motor that jumped up over the 200-hp marker to 205. By 1957 the Y-block was punched out to 312 inches. The optional dual-quad E-code cars and supercharged F-code cars are the stuff of legend.

But in the end, the small-block Chevrolet overshadowed the Y-block. The Y-block remained in production through 1962 and a bit later in trucks. When shopping for a Y-block start with at least 272 ci, the 292 and 312 are the preferred versions. Side motor mounts make them simple to install, and several companies manufacture engine adapters, which enable you to bolt up anything from a Ford AOD automatic to a 6-speed manual.

While the Ford Y-block never garnered the lasting appreciation of hot rodders the way the GM engines did, it is a natural for vintage hot rods. The engines are still plentiful and affordable, and there is tons of speed equipment in swap meets for these motors. Nothing looks better than a Y-block in a shoebox Ford or an open-bay Model A. So if you're a blue oval kind of guy, the Y-block is the motor you want under the hood.

1957–1966 Buick Nailhead

The Buick Nailhead has long been a popular engine with vintage hot rodders. While Buick was not new to the OHV concept, the company preferred to put its eight cylinders in a row. In 1953 when Buick decided to put those eight cylinders in an opposing V configuration hot rodders took note.

The Nailhead name speaks to the relatively small valves in these engines. While the small vertical valves may not make this engine a big breather in the high-RPM range, they produce torque—and lots of it! The vertical valve covers keep the motor narrow enough to fit between early frame rails with ease, but engine swaps are not without special problems.

Buick chose to mount the starter to the lower left side of the motor, which makes clearing steering boxes and routing exhaust a challenge. However, mounting the motor in most early Ford frames is fairly simple because motor mounts can easily be fabricated or purchased. The front mounts can be used to locate the engine atop the stock-style flathead biscuit-style motor mounts. The early motors all used a rather

A beautiful Nailhead engine powers this roadster, and it features great details such as center carb linkage, Weiand valve covers, and wire covers held in place with vintage Cal Custom wing nuts. Chrome headers and yes, a chrome frame are the makings of what could have been a mid-1960s cover car.

odd looking center sump oil pan, and for most hot rod applications, a later 1957–1961 rear sump pan has to be used along with the proper oil pumps.

Custom exhaust is almost a must on the left side of the motor, and while there are shorty headers available today, this style of header is too new for a period correct car. Having said that, if you're building a period flavor car, these shorty headers solve a lot of fitment problems.

All Nailheads were not created equal. As a matter of fact, like many things over the years, they became wider. The early 322/264 motors are 8¼ inches between the heads, measuring from the front intake bolt hole on one head to the same hole on the opposite head. That same measurement grew to 8⅝ on the 364-ci motors and the 401 engine takes that measurement to an even 9 inches. These changes can make buying vintage speed equipment a bit tricky.

The motor was a powerhouse from its introduction in 1953 with the 322-ci motor pumping out 188 hp. In 1954, a smaller 264-ci motor was produced for the Buick Special line, but the 322 would remain in production through 1956 when factory horsepower was rated at 255. The Nailhead family continued to grow to the famed 401-ci version introduced in the Invicta in 1959. The 364 remained in production until 1962 when the 401 became the standard engine for all full-size cars. By 1966 you could get 425 ci of Nailhead power in the Riviera with 340 hp on tap. The 1964–1966 motors had a modern TH400 automatic transmission bolted to them, and while the pre-1964 models don't bolt up to the TH-400, a crankshaft adapter makes this swap a simple one.

It is not unusual for hot rods with Hemi power to take on drag strip flavor with things like cheater slicks, zoomie headers, and blowers. The Hemi motor ruled top fuel at the drag strip. Vinny Santomarco's metal-flake coupe embodies the look of a radical rod of the early 1960s.

There is only one engine whose name is synonymous with power—the Hemi. This coupe has the ultimate combination of a GMC supercharger mounted to this Hemi. Size, weight, power—the Hemi has a lot of everything.

PERIOD POWER

When it comes to big, the 392 Hemi has everyone beat. Running smooth hood sides is out of the question, but who wants to hide a Hemi? The glass-beaded aluminum valve covers and intake and air scoops lend a business-like look to the engine.

The small-block Chevrolet is simply the king of all hot rod motors, and you can dress them up in any vintage you like. This vintage-flavor motor is stunning in gold and chrome. Six deuces top the small-block while very short zoomie-style headers must make quite a racket. The ground-smooth block, billet clamps on the fuel line, and modern-style coolant recovery are all permissible liberties taken on a vintage-flavor hot rod.

If you can handle a little extra length and find some room on the left side for steering, the Buick engine in your hot rod is a great choice. These engines enjoy the one of the longest period appropriate time frames, as hot rodders were installing Nailhead motors from 1953 into the 1970s. Speed equipment and dress-up items are available, and one look at a Buick motor with a finned-aluminum valley cover, valve covers, and ignition wire covers is enough to convince any hot rodder to build it better with a Buick.

Chrysler Hemi

Hemi. The word simply means power. No engine strikes fear into an opponent quite like having a Hemi under the hood. When Chrysler introduced the 331 Hemi in 1951, the 180-hp rating instantly captured hot rodders' attention. That was a huge amount of horsepower in stock form, but the power came in a big, heavy package making adapting it to early Ford frames a bit challenging. Hemi history is as simple as 1, 2, 3. In 1951, Chrysler introduced the Firepower Hemi motor with the 331, then in 1952 DeSoto brought out its own version of the Hemi, the Firedome 276-ci engine that was good for 160 hp. It became ever more powerful over the years with 291 ci in 1955 upped to 330 and 341 ci in 1956.

In 1953, Dodge brought out the Red Ram Hemi, a small 241-ci motor that delivered a respectable 140 hp. This motor is affectionately known as the "Baby Hemi" in hot rod circles due to its diminutive size. Like most babies, the Hemi grew quickly; in 1955 it was 270 ci and by 1956 it was up to 315 ci. A special dual-quad, solid-lifter motor could be ordered that produced 315 hp in 1957, arriving at that magical one-hp-per-inch level.

The Chrysler Hemi remained at 331 ci for five years, keeping pace with Cadillac until displacement grew to 354 ci in 1956. In 1957 the biggest Hemi of all was introduced, the elephant motor; the 392-ci Hemi went on to dominate Top Fuel drag racing for years, and occasionally found its way between the rails of a street-driven hot rod. It was an elephant motor in every sense of the word—size, power, and weight with the 392 tipping the scales at just under 750 pounds, which is a whopping 175 pounds more than the small-block Chevy, but a small price to put a Hemi under the hood.

If a Hemi is planned for your project, bear in mind there are virtually no shared parts between Chrysler, Dodge, and DeSoto engines, so find a complete engine and go from there. Rebuilding the Hemi will cost a lot more than a Chevy, but in the end you'll have a motor that will garner a whole lot more attention and bring nods of approval from vintage hot rod lovers. Consider the Red Ram as a better fit for many early hot rods, but I've seen the big 392 Hemi shoe-horned into everything from a Model T to a mid-1950 pickup trucks.

Remember the weight and provide springs and tire sizes designed to support the load. Speed equipment is out there, albeit often expensive, and transmissions can be adapted to the early motors.

Pontiac Motors

Pontiac motors were never as popular as many of the other GM offerings. This is because Pontiac was "a little late to the dance." While

This small-block Chevrolet motor is typical of a late-1960s hot rod. Single 4-barrel intake, finned valve covers, and white headers combine with yellow ignition wires for a real 1960s feel. That dual master cylinder would have been state of the art in 1967, when they were introduced on most cars. Billy Ray Long drives his coupe regularly.

The ultimate blending of old and new comes from Hilborn, the fuel-injection people. This may look like the same system you saw on top of junior fuel dragsters, but look closely and you'll see this is an electronic-fuel-injection system with completely modern controls. The finned-aluminum center fuel rail blends in perfectly.

PERIOD POWER

One of the most distinctive motors for vintage hot rods is the 348/409 series. These "W-head" motors look great and perform well. This motor appears to be a 409 because there is no dipstick on the driver's side of the motor. Modern A/C brackets and alternator brackets are available. These engines are wider and longer than a small-block Chevy, so plan ahead when building one. Jiggs Lindhorst put this 409 in a Deuce roadster.

Achieving the proper look often involves stair casing the carburetors with simple tubular spacers. It sure looks good on Paul Duval's flathead.

Pontiac engineers had begun development of a V-8 engine in 1946, the new V-8 was not in production until 1955, which was the same year that Chevrolet introduced the fabled small-block Chevy motor. While it was a well-designed engine with solid performance, it was seldom used in hot rodding because the lighter, quick-revving Chevrolet became the engine of choice. The 1955 Pontiac 287-ci motor grew the next year to 316 ci and then progressed through the 347, 389, 326, 421, and 428 motors.

In the late 1950s and throughout the 1960s, Pontiac took on a performance image, and while Pontiac cars were popular with hot rodders, the number of engine swaps using Pontiac engines pale in comparison to other offerings. Performance options from the factory were many and ranged from single 4-barrels to three deuces, dual quads, and even the early Rochester fuel injection on the first Bonneville models. Running such factory offerings is a great way to date your vintage hot rod.

Using a Pontiac engine in a vintage hot rod today is equally as rare, but the motors are available and affordable in comparison to other vintage motors. Speed equipment is available for the motors, and since they are externally the same, running a 326/389/421/428 engine results in the same look. The left-side starter is a bit of a problem on these motors, but they can be easily mounted to early Ford frames. Hurst made motor mounts for Pontiac in a Ford frame at one time, but today most people fabricate a set of modern-style side mounts. Pontiacs are great engines, and like any vintage motor, they are sure to start a bench racing session wherever you park.

Small-Block Chevrolet

The small-block Chevy was a mere 265 ci, but it was one potent package. Compact in size, light in weight, and suitable for just about any chassis, this motor quickly replaced the venerable Ford flathead. The little free-breathing, high-revving small-block responded to hot rod modification like few motors ever have, and it quickly became apparent there was a new king in the hot rod world.

There are many books dedicated to this engine, but for building a vintage hot rod the key is to find a vintage motor. Cubic inches ranging from 265 to 327 would be deemed appropriate with the popular 350-ci version being reserved for cars built after 1968. Visually there are subtle block and head differences. Yes, a 1969 350 is difficult to distinguish from a 1967 327 at a glance, but for the vintage hot rodder, the 283/327 reigns supreme over the later 350.

Today, many people think vintage hot rod means non-Chevrolet motors, but nothing could be further from the truth. If you were building the ultimate hot rod for 1955, the 265-ci motor would have been a natural. Today the 265 is best reserved for historically correct hot rods or restored 1955 Chevrolets. The early oiling system and lack of oil filter make these motors less than desirable. If you must have a 265, try a 1957 version, as they were the best blocks with improved oiling. The 265 engine only had front engine mounts.

The 283 is a far better choice for most hot rods, and while it was introduced in 1957, the first 283 also had front motor mounts only. This is a quick way to distinguish early motors, and if you are going for period correct, no part newer than 1957, any block with side mount castings would be inappropriate. However, if you can tolerate 1958 or newer parts, then all of the side-mount blocks are available. If possible, it is best to use 1959–1968 blocks as a neoprene rear main seal was introduced in 1959, which was a big improvement over the earlier rope seal. The casting number on these blocks is 3756519.

In 1962 the 327-ci small-block was introduced, so once again be certain this motor does not post-date your project goals. However, the 327 was the hot rod engine that put the small-block out in front. It is interesting to note that all 327 motors employ two-bolt main caps, with the improved four-bolt main cap being introduced with the 350 in 1967. For street use, the two-bolt main is adequate.

If there is any doubt the small-block was destined to be the performance leader, considers this: In the first year the motor was offered with a 4-barrel carburetor; by the second year, dual quads were available; and in 1957, fuel injection was introduced. Today, choices include all those and more—from early Hilborn injection to six deuces, and single 4-barrel carbs induction choices abound. One popular way to date the

It should come as no surprise that when you hang around a vintage emporium, like Honest Charley's Speed Shop in Chattanooga, Tennessee, you're going to come across some very cool parts like these SP carburetor air horns for the ever-popular Stromberg 97 carburetors. I could find little information about these pieces, but they sure are cool.

Used speed equipment is a bargain and a gamble. These finned-aluminum pans for small-block Chevrolets were very popular in the late 1960s, but many hot rodders have had the misfortune of hitting their cast-aluminum pan on the way out of a steep driveway and cracking it wide open. Maybe that's why you just don't see these around anymore.

The fenderwell headers on this 1940 coupe were built in the late 1950s in California, and somehow they have survived all these years. Bob Van Horn cleaned them up, made minor repairs, and had them coated to preserve them. It appears all welding was done with an oxy-acetylene torch. Nice work.

small-block is to employ Corvette performance parts from the correct period. While seldom seen today, a Rochester fuel-injected small-block is certain to draw a crowd. Dual quads can be arranged inline, on a tunnel ram, or a cross-ram intake according to the date of your motor. For the most part, tunnel rams and cross-ram intakes should be relegated to cars built in the late 1960s.

Attention to detail such as using iron heads with the better castings marks and double hump or camel heads add vintage flavor. Using a front breather tube on the intake gives the engine an early look. Many hot rodders know a lot about small-block motors, so take special care to select your parts carefully to fit the year of your car.

W-Head Chevrolet

In 1958 Chevrolet introduced the new 348-ci, Turbo-Jet V-8 engine. While the Turbo-Jet V-8 may be the corporate nomenclature, hot rodders simply refer to it as a W-head motor. One look at the valve covers explains the name.

The motor was powerful, with a stock 250 hp the first year. In 1961 the famed and feared 409 was introduced producing 360 hp. It was the 409 and the success it enjoyed at drag strips that would forever put the W-head motor on the list of all-time-great motors. By the time production ended, the "09" was making 425 hp.

Building a vintage hot rod with a 348/409 is a great way to capture the 1958–1962 feeling. Bear in mind these motors are heavier, longer, and wider than the small-block, and fitting one between the frame rails of a 1928–1934 Ford means hood side modifications. But why hide a cool motor with hood sides?

It is best to avoid the 1958 model as it was produced with rope rear seals, while 1959 and later models had a conventional two-piece neoprene seal. The easiest way to spot a 409 is by looking for the dipstick on the passenger side; the 348 has the dipstick on the driver's side of the motor. Prices on buildable 409 motors have skyrocketed in recent years, and with the introduction of several different aluminum heads for these motors, the popularity is certain to continue. Unless you simply must have a 409, I recommend going for the 348 motor. There are ample buildable motors available, and the core motor will cost you about 1/3 the price of a 409. Having said that, keep your eye out for 409 motors as they were also used in trucks.

Dress-up goodies for the W-head are available at swap meets, and Edelbrock, Moon, and Offenhauser offer finned-aluminum valve covers. The tin valve covers offer a factory performance look when chrome plated or simply painted silver.

Adapting the GM transmission of your choice is not a problem with the W-head family, making this a great motor for your vintage project. Factory three-deuce and dual-quad applications were available, but aftermarket manifold suppliers such as Edelbrock and Offenhauser offer new manifolds, and Sanderson has headers that work well with most hot rod applications.

Because most early hot rods were driven on the street and raced, accommodations were generally made to open the pipes when racing and cap them for street driving as seen on Lewis McMillan's roadster. This very traditional cap pipe is typical of the era. Later a variation on the theme, called lake pipes, were made available; the name indicated they were used when racing on dry lakes.

Building vintage motors often required ingenuity and craftsmanship. The fabricated stainless exhaust manifolds on this early Cadillac motor are similar to the stock units but hug the block to clear the steering.

Oddball Stuff

Hot rodders are a crafty bunch, and for that reason you may see almost any engine relocated in a hot rod over the years. This may have occurred because someone just happened to have a 1956 Packard 374-ci motor that pumped out 290 hp, so he put it in his 1946 Ford coupe. I put a blown 289 Studebaker motor in a 1940 coupe in 1971, after buying a wrecked Studebaker Golden Hawk for $100. They were rare then and even more so today, but using an obscure engine in your vintage hot rod can be fun and is almost guaranteed to be challenging. Be prepared to do all your own fabrication for motor mounts and alternator brackets. Transmission adapters will be non-existent and dress-up goodies may be limited to chrome plating stock items, but in the end you'll have one very cool vintage hot rod.

In Summary

Finally, regardless of the make and vintage engine deemed correct for your vintage hot rod, I suggest that you assemble the engine yourself. Few things are more rewarding than spending a weekend putting a hot rod motor together on an engine stand. This process gives you a direct connection to your hot rod and makes roadside repairs easier. While the crate motors of today are great items, painting a motor out of the box pales in comparison to actually touching every internal piece. Engine building at home is one of the great vintage hot rod traditions; one that we should strive to preserve.

A simple chrome fuel block is found on the Mallory 1940 coupe, but what's important is the use of flare fittings on the copper lines. I have seen extensive use of compression fittings on motors, but a single flare fitting is much safer due to the superior sealing ability of the flare.

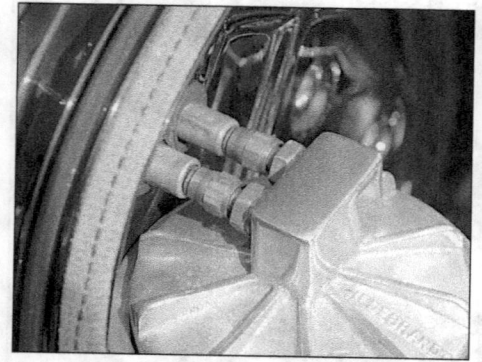

The Hildebrandt remote oil filters were a staple for hot rodders in the 1950s and 1960s, and while originals can be found, O'Brien Truckers makes a faithful reproduction that employs a modern canister-style filter, which provides full-flow filtering. The trick is to make your connecting hoses using vintage-style brass crimp collars and fittings.

Seldom seen today, but very typical of the early 1960s hot rod scene, is this simple chrome oil filter cover. Like many less-expensive accessories, they were not always the best quality but did provide that all-important splash of chrome.

CHAPTER 3

ROLLING STOCK: CHOOSING WHEELS, TIRES AND ACCESSORIES

Wheels and tires. Few pieces of the hot rodding puzzle provide more influence on the overall mood of the finished car than wheel and tire selection. It is imperative to get it right when choosing wheels for your hot rod. When shopping for that perfect wheel-and-tire combination, be certain you haven't missed your target date with the wrong-size whitewall, tire construction, or improper wheel selection. Beyond date, the proper diameter and width must also be considered; and a word of advice: Make no compromises on your hot rod wheels.

In the earliest days of hot rodding, the choices were simple—factory wire wheels or factory steel rims. The 1935 Ford wire wheels were popular with many of the early street-driven hot rods, but they were seldom seen at the dry lakes, Bonneville, or on the drag strip. The solid-steel rim was favored because it had superior strength; it remained true and was easier to balance. All of these attributes made it less likely to have any type of high-speed wheel shake. Since most hot rods were upgraded to hydraulic brakes, the 1936–1938 Ford rims were seldom seen, with the later 1939–1948 rims being more common.

Because racing over dry lake beds, drag strips on old concrete air strips (hence the term "drag strip"), or the salt flats all involved running high speeds over a less than perfectly smooth surface, hubcaps had a low survival rate. They would generally

No single hot rod component can dictate mood and period better than the wheel. Wheels allow a car to travel forward and back in time. For example, this black Deuce coupe just shouts vintage hot rod because of the Moon discs and whitewall tires, placing the car firmly in the 1950s. If this same car installed billet wheels and black walls it would move forward forty years in time.

HOW TO BUILD PERIOD CORRECT HOT RODS   37

fly off the wheel, leading to the practice of running no hubcaps on race cars, and many race sanctioning bodies later banned hubcaps during competition. Since many street rods were also part-time racers or at least wanted to look the part, the trend toward steel rims with no hubcaps became a popular look that lasted into the 1960s. Chrome lug nuts, dust caps, and stainless-steel trim rings were used to dress up the bare wheels. It was common to paint the wheels a bright contrasting color, such as red, orange, apple green, or yellow, and for a bit more money you could buy a chrome reverse rim. It's a look that is enjoying a resurgence as street rodders emulate the vintage style of early hot rods.

If you're building a pre-1958 hot rod, wire wheels, steel wheels, or early Halibrand wheels are the only choices. And as for accessories, hubcaps and whitewalls are are just the beginning.

Wire Wheels

Wire wheels don't seem to be very mainstream, yet they have always been a part of hot rodding. As mentioned earlier, the 1935 Ford wire wheel was popular with early hot rodders, and today a set of these wire wheels (new or original) wrapped with a set of bias-ply tires makes a real hot rod statement. When it comes to buying and refurbishing wire wheels, it is often a wise choice to buy new wheels. Truing a set of 75-year-old wire wheels can be a real chore, and if pitted, rust is a factor, and wheel strength and sealing capabilities may both be compromised. A new set of powder-coated wire wheels will save you time, look better, and be a safer wheel than the original.

Speaking of safety, it is common practice to see widened wire wheels on the back of a hot rod, and if you are running a set of bias-ply dirt tracker tires, you are probably just

The great looks of 1935 Ford wire wheels come from the fact that they are 16-inch wheels. However, all Ford wire wheels were designed for cars with mechanical brakes. When using 1928–1935 Ford wire wheels on a car with hydraulic drum brakes, a support plate must be run inside the wheel. This prevents the lug nuts from loosening and strengthens the wheel to prevent cracking around the spokes. The support rings are available from Speedway Motors, Honest Charley, and others.

The good news is brand-new 1935 Ford-style wire wheels are available today, and your options are many. This roadster owner opted for a black center and red rims, with stainless spokes connecting the two. It's a good look. Companies such as Wheel Smith can also help with mating wire wheels to large drum brakes, disc brakes, and other combinations. This is one instance when buying new makes sense.

A modern tire on a vintage wheel is a good combination for driving, and this owner added a gold line around the wheel at the tire bead for a very effective detailed look.

fine. However, if you're running a big set of radial tires, remember that a radial tire is capable of exerting much greater side force on a wheel than the bias ply, so those 75-year-old spokes might not be up to the loads exerted upon them.

This is a great-looking set of early Ford wire wheels; these are 17-inch wheels, probably off a 1934 Ford, and they appear to be in excellent condition. They measure 17x5 inches with a 5½-inch bolt pattern. While these wheels look great, there is no way to tell if they run true until they are installed.

If vintage wires are your choice, be prepared to run tubes in the tires and always be certain you have radial tubes for radial tires and regular tubes for the bias-ply tires. Although some tire experts say you can mix radials and bias-ply tires on the same car, I recommend avoiding that combination at all costs as it will affect the handling of your chassis.

In the 1950s, Buick, Cadillac, Ford Thunderbird, and Chrysler all had wire wheel offerings. These wheels were designed to carry a heavier load than the early wire wheels and for that reason they found their way onto some hot rods. Finding a set of good original Buick wire wheels can take some time, and unless you plan on painting the wheels, you are better off buying a set of reproduction wire wheels with brand-new chrome plating. Companies, such as Dayton Wire Wheel, have new wire wheels in many vintage and contemporary designs.

Steel Wheels

At first glance, you might think all steel wheels are created equally, but that is hardly the case. There are steelies, smoothies, and many in between. Some wheels have clips that hold the hubcap in place, while others have ears stamped into the wheel to lock the hubcap in place. Even the contour of the wheel center is different on a 1940s steel wheel than it is on a 1950s or 1960s wheel. Minor details, but these details are what make a vintage hot rod authentic. Unlike earlier wire wheels, if you can find a good set of rust-free steel wheels, they can easily be used on a hot rod today. Finishes are generally limited to paint or powder coating, as the popular chrome reverse wheel is generally best purchased new. If you have vintage wheels with attractive centers, the wheels can be widened and companies, such as the Stockton Wheel Company and others, can change the offset.

As cars became heavier more spokes were added to the wheels, and expensive cars of the 1950s had chrome wire wheels as options, including Cadillac, Chrysler, Buick, and Ford Thunderbird. These Kelsey-Hayes Thunderbird wheels are rare, but the good news is they are available in reproduction form from companies such as Coker Tire and others.

The steel wheel quickly replaced the wire wheel for most hot rodders. The added strength and ease of mounting and balancing tires made these wheels a big step forward, particularly for cars that would be racing on the rougher surfaces of a dry lake bed or dirt track.

Steel wheels came in styles beyond the smooth rim, and in the late 1930s the artillery wheel was very popular on new cars. Chrysler, Dodge, and Plymouth used these wheels extensively, and they make a great addition to any vintage hot rod. Due to minor differences from various years you must shop carefully to find a complete matching set. Since the band width of these early wheels is generally less than six inches, plan on having the rear wheels widened. If all this sounds like too much work, you'll be glad to know that reproduction artillery wheels are available from companies such as The Wheelsmith, and they come in 15-inch diameters with widths ranging from 4.5 to 10 inches.

Steel wheels can be used with or without hubcaps, and often the simple look of chrome lug nuts on a painted rim is the best choice. Spider Caps cover the five lug nuts and the center hub in an attractive manner, and they look particularly good with the small center trim ring.

Birth of the Mag Wheel

The first dedicated magnesium race wheel can be traced back to Ted Halibrand. After working in the Southern California aircraft industry during World War II, he became familiar with new and exotic aircraft metals, such as magnesium. He was quick to realize that the light weight and strength of magnesium would make it an excellent choice for race car parts. After the war ended, it didn't take Halibrand long to cast his first 18-inch-diameter racing wheels for championship race cars.

Those first wheels were cast in 1946, and that year a set of Halibrand wheels rolled to victory at the Indy 500. The wheels became an instant hit with racers because of the weight savings and strength. These early wheels were located on the hub by six blind studs, with a knock-off holding the wheel tightly against the face of the drum. Not long after, Halibrand offered bolt-on wheels for virtually every type of race car.

Later the company manufactured kidney bean and 12-spoke spindle-mount wheels for both early Ford spindles and Anglia spindles. These spindle mounts became the wheel of choice for winning drag race teams from the gasser wars to altereds and some early top fuel cars. Of course, wheels of this caliber didn't come cheap, so only the top-tier racers and hot rodders were able to afford the real Halibrand mag wheels.

Halibrand wheels were racing and winning around the world and quickly became known for their high quality, and it is from this very wheel that the term "mag wheel" was

Since hubcaps tend to fly off during race events, the bare steel wheel was the look of many early hot rods that doubled as race cars. Chrome lug nuts dressed up the wheel a bit.

The chrome reverse wheel is a standard among hot rodders and was originally just that, a wheel that had the outer band reversed to provide more offset. Today the chrome reverse is available in myriad sizes and offsets and still looks great on a hot rod. Grooved slicks are a wise choice for street driving.

Spider Caps were a popular accessory that covered the lug nuts and the spindle on the front wheel. Beauty rings dress up the wheel even more, and in this case double pinstripes were added. Pinstriping wheels involves a stationary brush and rotating wheel.

Artillery wheels are generally associated with Chrysler and GM products. They look great on vintage hot rods of any make. Steel wheels and bright colors just seem to work well together.

How To Scallop-Paint Wheels

When Larry Shoaf chose the wheels for his 1927 Chrysler roadster, he wanted to keep that Chrysler flavor alive, and to that end a set of artillery wheels were used. After trying to find four matching 1936 Chrysler artillery wheels, he found two slightly different style wheels, possibly illustrating that different suppliers made slightly different centers. A call to Wheelsmith ended the frustration with a set of four new wheels.

The Shoaf roadster was originally going to have cream scallops over the blue paint, but when Larry painted the blue, he decided he just liked the simplicity of a single color, but that didn't mean he had forsaken scallops on the car. He thought maybe a little splash of color on the wheels would look good, and the wheels were scalloped in burgundy.

First the wheels were painted tan, and then tape was put down on the wheel. Pieces of tubing were used to draw the radius on the wheels, which were then colored in to see if the scalloped wheels would look appropriate. Satisfied that the scallops would be a good addition Shoaf made a small template of the proper radius. He then went to his local vinyl sign shop and had them computer generate a sheet of vinyl radius pieces to be the negative image of the scallop. The vinyl was carefully laid up on the wheel. Conventional masking tape covered the rest of the wheel before spraying the burgundy single-stage urethane paint on the wheel.

When the paint was dry, the tape and vinyl were removed, exposing scallops that were exactly the same shape. A simple pinstripe added to the finished look of the wheel. If you are wondering where Shoaf managed to come up with Chrysler embossed hubcaps, the same sign shop produced those red logos. When I asked Larry how he managed to measure and center the logo he said, "The fellow at the sign shop just eyeballed the location and laid them down." Later measurements indicated that a good sign man has an incredible eye, as the logos are nearly exactly in the middle of the hubcaps.

Here's a great tip for scalloping your artillery wheels. First paint the base color and mount the wheels and, tires on the car. Then mask off the rim area and, using a piece of tubing or other suitable radius, draw out the scallop on the wheel. To be certain each scallop will be the exact same size, make each scallop point end in the exact middle of each spoke. Once satisfied with the look (coloring the scallops with a Sharpie helps) take this radius measurement to your local vinyl sign shop and have them generate a couple sheets of semi-circles. Now just apply the vinyl to the wheel, tape off the rest of the outer wheel, and spray your color.

Add a little pinstriping around the scallop if you like, and then pop the hubcap in place for a very nice custom-finished wheel. That Chrysler logo on the hubcap came from the same vinyl sign shop. Like any modification, patience is the key here, and the rewards are obvious.

coined. From LeMans to Indy to the local drag strip and oval track, Halibrand wheels were popular with road racing, oval racing, drag racing, and even salt flat racing, so today any automotive enthusiast recognizes the Halibrand name. The wheels were not only strong and light, they were beautifully designed to incorporate form and function in a most distinguished manner. As time went by, the term mag wheel was applied to many aluminum wheels as well, but as long as Ted Halibrand owned the company, he only cast wheels in magnesium. When Halibrand was sold in 1979, the new owners began to cast the famous Halibrand Kidney Bean (small window) and Sprint (big window) wheels in aluminum.

Later, when the aluminum versions became widely available, more and more street rods were seen running the iconic Halibrand wheels. Since magnesium oxidizes quickly, particularly in the presence of moisture, running a set of real magnesium wheels brings serious maintenance problems. Many of the original wheels were coated with Dow #7 to help protect against oxidation, a coating that gave a gold cast to the wheels. While it was not particularly durable, it did help fight moisture-related problems, and many hot rodders relate that soft gold hue to magnesium today.

Halibrand wheels were made in many bolt patterns based on

By the 1950s, Halibrand Engineering was manufacturing lightweight and strong magnesium wheels. They were cast of real magnesium and designed for racing. Hot rodders were quick to notice, and these great looking wheels found their way on to many fine street rods of the day.

The lightweight wheels and lack of front brakes on many race cars made the 12-spoke spindle-mount wheel the choice of many winning altered and gasser drag cars. Like all Halibrand products, they had a perfect blend of form and function—they worked well and looked beautiful doing it.

As tire technology changed so did Halibrand mag wheels. These monsters were no doubt designed for the rear of a Top Fuel car, but today they reside on the rear of Bob Sargis' fenderless 1940 pickup. They measure 16x14 inches, wrapped with Firestone dirt track rubber.

Halibrand wheels are still out there at swap meets, and they command a hefty price. This 15x6-inch wheel was priced at $400, but it has the all-important Halibrand name cast in the wheel.

Because Halibrand never produced aluminum wheels until after Ted Halibrand sold the company in 1979, to be period correct a 1950s, 1960s, or 1970s hot rod should run magnesium wheels, which means hitting the swap meets for a find like this. However, since the aluminum wheels are identical in design and better suited for street use the aluminum wheel is generally accepted as proper for everything except the most stringent restorations.

ROLLING STOCK: CHOOSING WHEELS, TIRES AND ACCESSORIES

Bring plenty of cash if you're in the market for real magnesium wheels. On the left is a set of spindle-mount Halibrands carrying a price tag of $1,500. The twelve-spoke magnesium American Racing wheels on the right were listed for $1,100.

Mag Wheel Manufacturers

While select hot rods ran real Halibrand wheels, it is safe to say that the real transformation from steel rims, hubcaps, and wire wheels took place in the early 1960s when mag wheels were mass produced in aluminum to fit virtually any application. From Corvettes to muscle cars and traditional hot rods, it seemed by the mid-1960s every car was rolling on mag wheels of one brand or another. Some dealers were even offering dealer-installed options of mag wheels. Hot rodding had reached fever pitch. The car manufacturers were making ever more powerful cars, and hot rodders were responding by purchasing the cars and also by purchasing these new engines and mag wheels for their hot rods.

15-inch-diameter wheels with widths ranging from 4½ inches to 8 inches. Huge rear Sprint wheels for Top Fuel and Funny Cars measured 16x13 inches.

Today's Halibrand wheels are only available in aluminum, and after a series of financial woes it appears the wheels are again being produced under the Halibrand name. There are any number of Halibrand-style wheels being manufactured by other companies that provide the look and attitude of the original.

American Racing Wheels

When American Racing came on the scene in 1959, it focused on race applications. Competing with Halibrand, American Racing was casting

While Halibrand was the early leader in true mag wheels, the American Racing five-spoke wheel launched a new wave of mag wheels, even though most of them were cased in aluminum for the street. These are wrapped with Hurst slicks.

The Ansen Sprint and similar wheels came on the heels of the five-spoke mag and were very popular through the 1970s and 1980s. These wheels are plentiful at swap meets and are appropriate for 1970s-style hot rods.

HOW TO BUILD PERIOD CORRECT HOT RODS

wheels in magnesium, with the five- and twelve-spoke designs being very popular with racers. These very early magnesium wheels have a smooth rim face and the spokes were round. In 1963 the five-spoke aluminum wheel called the Torque Thrust was introduced. They were available in a limited number of sizes, but in the early 1960s wheel widths were not as varied as today. The original Torque Thrust wheel came in either 14- or 15-inch-diameter wheels with widths of 6, 7, or 8½ inches available. There was a thin lip added to the face of the rim, and the spokes had a center peak line sometimes referred to as an A-spoke. On the inside of the American Racing Torque Thrust wheel, you will find the company name cast in script. If it doesn't say American Racing Equipment on the aluminum wheel, another company made it.

In 1965, when disc brakes were available on Corvettes, the wheel had to be modified to clear the brake calipers. These wheels were named the Torque-Thrust D, with the "D" being an obvious reference to the disc brake application. These wheels proved to be very popular with Corvette owners, as they were one of the

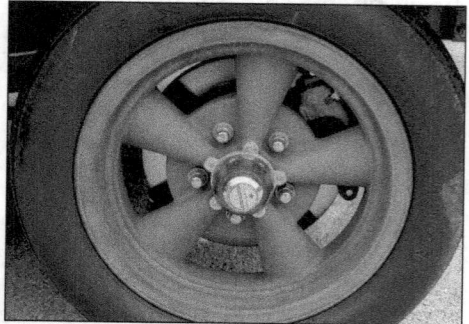

This is an early American Racing wheel with the round spokes and what appears to be mildly oxidized magnesium. Keeping magnesium polished is a full-time job if there is humidity in the air.

While many people believe all early American Torque Thrusts have a five-screw flange, that is inaccurate. Some wheels were manufactured with a round center. This wheel is 14x7-inch on 4¾-inch bolt pattern. I also had a set of 15x6-inch in the same design.

With the Etchison Machine center in place, the wheel takes on a certain spindle-mount appearance. My guess is these wheels came out in the late 1960s or 1970s, as the spokes are peaked but not D-spoke style.

American Racing also made some spindle-mount wheels; they are rather rare today. Also keep in mind there are a limited number of brakes that will work with spindle-mount wheels.

The back side of this wheel clearly shows the American Racing logo. All aluminum wheels from American Racing have a similar cast name somewhere on the back side of the wheel.

Today, the fully polished American Racing Torque Thrust wheel is king of the hill again. This is the most popular wheel on the hot rod scene today, and while it is a great-looking wheel, there are other options that might help make your next project unique. An aftermarket center cap replaces the standard plastic cap on this wheel.

first aftermarket wheels designed to clear the new disc brakes. And oh yeah, they looked great on Corvettes.

Today, American Racing has reintroduced the classic Torque Thrust in a larger variety of back spacing and rim widths. If you are building a true 1960s hot rod, it is best to search out a set of the early wheels as there are minor differences in the cap spacing, lug nuts, and spoke shapes that a real vintage hot rodder will appreciate.

Cragar Wheels

Production of the Cragar mag wheel (generally referred to as the Cragar S/S) began in 1962, but the company's roots go all the way back to the 1930s when Cragar was part of George Wight's Bell Auto Parts, one of the first speed shops in the country. Roy Richter worked at Bell and was an immensely talented pattern maker, designer, fabricator, and mechanic. It took two years of design and testing for Richter to perfect the final Cragar S/S. He later went on to own Bell and Cragar.

The Cragar S/S was one of the first wheels to employ a cast-aluminum center joined to a steel rolled rim. The entire wheel was chrome plated, making it the first all-chrome five-spoke wheel. It proved to be very popular, and today the Cragar S/S is nearly as iconic as the American Torque Thrust. Cragar wheels gained popularity with the muscle car and pony car set and were available in all popular 14- and 15-inch-diameter sizes with widths ranging from 4½ to 10 inches. These wheels were designed for street cars, but many gassers and other race cars employed them. Over the years, there were variations of the Cragar S/S, including some uni-lug wheels and other applications, but none of the vintage wheels were ever larger than 15 inches in diameter.

The classic Cragar S/S is still being produced today, and they are now available in 14-, 15-, and 17-inch diameters. Building a true 1950s or 1960s hot rod will limit you to the use of 14- and 15-inch wheels with the most common wheel combination being 14x6 inches up front and 15x7 or 8½ inches on the rear. Cragar S/S is still a great-looking wheel today and a perfect fit for any hot rod looking for a 1962 and later flavor.

Of course, that's the easy way, since the S/S is still in production. But for those who either have an authentic 1960s hot rod or want that something extra on their car, Cragar built other more obscure wheels in the 1960s. In the late 1960s the company produced the Cragar S/X, a very rare one-piece cast wheel resembling the Torque Thrust, but with a rounded lip leading to the spokes. The wheels were available in 14x6; I know that only because I have seen a set. The wheels are so rare that I have not been able to find any information on other available sizes.

I personally owned a set of Cragar S/S wheels that I purchased in 1966. They were the classic S/S wheels, but the spokes were polished aluminum, not chrome plated. I have never seen another set of these since, but I bought them used in 1966 and can vividly remember having to polish the aluminum spokes. They were great-looking wheels. So, if you have the patience, there are some super-rare Cragar wheels that are certain to start some great bench racing stories, and set your hot rod apart from the crowd.

Rocket Wheels

Although Rocket Wheels were one of the many wheels to come on the scene during the mag-wheel heyday, I mention them mostly because the company name has resurfaced with a line of wheels that are well

Cragar wheels are yet another icon of hot rodding. These high-quality wheels are distinct due to the complete chrome-plated finish. Cragar wheels are still manufactured today and make a great wheel for any vintage hot rod.

Rocket Wheel was one of many manufacturers in the late 1960s with a style similar to the Torque Thrust. It is back in a big way with a full line of great-looking wheels, with popular offsets and sizes. This is the Rocket Igniter wheel, and once again it seems all mag wheel styles can be traced back to either Halibrand or American Racing.

suited for vintage-flavor hot rods. While the wheels look period correct, they have been altered from the original—maybe improved from the original wheels would be more accurate. Today, Rocket Wheels are one-piece cast wheels with far superior finishes, machining, and size selection than the original 1970s wheel. If you are building a vintage-flavor hot rod, these wheels allow you to have a very traditional look but with modern tire sizes and at a surprisingly affordable price. Of course, they are available in the more traditional sizes too.

The Rocket five- and ten-spoke offerings are great-looking wheels, and Rocket has done its homework during the building process and can fit all popular offsets and widths. The Rocket Igniter carries a heavy Halibrand influence, while the Rocket Launcher is its ten-spoke wheel. The other great feature of these wheels is the diverse finishes, ranging from as cast to fully polished, full chrome plating, or machined finish. And there are a myriad combinations of the finishes available too.

Rader Wheels

Dick Rader started this company in 1961 and was one of the early entries in the new mag-wheel market. The wheels were marketed in conjunction with Mickey Thompson from 1964 to 1966 as M/T Rader wheels and were offered in more different finishes than most wheels of the day, including polished, cast, chrome, polished rim, unpolished spokes, and even painted spokes in several different colors. This makes Rader wheels a unique opportunity for a different, yet correct wheel for vintage hot rods. In 1967 Rader reintroduced the original Rader wheel along with other styles, and the M/T was dropped from the name. Competition in the wheel market was intense at this time, and Rader closed its doors in 1969.

The new Radir Wheel Company, established in 1995 (note the slightly different spelling), put the wheel back into production. The new wheel is a one-piece cast unit that is available in 14x6-inch and 15x4-, 6-, 7,- 8-, and 10-inch widths. Radir also makes a very nice 12-spoke aluminum spindle-mount wheels that is popular with vintage hot rodders and drag racers. Speaking of drag racing, Radir also offers classic 2¼-inch whitewall slicks produced in conjunction with Mickey Thompson, so as you can see, things in the hot rodding community tend to come full circle.

The Radir wheel is period perfect for your 1960s-style hot rod, and the new wheels are of higher quality than the early wheels. Finding a set of early M/T Radar centers would make the wheels more period correct.

This is simply the ultimate hot rod rear wheel. Today, the ET III is manufactured as a one-piece cast wheel, but the original iteration was a two-piece wheel that interlocked in the middle of the band. This design was brought about for drag racers to make it faster and easier to change those big slicks between rounds. The

Rader wheels were fairly short-lived in the 1960s, and were sold as M/T Rader wheels for a couple of years before the company closed in the late 1960s. The wheels are back in production today by a company called Radir, a slight variation on the name.

Team 3 Wheels produces the ET line of wheels, and this is its new Dragmaster. Available in several finishes, it is a great-looking wheel and built to a very high standard. There are also a spindle-mount and a five-lug-mount version of this wheel.

ROLLING STOCK: CHOOSING WHEELS, TIRES AND ACCESSORIES

Size	WW Width	Construction	Load Capacity	TW	CS	OD
520-13	2	4 PLY POLY	770@32PSI	3.80	5.50	23.10
560-13	2 1/4	4 PLY POLY	850@30PSI	3.55	5.94	23.66
700-13	5/8	4 PLY POLY	1270@32PSI	4.70	6.90	24.78
750-14	2 1/4	4 PLY POLY	1580@32PSI	4.25	7.52	26.89
775-14	7/8	4 PLY POLY	1580@32PSI	4.50	7.65	27.02
775-14	3/8 RED GLD	4 PLY POLY	1580@32PSI	4.50	7.65	27.02
560-15*	1	4 PLY POLY	970@32PSI	3.80	5.96	25.79
560-15*	2 3/4	4 PLY POLY	970@32PSI	3.80	5.96	25.79
640-15	2 1/8	4 PLY POLY	1190@32PSI	4.45	6.61	27.01
670-15	1	4 PLY POLY	1450@32PSI	4.50	7.01	28.58
670-15	2 1/4	4 PLY POLY	1450@32PSI	4.50	7.01	28.58
670-15*	2 11/16	4 PLY POLY	1450@32PSI	4.50	7.01	28.58

Size	WW Width	Construction	Load Capacity	TW	CS	OD
670-15*	3 1/4	4 PLY POLY	1450@32PSI	4.50	7.01	28.58
700-15**	4 1/8	4 PLY POLY	1700@32PSI	5.38	7.40	29.29
710-15*	2 3/4	4 PLY POLY	1550@32PSI	4.50	7.70	28.88
710-15*	3 1/4	4 PLY POLY	1550@32PSI	4.50	7.70	28.88
775-15	5/8	4 PLY POLY	1490@32PSI	4.70	7.28	27.36
775-15	7/8	4 PLY POLY	1490@32PSI	4.70	7.28	27.36
775-15	3/8 RED, GLD	4 PLY POLY	1490@32PSI	4.70	7.65	27.24
820-15*	3 1/2	4 PLY POLY	1920@32PSI	5.00	8.35	29.56
820-15*	4 1/4	4 PLY POLY	1920@32PSI	5.00	8.35	29.56
890-15	3	8 PR POLY	2500@40PSI	5.00	8.80	31.00
890-15	5	8 PR POLY	2500@40PSI	5.00	8.80	31.00
450/475-16**	2 1/4	4 PLY POLY	660@30PSI	3.80	4.75	26.20

Size	WW Width	Construction	Load Capacity	TW	CS
500/525-16	2 1/4	4 PLY POLY	1070@32PSI	3.75	5.26
550-16	2 1/2	4 PR POLY	840@32PSI	4.25	6.06
600-16*	3 1/4	4 PLY POLY	1400@32PSI	4.63	6.26
600-16*	3 1/4 DBL WHITEWALL	4 PLY POLY	1400@32PSI	4.63	6.26
600-16	KNOBBY	4 PLY POLY	1400@32PSI	4.63	6.26
185HR16	CAVALINO	4 PLY POLY	1355@35PSI	4.75	7.44
650-16	3 1/4 nonscript	4 PLY POLY	1580@32PSI	5.10	7.00
650-16*	4	4 PLY POLY	1580@32PSI	5.10	7.00
650-16	KNOBBY	4 PLY POLY	1580@32PSI	5.10	7.00
670-16	-	6 PR POLY	1130@30PSI	4.75	6.77
700-16*	4	6 PR POLY	1800@36PSI	5.60	8.09

Size	WW Width	Construction	Load Capacity	TW	CS
750-16*	4 1/2	8 PR POLY	1660@40 PSI	4.96	8.28
525/550-17*	3	4 PLY POLY	955@32PSI	4.00	5.91
525/550-17*	3 DBL WHITEWALL	4 PLY POLY	955@32PSI	4.00	5.91
600/650-17*	4	6 PLY POLY	1320@36PSI	4.38	7.20
700-17*	4 1/4	6 PLY POLY	1480@36PSI	5.66	8.25
700-17*	4 1/4 DBL WHITEWALL	6 PLY POLY	1480@36PSI	5.66	8.25
750-17*	4 3/4	8 PLY POLY	1870@40PSI	6.32	8.25
750-17*	4 3/4 DBL WHITEWALL	8 PLY POLY	1870@40PSI	6.32	8.25
12/13/14x45		4 PR POLY	1000@50PSI	3.75	4.90
550-18*	3 1/4	4 PLY POLY	1125@32PSI	4.30	5.94
550-18*	3 1/4 DBL WHITEWALL	4 PLY POLY	1125@32PSI	4.30	5.94
600/650-18*	3 3/4	4 PLY POLY	1205@36PSI	4.50	5.75

Size	WW Width	Construction	Load Capacity	TW	CS	OD
700-18*	4 1/4	6 PLY POLY	1520@36PSI	5.66	8.00	32.50
700-18*	4 1/4 DBL WHITEWALL	6 PLY POLY	1520@36PSI	5.66	8.00	32.50
750-18*	4 3/4	8 PLY POLY	1930@40PSI	6.23	8.60	33.80
750-18*	4 3/4 DBL WHITEWALL	8 PR POLY	1930@40PSI	6.23	8.60	33.80
450-19		4 PLY POLY	900@32PSI	4.00	5.00	29.50
475/500-19*	2 5/8	4 PLY POLY	895@32PSI	3.90	5.63	29.80
550/600-19*	3 1/2	6 PR POLY	1255@36PSI	4.80	7.30	32.00
700-19*	4 1/4	6 PLY POLY	1570@36PSI	5.60	8.00	33.40
700-19*	4 1/4 DBL WHITEWALL	6 PLY POLY	1570@36PSI	5.60	8.00	33.40

Size	WW Width	Construction	Load Capacity	TW	CS	OD
750-19*	4 3/4	8 PLY POLY	1980@40PSI	6.25	7.60	35.00
14/15/16x50		4 PR NYLON	1100@50PSI	4.00	5.15	31.15
475/500-20*	2 3/8	4 PLY POLY	1170@32PSI	3.63	5.39	30.59
600-20 (30X5)	3 1/2	6 PR POLY	1400@50PSI	4.88	6.30	32.63
650-20* (32X6)	3 3/4	6 PR POLY	2120@60PSI	5.20	7.82	34.58
650-20	truck black	6 PR NYLON	2120@60PSI	5.20	7.80	34.60
700-20	4 1/4	8 PLY POLY	1930@40PSI	5.40	7.35	34.20
440/450-21*	2 3/8	4 PLY POLY	855@32PSI	3.75	4.69	30.79
525-21*	3	6 PR POLY	1120@36PSI	4.25	5.12	31.50
700-21*	4 1/4	8 PLY POLY	1930@40PSI	5.60	8.00	35.60

Provided by Coker Tire.

Talk about the ultimate new vintage wheel, this wheel was milled from billet aluminum in a design with clear ties to the early Halibrand wheels used on Indy cars of the 1950s. The design is original and the aluminum was finished perfectly to resemble the Dow #7 gold anodized finish on the early magnesium wheels. Mike Curtis made the wheels for Pinkee's Rod Shop, and they are nothing short of stunning. Real knock-offs require safety wires.

E-T Wheels is now Team III Wheels, and they are turning out some of the finest quality wheels on the market. The original ET-III was a two-piece wheel designed to make changing slicks on dragsters easier. While the vintage wheel is sometimes used on the street, the new ET-III wheel meets or exceeds all standards for street wheels, something the old wheels can't do. For that reason using the new ET-III wheel is the way to go.

stepped center seam fits well, but inner tubes must be used with these wheels. The original ET III wheel was a one-size-fits-all wheel, and that size was 16x10 inches.

Today, Team III Wheels manufactures the ET Wheel. Although the new wheels are two-piece design, they are two completely different pieces. This time the one-piece rolled aluminum band mounts the tire while a cast-aluminum center is mounted to the band. While the building of a vintage hot rod is almost always best accomplished with true vintage parts, the Team III Wheels do not require tubes and are an overall superior design to the early wheels. If I wanted the ET-III look on a vintage hot rod, I would use the new Team III Wheels. Proper offsets and rim sizes are yet another plus. While the company name has changed to Team III Wheels, the wheels still use the vintage ET logo on the center caps, making them picture perfect for a vintage hot rod. These are very-high-quality wheels and meet or exceed all modern safety standards.

Hubcaps

There are myriad hubcaps deemed appropriate for the pre-1962 hot rod including the 1953 Oldsmobile Fiesta spinner hubcaps, Dodge Lancer, and most 1939-1948 Ford hubcaps and trim rings. Performance hubcaps came in one form, the Moon disc. These discs were used to minimize air turbulence around the wheels at high speeds, and of course, if it was good for race cars, it was good for street-going hot rods too.

Finding a good set of vintage hubcaps used to be a real challenge. Just removing and installing hubcaps accounted for many of the dents and scratches found in original caps today. The rigors of rolling for a couple hundred miles takes its toll on a hubcap too, but, happily, damaged hubcaps are no longer a problem. Once again the hot rod aftermarket has stepped up by reproducing many of the popular hubcaps from the 1950s and 1960s. Everything from the Olds Fiesta and Dodge Lancer spinner hubcaps to the more mundane small hubcaps for Chevrolet, Ford, and Chrysler products is available.

Full Moon discs are the oldest hot rod specific hubcap that I know of; and yes, Moon still spins out these hubcaps brand new. The smaller, Baby Moon or Baldie hubcap was also a popular hubcap that looks particularly good with either a smooth or ribbed beauty ring or mounted atop a chrome rim. Add a custom valvestem cap, and your wheels are fully dressed. Some of the more popular valvestem caps included miniature dice, eight-balls, and the

Cadillac built world-class cars all through the 1950s and 1960s and had hubcaps to match. The 1948–1952 Cadillac Sombrero hubcap is a study in simple elegance. The good news is they are reproduced today, and the good ones are even made in the United States. They have a special mounting system. So go reproduction and get all the right stuff, but be forewarned: They're not cheap.

When it comes to traditional hot rodding, it is still hard to beat the basic look of a steel wheel, beauty ring, and early Ford hubcap. They work well with virtually any tire and any Ford.

One of the earliest performance-only wheel accessories was the spun aluminum Moon disc. Made by the company of the same name (and, no, the name has no planetary roots), these lightweight discs were designed to reduce turbulence and drag at high speeds. The fact that they look so cool was an added bonus.

The 1950 Mercury hubcap has been a hit with hot rodders since 1950. Often referred to as pancake hubcaps, the smooth look is timeless by design. They are now available to fit both early Ford and later Chevrolet wheels from companies such as Night Prowlers.

The single-bar Hollywood is the essence of simplicity. The chrome hubcap works best with whitewalls, and painting the steel wheel red before mounting the hubcap provides the perfect splash of color.

chrome or red crown valve-stem cap. These accessories can spice up your wheels and add 1950s flavor, but like all spices they were meant to be used in moderation. Often restraint goes a long way to giving your car a clean appearance.

Evolution of the Whitewall

When talking about when the first white sidewall tire was introduced, people really have it backward. It would be more accurate to ask when the first black-wall tire was introduced. Since latex rubber in its natural state has a white color, the earliest tires were white—all white from the tread to the rim bead. The all-natural rubber proved to be too soft to last in the tread area, so carbon black was added to the tread area to toughen it up and handle the rigors of the road. The sides of these early tires remained white because the black rubber was more expensive and not needed on the sidewalls.

Since the whitewall was not yet a styling or status symbol, black tread and white sidewalls were standard fare in the teens and early twenties. Of course, keeping tires clean on those early roads was nearly impossible, so the more expensive automobiles began to offer all-black tires.

All that changed in the 1930s when automobile designers used the white sidewall as a way to brighten and enhance the wheel and tire package. This design element symbolized expensive cars, and soon all car makers were offering white-sidewall tires as options again. Since many 1930s cars had open-face fenders and non-skirted fender sides, many of the early whitewall tires were whitewall on both sides. This was particularly attractive on these early cars, and some early hot rods followed suit with whitewalls on the inside too.

Whitewalls in the 1950s and 1960s were an extra cost option, so many budget-minded rodders went to the local auto accessory store to buy a product called Port-O-Walls. Basically this was a rubber whitewall circle that was held in place by the tire bead against the rim. When installed properly they did a fine job of looking like real whitewall tires, until you scrubbed a curb. It was not uncommon to see some pretty neat cars cruising through town with a

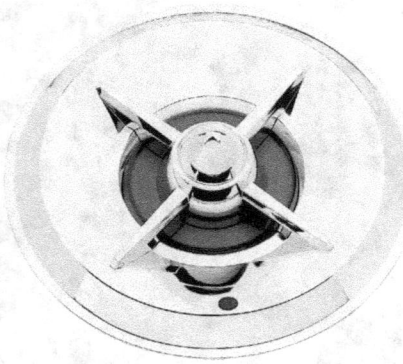

In 1957 the Dodge Lancer came with spinner hubcaps. Finding originals in good condition is tough, but luckily you can purchase them new in both 14- and 15-inch diameters. This means you can run big and littles with Lancer caps.

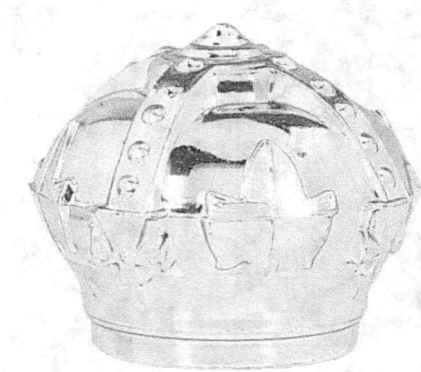

The crown air stem cap has been a favorite detail piece since the 1950s. They come in red, gold, or chrome. It seems most folks remember seeing the red ones more than the chrome.

Adding a bit of 1950s flavor can be done anywhere, and items such as these valve stem caps can dress up a wheel. They should be limited to steel wheels and hubcap applications and always use such trinkets on a car with restraint.

ROLLING STOCK: CHOOSING WHEELS, TIRES AND ACCESSORIES

I thought it would be interesting to do a timeline on the evolution of the white sidewall tire in the post World War II era. None of the measurements or dates are cast in stone, as some high-end automakers had tires made for special models, but this guide is correct for hot rods. Of course, whitewalls were just an option, and many hot rods rolled on blackwall tires too.

1) Pre-1954 hot rods should employ a tire such as this with a whitewall that is a minimum of 3 inches. 2) From 1954 through 1956 whitewalls were 2½ to 2¹¹⁄₁₆ inches, and it is worthy to note that the tubeless tire was introduced in 1954. 3) The 1957 through 1961 time period had whitewalls ranging from 2¼ to 2½ inches, and for the first time a line of black could be showing against the rim (as shown), or not. The most common being the 2½ whitewall that began at the rim's edge. 4) Generally speaking 1962 was the introduction of the narrow whitewall that measured 1½ to 1¼ inches. Bear in mind that 1962 was the beginning of the mag-wheel era too, and many hot rods running mag wheels preferred blackwall tires. 5) By the mid 1960s the whitewall had become literally pencil thin, with variants ranging from double thin lines to even triple thin lines. These thinline whitewalls never caught on with the hot rod set and are generally not seen on hot rods of any period. 6) The muscle car wars of the 1960s brought with it the redline tire. An attractive tire for muscle cars, it is seldom seen on hot rods. Raised white letter tires and blackwalls dominated the scene beginning in the 1970s.

wrinkled or, worse yet, torn Port-O-Wall. But an even better use for this product was to mount the Port-O-Wall on the inside of the tire, giving you the double whitewall look. This was particularly effective on fenderless hot rods. Port-O-Walls are still available today if you are contemplating inner whitewalls on your vintage hot rod.

When it comes time to choose a whitewall for your vintage hot rod, determining the correct width for your time period is a little tricky. Different tire makers had slightly different styles and widths, and in some cases an automaker could have tires made especially for a certain make and model. As a general guide, whitewall tires prior to 1954 were 3 inches or wider, while 1954–1956 cars sported the 2½- to 2¹¹⁄₁₆-inch-wide whitewalls. In 1957 to 1961 the wide whitewall measured 2¼ to 2½ inches, and these are the tires most suitable for 1950s style hot rods. By late 1961 the narrow whitewall was showing up on new cars, ranging from 1½ to less than 1 inch by 1964. For the most part, 1962 is the first year of the narrow whitewall, yet in 1957 the Cadillac Eldorado came from the factory with narrow whitewalls. Next came pencil-thin whitewalls and then triple-stripe whitewalls, redline tires, and whitewalls with a gold stripe.

For the hot rod set of the 1950s and 1960s whitewall tires were generally the way to go, and since many hot rods saw dual duty as both show and weekend racers, it was not unusual to see whitewalls at the drag strip. As a matter of fact, even whitewall slicks were available at the time, and they are reproduced today.

This bias-ply whitewall tire is a Coker Classic, and the tread pattern is perfect, while the fluting on the sidewall has been replaced with a more ornate pattern better suited to a whitewall tire. It's a great-looking tire for a vintage hot rod, but name brands, such as Firestone, Goodyear, and B.F. Goodrich, are period correct.

Many early hot rodders couldn't afford whitewalls, an option that could add $5 to the cost of each tire. So the Port-O-Wall was born, a white rubber circle held in place by the tire bead against the rim. Properly installed they worked great, but hit a curb and the wall buckled. It is also difficult to keep Port-O-Walls tight on a radial tire due to sidewall flex and squat (as seen here).

Cheater slicks are becoming very popular among street-driven cars, and these high-quality Firestone Dragsters are among the best. Unlike most cheater slicks, these are not recaps, but that twin-groove tread pattern still makes them tricky in the rain.

Selecting The Right Vintage Tires

For those enthusiasts building an accurate pre-1970 hot rod, the tire choices are limited. Hot rodders were slow to make the change to radial tires, so bias-belted tires are the only authentic tire to run on a true vintage hot rod, but that is not to say it is your only choice. Many hot rodders opt to have two sets of wheels, one with bias-ply tires for around town and another set of radial tires for longer drives. There is a lot of talk about bias-ply tires and how horrible they are to drive. While there is no arguing the fact that radial tires are a vast improvement, driving your hot rod on a set of good-quality bias-ply tires is not as bad as you may think. But before I discuss tire construction, maybe it is time to look at the typical sizes selected for hot rods.

The single biggest contributor to hot rods having less than sports car–like handling is the whole big-and-little tire combination. While mixing sizes degrades handling, it is an integral part of the hot rod look. The tall rear tires and small front tires go back to the early days of hot rodding when the tallest rear tire available was installed on the back of a hot rod. This tall tire gave a higher rear gear ratio (lower numerically), which in turn provided a higher top speed—just what the hot rodder running on the dry lakes or salt flats was looking for. Think of it as a poor man's quick change.

Meanwhile the front tires were small and narrow to reduce rolling resistance and weight, hence the term big 'n littles. Like all things associated with racing, "the look" was adopted by the street going crowd, and today big 'n littles are an important part of the proper hot rod look. Of course, this rubber rake also pitched the car forward on an eye-pleasing forward rake, which in turn put more weight on the intentionally small front tires. Such a combination is a sure way to induce understeer or push, but then, for the most part, hot rods were designed to go fast in a straight line.

Now that you understand some of the inherent handling traits induced by the tires on your hot rod, it is time to select the best rubber for the car. To make these choices wisely, a little history may help. From the discovery of vulcanizing rubber in the late 1800s until the early 1960s, bias-ply tires were the order of the day on American cars. European cars, referred to simply as foreign cars by most hot rodders, had radial tires as early as 1948 when Michelin introduced the new radial technology.

A bias-ply tire is constructed using layers of rubber over layers of cord that overlap on an angle from either side of the tire. These overlapping cords are on angles that vary depending on the manufacturer, but they are generally around 45 degrees give or take 10 degrees. Bias-ply tires evolved using cotton cords very early on with nylon, steel, and finally fiberglass. Bias-ply tires were often referred to by the number of plies used in construction, ranging from a low of 2-ply up to some truck tires that were 10-ply or more—the more plies, the stronger the tire, the stiffer the ride. Since the sidewalls had the same number of plies, there was virtually no squat to the tire. The stiff sidewalls provided very little flexibility in hard turns, which led to the tire breaking loose and sliding on the pavement at a lower threshold than a radial tire.

The good news for the bias-ply tire is it supports more weight than a radial of the same size. The bad news is it has a higher friction rate and rolling resistance. You will find that strong bias-ply tires wear faster due to the higher operating temperatures caused by the increased friction rate and bias-ply tires provide lower gas mileage because of the rolling resistance.

Overall grip or traction is best with the radial design too, as the design of the tire allows a squat factor that puts more tread on the pavement. This larger patch on the pavement produced by radial tires can add some steering resistance at low speed, making parking a vintage car with no power steering a

Here's the real deal: a B.F. Goodrich Silvertown blackwall tire. This is a true bias-ply tire. Note the attractive fluting on the sidewall of the tire and the simple tread design. For vintage accuracy there is no substitute for bias-ply tires.

bit more of a task, but that is a small price to pay for the added grip of the radial. And remember, grip does not just help a hard launch, grip also dramatically shortens your braking distances.

When radial tires first became popular in the early 1970s, many people viewed the sidewalls and thought the tire was running soft (low on air) when it was actually the design of the tire. There is no doubt the radial tire is superior to the bias-ply tire in every way, but if you're going for authentic 1950s style you are locked in to bias-ply tires.

For those who strive to be absolutely accurate in their build, bear in mind the tubeless tire came on the scene in 1954, so technically most hot rods 1955 and older should be running tubes too. Beyond the construction of the tires, the bias-belted tires simply have the proper look, with unique sidewall construction and fluted edges on the tread. The look of these tires provides a very important connection to the era the car represents, and few things kill the mood of a vintage hot rod quicker than inappropriate tires; and please, no raised-white-letter tires.

One good compromise comes in the form of specialty tires that have early-style tread patterns and sidewalls but are still of radial construction. I found just such a radial tire at Coker Tire, and it would make an excellent choice for a car that needs the early look and is going to be driven long distances. It is a compromise product that doesn't look exactly like a bias-ply but it does have a more vintage appearance than the modern radial tires.

Other Visual Options

Selecting tires and wheels with the correct appearance is crucial. You want the tires and wheels to enhance the particular theme of a hot rod and not detract from it. Pay close attention to paint, finish, hub caps, tread pattern, and sidewall height.

Tire Paint

No discussion of dressing up tires would be complete without talking about tire paint. Painting on whitewalls doesn't even sound like it should work, so I'm not sure why people continue to try, but painting letters on the sidewalls does work. I can remember painting the Firestone letters on my car gold with a tiny brush and a small jar of tire paint purchased at the local accessory store. The letters were small, but it gave my Firestone tire what I perceived to be the same look as the tires running in the Indy 500. It was not uncommon for hot rods, show cars, and even race cars to paint the raised letters of the manufacturer's name on the sidewall, and this was long before raised white letter tires. As with pinstriping, to be effective with tire painting restraint is called for, and when done properly it is a vintage-appropriate detail. Today, tire paint is available in paint pens from companies such as Summit Racing.

Tire Finish

For those highest level restorations or survivor hot rods even tire finish must be considered. These are products known as rubber protectants. These tire treatment products

Making the choice between bias-belted and radial tires can be difficult. The radial is a superior tire in every way, but the era-correct look of the bias-ply tire is important. There are some new tires coming out that combine the best of both worlds, almost. These new breeds have a simple tread pattern like the bias ply, with some fluting on the sidewalls, and at a glance they do have that vintage look and they perform like only a radial tire can. However, they don't quite have the look of the bias ply, but frankly I'd run this tire on my old hot rod and leave the bias-ply tires for show only.

are relatively new, so applying the latest "Extreme Maxi-Super Wet Tire Shiner" to your Firestone dirt tracker or 16x6 bias-belted tire is just completely out of place. On a personal note, I never understood the concept of a shiny tire, rather the goal of a good tire treatment is to make the tire look new and clean.

After trying many different products over the years, my current favorite comes from Adams, called VRT (vinyl, rubber, tire) dressing. This product is wiped on a clean tire and produces a rubber finish that looks like a new tire with no shiny or oily finish. It does the same for weather stripping, radiator hoses, and vinyl upholstery.

Recaps

Speaking of slicks, the ever popular cheater slick, or full slick, in whitewall and blackwall versions, is quite popular today, and these tires are recaps. Be advised even the cheater slick is a competition tread style that does not evacuate water; driving in a heavy rain with these tires is treacherous at best, tragic at worst. If you simply must have the "pie crust slick" look, it may pay to have a set of full-tread tires for long-distance running. The pie crust name is a reference to the heavy fluted cap around the outside edge of the slick. Another consideration is the fact that recap tires are illegal in many states, although it is unlikely the average police officer would recognize a recap tire today.

If you like the look of a competition tire with safety for all-weather driving the Firestone dirt tire is the way to go. These tires are basically slicks that have been cut in a crosshatch pattern, just like the sprint car tires. The good news is these tires have the aggressive look of a competition tire, but the big channels cut in the tire prevent dreaded hydroplaning on wet roads.

Tread Pattern

The tread pattern is an important consideration with hot rods and becomes even more important with open-wheel cars. Other than cheater slicks or dirt track tires the tread pattern should not draw attention, and while the new directional tread designs of modern tires are a big step forward in handling they simply should never be used on vintage hot rods. Even the new flame pattern tread should be reserved for the most contemporary Highboy cars.

Sidewall Height

Sidewall height is another visual aspect to consider. Remember the taller the sidewall of the tire, the smaller the wheel appears. So, if you have a tire with a very large sidewall on the rear, the rear wheel visually looks smaller. If you put a low-profile tire on the front and a tall tire on the rear it is possible to produce the illusion that the front wheel is larger than the rear wheel—a look that is not desirable on any hot rod.

Generally speaking there is no application appropriate for modern low-profile tires such as 235/35-16 or similar sizes. The second number on the sidewall is the aspect ratio of the tire. Here 35 means the sidewall is 35 percent as high as the tire is wide. This is a very small sidewall, not proper for a vintage hot rod. However, if you change that second number to 70, as in 235/70-16 you now have an appropriate sidewall. Vintage tire markings do not include an aspect ratio at all, rather they are simple measurements in inches. For example, 8.50-15 is a tire for a 15-inch rim with a tread width of 8.5 inches.

The real joy of hot rodding is creativity, and these great wheels demonstrate craftsmanship, style, and period perfect finish, not to mention they're brand-new, one-off wheels from Pinkee's Rod Shop. Safety wire prevents the real knock-off from loosening while driving. I'm sure more than one hot rodder thinks they remember seeing these wheels years ago, and that's what makes them great.

In Summary

The American Torque Thrust wheel was the leading edge of a wave of mag wheel manufacturers. Some blatantly copied the design while others were obviously inspired by the design. But one thing is sure: Five was the designated number of spokes for the hot rod wheel, and there were thousands upon thousands of them manufactured during the 1960s, 1970s, and 1980s. Rader, Cragar, Fenton, Rocket, Keystone, Appliance, Superior, and others, flooded the market with mag wheels. Some of these companies were long-time hot rod manufacturers finding themselves in the booming wheel market, while others sprouted up to capitalize on the market. Quality varied greatly, but for the most part all of the popular wheels of the 1960s were a variation on the five-spoke theme.

Some of these companies continue making wheels today; others were gone by the early 1970s. For the vintage hot rod builder, the natural choice is the Halibrand, American Racing, or Cragar wheel as they have the longest legacy and are easily recognizable as wheels of the era. But for building a bit more interesting piece take the time to search out some lesser-known brands of wheels from that time period. Wheels, such as Morbec or even an old set of Keystone or Rocket will keep your hot rod 1960s perfect but just outside the standard-fare group. Another thing to remember is mixing wheels was entirely okay in the 1960s. It was not unusual to see five-spoke wheels on the front and chrome reverse wheels on the rear. This was no doubt more of the drag race influence, as many drag cars ran similar mismatched wheels.

In the end there are many tires to choose from for your vintage hot rod. First narrow the search to tires produced during the same time period as your hot rod. If your car was built in 1958, look for those 2¼-inch whitewalls or a simple blackwall tire. Bias belted would be the authentic tire for a true 1958 hot rod, but a vintage-look radial may be the wiser choice.

Once you have a list of correct available tires you must make the tough decision. For many people building vintage hot rods it is all about experiencing hot rodding of a certain era, and if you fall into that category then you will want bias ply tires. But for those hot rodders who simply love the look, a modern tire will give better service. The choice is yours—talk with fellow hot rodders who run wheels and tires that you are considering, then consult tire professionals before making that final decision.

The five-spoke wheels became wildly popular by the late 1960s, and it seemed everyone was making one. This wheel is the Appliance Wheel version of the five-spoke. There is no denying the American Racing influence on all of these wheels.

The Morbec wheel was produced in the Fort Worth area of Texas, and they are very rare today. The one-piece center can make them difficult to mount tires, and the valvestem is on the back side of the wheel. They were originally built with chrome bands and polished-aluminum centers; this wheel has been painted because the chrome rusted away over the years.

CHAPTER 4

BUILDING A VINTAGE CHASSIS

Building a vintage chassis is a real gut check—just how tough are you and can you stay within the confines of an early period hot rod? You might think you can build a vintage chassis, but let's look at an example scenario: Suppose the plan is to build a very cool, very vintage, Model A coupe. You have found a good body for the project, but now you need a frame. Luckily finding an original Model A frame is still quite easy. As a matter of fact, there are so many of them around it pays to shop for price and find a good frame. A quick check of online sites and swap meets was it all took to find several original frames in decent condition for less than $300. This would seem to indicate that an original frame is a great way to start that vintage project, until you discover you can purchase a complete, new perimeter frame for $599.

The problem is you can buy a stronger new frame manufactured from box tubing for about the same amount of money it takes to buy an original frame and boxing material, and you still have all that work to do. So, many hot rodders opt for the new perimeter chassis to hang their vintage suspension on, but if you are building the real deal vintage hot rod, there is only one way to go and that is beginning with a frame that was found under your particular car when new. Be it a 1940 Ford or a 1937 Chevy, the original frame should be used for true period correct hot rodding. I'm not saying the new frames aren't equal or even better than an original platform, but you must transport yourself back in time, and guess what? In 1957 there were no reproduction frames for hot rods.

If, however, you are simply building a hot rod with great vintage flavor, rather than a period correct car, you can know the joys of 1-800-hot-rodding and order up that nice, new perimeter frame. The good news is you can purchase a new chassis built for virtually any vintage car. Having said that, I must say the rewards of building your own chassis are great and few things are more satisfying than saving an old frame and modifying it in time-tested ways to handle the horsepower of your favorite hot rod motor.

Vintage hot rod chassis are a study in simplicity. Building a vintage-style frame at home is within reach of advanced shade-tree mechanics. The key to an authentic early hot rod is combining all the right parts.

Boxing Plates

Most early Ford frames from the Model T through 1934 require boxing to strengthen the outer rails. This involves cutting boxing plates from 1/8-inch steel plate. Some hot rodders move up to 3/16-inch plate so they have more material to tap threads for brake-line clamps and other accessories, but 1/8 inch is all that is needed to strengthen the frame for most hot rod motors.

Hardcore hot rodders might want to cut their own boxing plates to fit the frame rail, but there are any number of suppliers who provide laser-cut boxing plates for an entire Model A frame for $150, which is entirely reasonable considering the time savings. The cost for larger frames like the 1932 or the 1935–1940 Ford frames is slightly higher.

Boxing the frame involves welding the plates in place. To do this you alternate welds from side to side in short spans until the plates are fully welded. This is a lot of welding and with properly fitted boxing plates the fastest way to complete the job is with a MIG welder. Since the welds will be ground down a MIG or TIG welder can be used on this portion of the job, but for brackets where the weld will be showing, a stick welder is a more accurate weld if you are building a period correct car. Shock brackets, motor mounts, and such were all stick welded in the 1950s and 1960s. TIG or Heli-Arc welding was downright exotic stuff reserved for the aircraft industry; virtually no backyard shops had access to TIG welding in the early 1960s. While this may sound like a minor detail, at the end of the day, great hot rods differ from good hot rods based almost entirely on attention to detail. It should also be noted that a good welder can lay a bead with a modern machine that looks much like old gas welding or even stick welding.

It should be noted that many mid-1930s GM products were resting on a frame that was a fully boxed unit from the factory. The frames have a flange on the bottom, and the top U-shaped frame rail is joined to the bottom plate. This brings with it other fabricating challenges, and it is important to find a rust-free frame as repair tends to be more difficult with these frame rails.

Procedures like Z-ing the frame are a bit more complicated with a GM frame than it is with a Ford frame rail. For that reason, it was not uncommon to see an early-1930s Chevy coupe body mounted to an early Ford frame, so the owner could use many of the suspension and motor mount adapters available for Ford frames. It is also easier to get a low hot rod stance with Ford suspension, as GM used parallel leaf springs that can be clumsy looking on a fenderless car.

Motor Mounts and Brackets

Early motor mounts were generally fabricated pieces, and when the chassis was an early Ford frame these fabricated mounts often involved using the stock motor-mount rubber biscuits located on the front mounts. Because bellhousings and automatic transmissions were made from cast iron, the front mounts on the motor were fine, as the transmission became a structural mounting point. Later when aluminum bellhousings and transmissions became popular, side-mount motor mounts were developed to eliminate loads on the bellhousing or transmission.

Hurst made a huge number of different motor mounts for engine swaps in the 1960s, most constructed from angle iron with flat stock braces. They worked well for anything from putting a hemi in a 1940 Ford to the famous front-engine-mount cradle that mounted 90 percent of all small-block Chevrolets in the early days.

If you are building a "vintage-style" hot rod the use of a reproduction frame will speed the building process dramatically. A reproduction frame with vintage hardware is very hard to detect from an original under a well-built hot rod and it saves a lot of work.

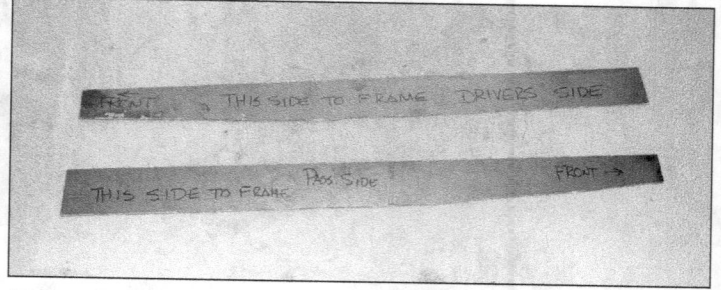

Since original frames were designed to hold engines producing less than 100 hp, the frame rails must be boxed to reduce flexing. Boxing plates made of 1/8-inch steel are fitted and welded to the inside of the channel.

BUILDING A VINTAGE CHASSIS

While these engine swap kits from Hurst are no longer available, there is a wide array of shops making motor mount kits for most popular hot rod engines.

The engine you select should dictate what style motor mounts are suitable. If your engine was manufactured with side-mount castings, then it is entirely appropriate to use them. Although some people prefer to use early front mounts for the vintage look, the side mounts are a superior method of mounting an engine. Since Chevrolet introduced side motor mounts in 1958, using a side-mount-style motor mount is entirely acceptable for vintage cars.

Crossmembers can be fabricated from angle iron, channel iron, and flat stock. Box tubing was the stuff of exotic race cars, so only high-end hot rods used such material in the 1950. It was not uncommon to simply modify the existing crossmember using flat-stock steel and angle iron, or even using a tubular crossmember from a later-model car.

When I built my first hot rod, I used a cut-down tubular transmission crossmember from a late-1950s Chevrolet to support my transmission. The ends were trimmed off, and

One method of lowering your hot rod is to Z the frame. This is simply stepping the frame up in the suspension mounting area, lowering the rest of the chassis in the process.

Motor mounts on early hot rods were often designed around a cradle that bolted to the front of the engine, then early Ford motor-mount biscuits were used on the frame adapters. Speed holes in this Oldsmobile mount add hot rod flavor.

Side mounts were introduced in 1958 for the small-block Chevy, so side mounts are perfectly cool on a vintage hot rod. This particular side mount is artistically designed and employs a urethane rod end as a vibration insulator. This piece is strong, good looking, and carries nice vintage flavor.

Frame adapters were fabricated and welded to the top of this Model A frame rail, then the flathead V-8 motor mount was used to bolt the motor in place. This is a very clean and simple approach to mounting the motor.

CHAPTER 4

Transmission crossmembers were generally fabricated from channel iron or tubular steel. The universal, dropped-tube crossmember has been around for a long time and works well in traditional hot rods.

Building a modern rendition of a vintage hot rod combines modern techniques with vintage style. The Alan Johnson Hot Rod Shop aluminum wishbones capture the early hot rodding mood in high style. The Winters quick-change rear end with tapered tubes also has early flavor but uses all new parts.

new end plates were fabricated and welded to the crossmember, so they could bolt to the side-rail boxing plates. This was typical of modifications in the late 1960s.

The real key to building an authentic-looking vintage hot rod chassis is to keep the frame and brackets clean and simple. Lots of sculpted and molded brackets and such are things of later, highly detailed cars. For a vintage hot rod, the beauty comes from the simplicity of the bracket performing a job with minimal frills attached. Speed holes, rounded corners on brackets, and either good welds or welds ground smooth were all hallmarks of a quality built hot rod, so do tend to the details, but resist overworking the brackets.

Suspension Choices

Building a period correct hot rod helps to lessen the number of decisions required during the build. If you are building a 1948-or-older hot rod, chances are your front suspension is going to involve a straight axle and a single transverse-mounted spring on all Fords, with some straight axles and some independent suspensions on GM and Chrysler products. Since Ford clung stubbornly to the straight axle until 1949, setting up a Ford hot rod was really quite simple and the methods used today are the same methods used 50 to 60 years ago.

One problem with installing a later V-8 motor in a Ford frame came from the radius rods that located the front axle. These two rods extend rearward and locate the axle front to rear. The two rods are actually one assembly joined in a triangle configuration with a forged pivot ball that was the rear center mounting point. Quickly dubbed wishbones because of their resemblance to turkey parts, the pivot ball mounted directly under the transmission. This was fine if you were using a flathead and associated transmission, but if an engine and transmission swap was in order the rear wishbone mount was almost always in the way, and often the wishbones themselves would come in contact with oil pans, starters, or exhaust manifolds. The solution was to split the wishbones.

Splitting wishbones involves cutting the two radius rods free from the central rear mount and swiveling the rods out toward the side rails. Many early hot rodders heated the radius

When it comes to simplicity, it is hard to top the early Ford suspension. A single-transverse "buggy" spring, two shock absorbers, and two radius rods to locate the axle fore and aft make up the entire front suspension.

rods and bent them to align under the frame rail. In the ends of the cut-off rods, a cut-off piece of tie rod was welded into the wishbone, and the associated tie rod end was screwed into the end of the now-modified wishbone. A bracket under the frame was used to locate the wishbone, and the splitting of the wishbones was complete.

More sophisticated hot rods used a tapered cup (or the end off a steering arm welded to the bracket) to act as a receiver for the tapered shaft of the tie rod end, while others simply used a hole in the bracket. A tapered receiver is the proper way to ensure the strength of the tie rod end.

Another method of attaching the wishbone or radius rod end to the chassis was employing a spherical rod end, often called heim joints. These rod ends were used in aircraft, and the high-quality units are strong and easy to use. Spherical rod ends have largely given way to urethane rod ends that rely on a captured urethane bushing and sleeve to mount the radius rod. For early hot rods, the tie rod end is the most common and accurate piece, but spherical rod ends can be used on cars beginning in the 1960s, with the urethane rod end finding its way into production in the early 1970s.

For those of you considering independent front suspension on prewar hot rods, it was nearly nonexistent. That's not so say some racecar-inspired hot rods didn't use the technology, but for the typical traditional hot rod, solid axles, front and rear were the order of the day. As early as 1934 GM products were offered with a big, heavy, clumsy front suspension commonly referred to as knee-action suspension. Hot rodders never embraced this suspension, but variations on that suspension found their way under Chevrolets of the 1940s. Many standard-model Chevrolets used a straight axle, but it was mounted with two parallel-leaf springs. The simplicity of working with a solid-axle suspension and the flathead V-8 were two major reasons why Fords remained more popular than GM or Chrysler products through 1948.

In the 1960s some forward-thinking hot rodders were adapting Jaguar independent suspension to their hot rods. This brought all kinds of new technology with it, such as inboard disc brakes on the rear and adjustable coil-over shocks on all four corners along with rack-and-pinion steering. This was all pretty exotic stuff in an era when Americans hadn't even embraced the radial tire yet. The fabrication was extensive and the parts were expensive, but in the early 1970s the look of a fully polished and plated Jaguar rear suspension was a big hit with many hot rodders, and if you ever have the pleasure of following a fellow hot rodder with

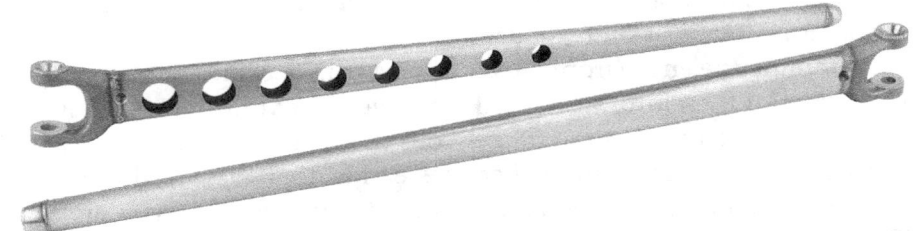

The joy of modern-day hot rodding is so many vintage parts are available in reproduction form, like these high-quality early Ford wishbones from Speedway Motors. Available plain or drilled with a threaded bung for a rod end these pieces are perfect for a vintage hot rod.

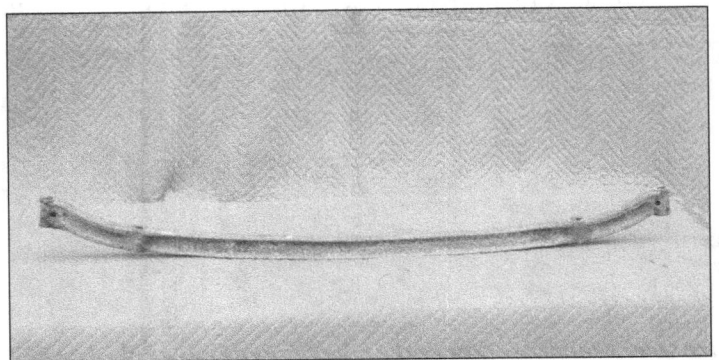 

Early Ford axles changed over the years, from 1928–1934 the spring was located directly over the axle, while the 1935–1948 axles placed the spring on hangers in front of the axle. A dropped axle is still the preferred method of lowering a vintage hot rod.

a Jag rear, the effect is nothing less than mesmerizing.

Independent front suspension started to become popular in the 1970s. In 1971 Ford introduced the Pinto, an economy car that was small in stature, having similar measurements to a mid-1930s automobile. Hot rodders soon discovered this combination of a narrow front track and independent suspension. Pinto front suspension was finding its way under all types of hot rods.

In 1974, Ford introduced the Mustang II, which was basically built around the Pinto platform. Given the choice of having Pinto suspension or Mustang II suspension, hot rodders quickly changed the name of this suspension to Mustang II. It is a remarkably versatile suspension that can be adapted to almost any frame due to the short upper and lower control arms. At first hot rodders were trimming the entire front crossmember out of the Pinto/Mustang II and notching it, so the hot rod frame rails would fit into the crossmember. I did exactly that in late 1970s on my 1934 Pontiac and achieved a very aggressive stance with a good ride and reasonable handling.

It wasn't long before the aftermarket picked up on this versatile suspension system and began building crossmember kits for specific cars. These kits seemed to be particularly popular with the GM and Mopar crowd, as they were in need of a front suspension swap more often than an early Ford with the traditional dropped axle. Today, the Mustang II suspension is very popular under all makes of cars.

If you are considering building a 1970s-style car, which very well could be a nice resto-rod approach, the use of the Mustang II suspension is accurate, although it is period correct with the factory-style, stamped-steel control arms, as the tubular items did not come on the scene until later. And for those thinking a 1970s hot rod is not vintage, bear in mind a 1970s-built hot rod was modified more than 35 years ago.

Rear End Choices

When it comes to selecting the rear gear for your hot rod, it is obvious that you must choose a rear axle assembly that was available during your target period. If you are building a car to pre-1955 standards you can choose from the most popular of the period, an early Ford rear, or you could go with a vintage Olds rear. If you get into the mid-1950 era, the popular and strong 9-inch Ford rear axle housing was in production, so it would be appropriate under a hot rod of that era. Since there are several companies, such as Currie Enterprises, that manufacture complete new 9-inch Ford housings, this will solve that problem. However, do take the time to research details, such as the location of the drain and fill plug, and have them in the proper location, or simply find a 1957 housing and fill it with all new parts. Real sticklers for detail will want a carrier with proper casting numbers that match early production figures, but that would apply to only the most stringent restorations or replica builds.

The lure of the 9-inch Ford comes from the fact that it is a bulletproof rear with literally tons of new parts available, including the housing. However, if your project is a car inspired by one that saw duty on the drag strip, there is no substitute for the giant Olds rear ends from the mid 1950s. Commonly found under gassers, altered, and dragsters of the day, these rear axle units make a real statement. If you add chrome plating it becomes even more impressive.

And, of course, I cannot talk about hot rod rear axle assemblies without mentioning the ultimate rear axle, the quick-change rear.

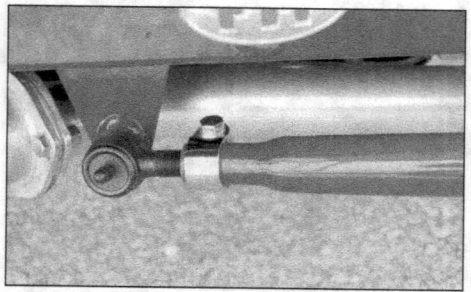 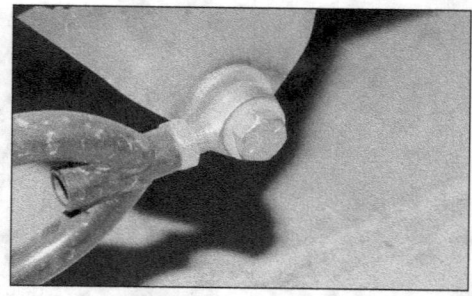 

Rod ends were used in both front and rear radius rods to attach and adjust the fore and aft location of the axles. Early hot rods used tie-rod ends (left), then spherical-rod ends (center) became popular, and later the urethane-bushing rod end (right) became the preferred piece. For a period correct car use tie-rod ends; for vintage-flavor cars the urethane busing rod end is far superior.

Originally designed by Ted Halibrand, his company, Halibrand Engineering, provided quick-change rear ends for racers of every type, and many street-going hot rods also used them. Not only are these rear ends functional, they are works of art. To be period correct, find early Halibrand parts from the Culver City days, but if you're building a hot rod with heavy traditional flavor, quick-change rear axles are available from Winters, Franklin, Speedway, and others. The good news is for street use all of these units have the same great looks and gear whining attributes of the original Halibrand. Winters even has a series of quick-change rear axles for hot rods with traditional tapered tubes for that vintage look. These are all viable quick-change options, and let's face it, a quick-change rear is the ultimate hot rod rear end, bar none.

Building a vintage hot rod chassis is rewarding. While today's modern rod shops employ full chassis fixtures, surface plates, and other high-tech means of ensuring a perfect chassis, a good hot rod frame can be built at home using nothing more than a tape measure, level, plumb bob, and square for measurements and large C-clamps, vise grips, and bolts to hold things together during the fabricating process.

With the axles located in the proper position, it is time to adjust the ride height and add some modern shock absorbers. Early hot rods did not sit as low as the modern versions; today's hot rods are ground-hugging cars that have seen 6 and 8 inches of suspension lowering. Many early hot rodders were content to have a 2- or 4-inch drop by using a dropped axle and then picking up another inch by reversing the front spring eye or other tricks, such as using a Model A front crossmember in a 1932 chassis. Modern hot rods have the luxury of coil-over adjustable shocks that allow you to adjust ride height, whereas early hot rods are, for the most part, non-adjustable so the ride height must be built into the car using the correct components.

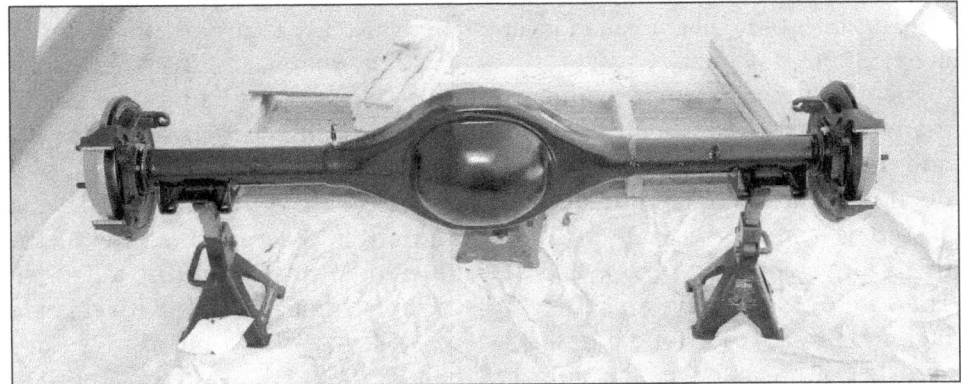

The nine-inch Ford rear is the mainstay of hot rod rear gears. The clean and simple housing holds a rear gear set that is simply bulletproof. Brand-new housings are available from companies such as Currie Enterprises. If you are looking for a narrow vintage rear, the 1957 Ford station wagon or Ranchero rear axle is an excellent choice for vintage hot rods.

Chevrolet used two springs to locate both the front and rear axles; this straight-tube axle is mounted using parallel leaf springs on a vintage Chevrolet-built, nose-high, gasser style.

The rear axle combines suspension with gears to drive the rear wheels, so brackets and attachment points must be well engineered and structurally strong. On vintage hot rods, the design and execution is still extremely simple.

Appropriate shock absorbers are early-style lever actions, which include friction shocks, the original Houdaille hydraulic lever shocks, early Armstrong aluminum hydraulic lever-action shocks as found on MGs and other imported cars, and of course, the now-conventional tubular shock absorber. While C.L. Horock conceived the basic design of the tube shock in 1901, it didn't become popular on modern cars until the early 1950s when independent suspension became standard fare. Prior to 1949 all Fords had lever-action shock absorbers.

Houdaille, a French company, manufactured these shock absorbers and installed them on many production vehicles. Today, these shock absorbers can be reconditioned or there are reproductions available. The ease of installation and the vintage style make the Houdaille shock absorber an attractive solution to spring damping. There were several different models from the Model A through 1948 with some of the shock absorbers mounting on the side of the frame rail while others were designed to mount under the frame rail. The side-mount units tend to be more popular as there is no interference with the front wishbones. A link from the lever arm to the axle is the final connection and these arms, often called dog-bone links, are available in reproduction form. Alan Johnson's Hot Rod Shop in Gadsden, Alabama, also makes aluminum dog-bone links for hot rod applications.

Many early hot rodders opted for the more modern tube shocks, and these are easy to mount and come in a wide variety of lengths. The vintage tube shocks often had a flare on the bottom of the dust cover, and it is a detail that real hot rodders will pick up on. While you may not be able to find an NOS set of shocks with the flared dust covers, putting a flare on the bottom of a new dust cover could be achieved with a bit of ingenuity. In the 1950s, these shock absorbers were often referred to as aircraft-style tube shocks, but companies like Monroe had been supplying shocks for car manufacturers since 1951, so they are really automotive pieces. Chrome plating seemed to be very popular on the tube shocks, and they were often mounted using the upper mount from an F-1 Ford pickup and then had a hole drilled in the web of the front axle.

Brake Choices

Since Ford did not introduce hydraulic brakes until 1939, all Fords built prior to that date require a brake upgrade. The good news is the spindles and associated hydraulic drum brakes are an easy swap, and aftermarket vendors have an endless supply of reproduction spindles and brakes to facilitate this swap.

If you're building or restoring a 1960s or earlier hot rod, your brake choices are almost all the same, drum brakes all around. One of the difficult decisions to make when building a vintage hot rod is ignoring safety advances that have occurred over the years. To be accurate, a single-reservoir master cylinder is correct, yet there is no denying that a

The ultimate rear gear for any period correct hot rod is the quick-change rear. While quick-change rears are available new today, there are still many vintage units to be found at swap meets or online.

The rear cover of the Halibrand quick-change is all-important when it comes to dating a hot rod. The most desirable rear cover is the Culver City unit, as that was the first home of Halibrand; later covers had Torrance, California, cast into the plate.

dual-reservoir master cylinder is a superior unit. The only advice I have here is to increase the maintenance schedule on old systems. If you're running a single-stage fruit jar master cylinder (so named because of the screw-on lid), be certain to change your brake fluid annually; this prevents moisture from contaminating the system and goes a long way to preventing pitted cylinder walls and leaking seals.

Today, early Ford drum brakes are available brand new, and a nice upgrade is to use the early Lincoln brakes because they are self-energizing, meaning they bring themselves into contact with the drum when pressure is applied. This feature minimizes the number of adjustments required, while the early 1939–1948 Ford drum brakes tend to require periodic adjustments to keep them working properly.

For the GM crowd and for some aftermarket straight axles, the use of 1954 Chevy-style drum brakes and spindles is the answer. These brakes are modern enough to work well on a hot rod, and since most hot rods are lighter than a 1954 Chevy, the hot rod has slightly oversize brakes. The use of the early Chevy brakes also provides the popular 4¾-inch on five-lug bolt pattern. This is also a very common swap on early Chevy trucks as they have six-lug wheels. Swap in a 1955 passenger car rear end and a set of 1954 Chevy drum brakes up front, and you have the same bolt pattern all around and a wide choice of wheels for your hot rod truck.

Using 1953–1962 Corvette parts is an easy way to find all new parts for your early Chevrolet axle.

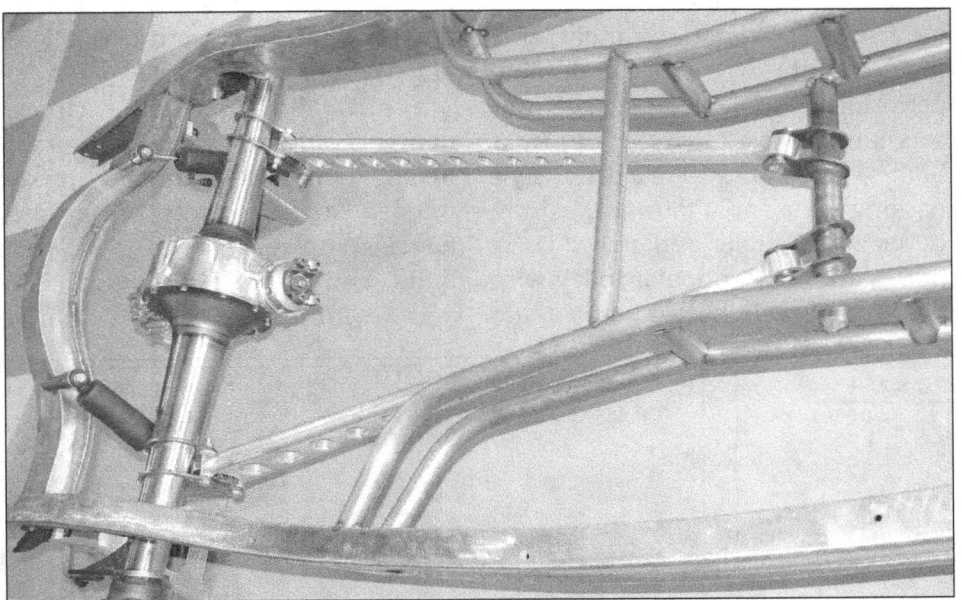
Once again, it is entirely possible to build a hot rod with a tremendous amount of vintage flavor and use virtually no old parts. This Alan Johnson chassis is graphic proof.

Friction shocks were one of the earliest methods use to control springs. Simple leather discs were sandwiched between steel discs and the lever was attached to the axle. The friction between the discs controls the axle, and tightening the nut stiffens the shock absorbing action.

While most early shock absorbers employed an eyelet-type mount, the Conley roadster used a stud mount. Note the sturdy bracket that was built in 1958, formed from flat stock with gussets welded and ground smooth on the sides to prevent flexing. The acorn nut is a perfect fastener for the car.

CHAPTER 4

Corvette suppliers, such as Eckler's, offer all-new parts for the front brakes, and since 1953–1962 Corvette front brakes are the same as 1953–1954 standard Chevrolet cars, it all fits, and you can honestly say you're running Corvette front brakes. Even the 1949–1954 Chevrolet front spindles and kingpins are available from Speedway Motors, making the conversion a simple new-part installation.

Disc brakes were limited to the rare Kinmont disc brakes that were designed for race cars. Some enterprising hot rodders adapted the early Jaguar and other import cars to early Ford spindles, but disc brakes were seldom seen until the 1970s, and if you are building a car dedicated to a certain year, use only disc brakes available during that time period. While things like aluminum monoblock calipers with cross-drilled rotors are awesome brakes they simply were not available in 1972, so let the date be your guide.

However, if you are simply looking for vintage flavor and modern performance, many vintage-style cars embrace disc brakes, or run "fake brakes," a system where a drum-style backing plate and a faux brake drum cover a disc brake and rotor. These brakes are wildly popular today with the vintage-style hot rod crowd and for good reason; they look great and stop well.

For those hot rodders concerned with using drum brakes, remember: Most hot rods see limited mileage and most drum brake systems were designed for cars heavier than the average hot rod. By using all-new parts to begin with and a good maintenance schedule, drum brakes provide years of good service.

Other brake system components should also be date-correct items. Rubber hoses are appropriate. Braided stainless steel brake lines have no place on a 1950s-style build, and even stainless steel lines and AN fittings are best left to more

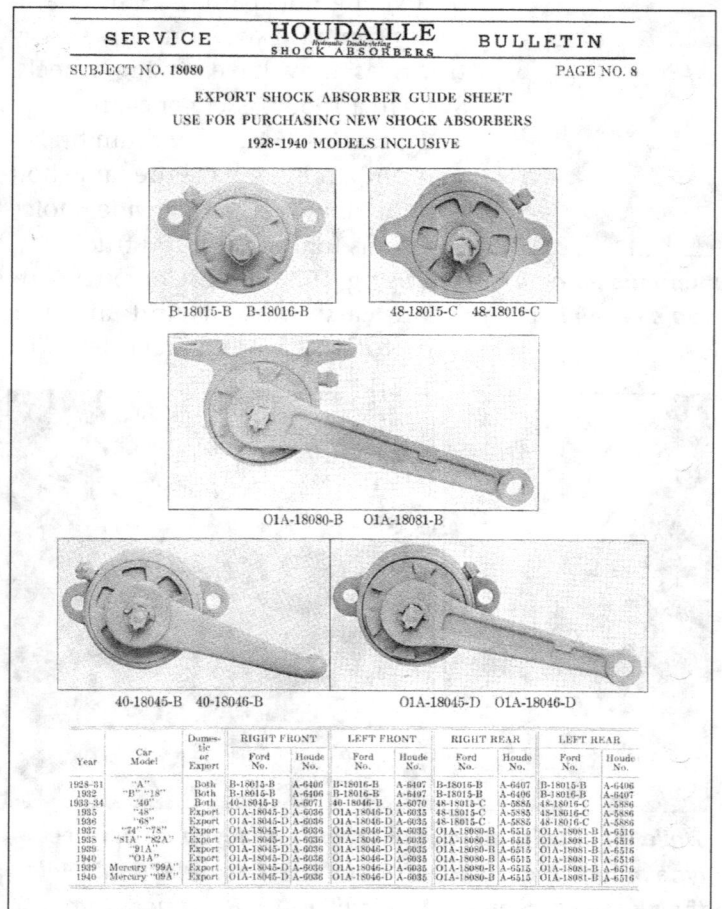
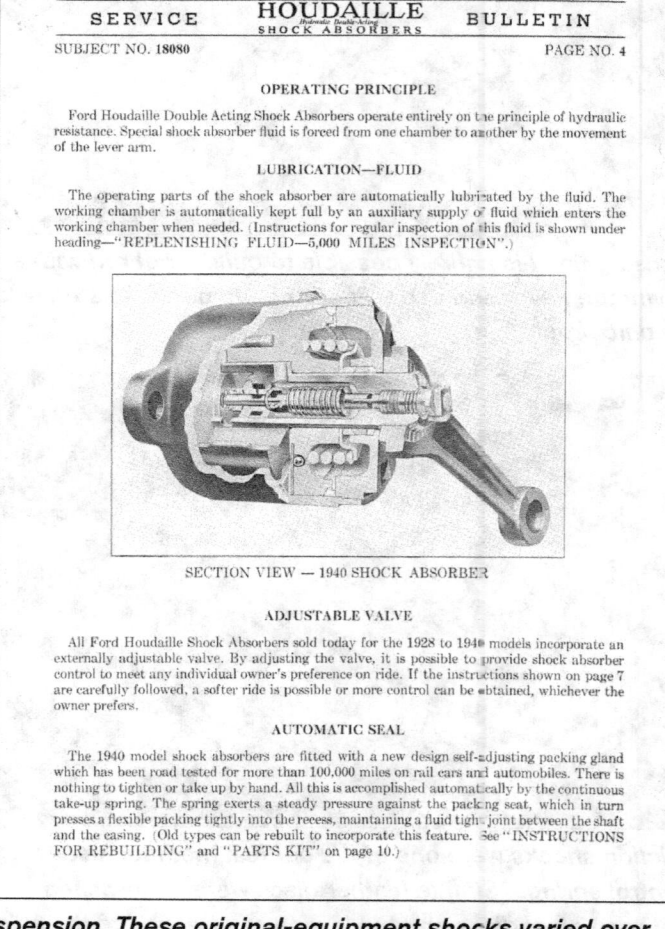

Hydraulic lever-action shocks work well with the early Ford suspension. These original-equipment shocks varied over the years and some reproductions are available, but originals can be reconditioned. These are pages from a Houdaille rebuild catalog. (Photos Courtesy of The Old Car Manual Project)

contemporary hot rods. Sure, stainless steel tubing is superior to the steel Bundyweld-type tubing, but the double-inverted flare fittings and steel tubing last a very long time on a car that is not subjected to the ravages of Mother Nature. Another plus is the mild steel tubing is easy to work with and employs vintage-style brass fittings, making it very affordable and accessible.

Steering Choices

Steering a vintage hot rod usually involves either rebuilding the stock box or upgrading to a newer steering box from the same car make. A popular swap for early hot rods is the F-100 to F1 Ford truck boxes. Most steering box swaps in early hot rods were precipitated due to a worn-out original box or to relocate the steering gear for engine clearance.

Ford steering from the Model T through 1934 was the simple drag-link steering. A near vertical Pitman arm connects to a bracket on the backing plate. As the arm moves fore and aft, the front wheels turn as they are connected by a tie rod on the steering arms.

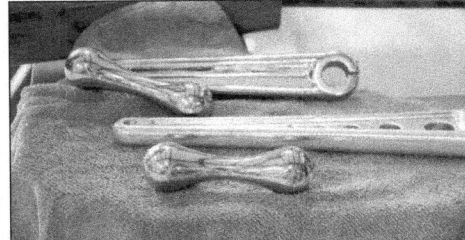

The links from the original Houdaille shocks to the axles were affectionately dubbed dog-bones for what should be obvious reasons. Today Alan Johnson makes these great-looking aluminum dog-bone links for use on sway bars or lever-action shocks.

Beginning in 1935 Ford went to cross steering whereby the Pitman arm is on a near-horizontal plane and the drag link goes across the car to the right-hand spindle, thereby explaining the term cross steering. On this system, the Pitman arm moves left and right to move the wheels. If you adapt cross steering to a 1923–1934 car you have to replace the steering arms to provide a drag-link attaching point. Cross steering is considered to be a superior system.

If you are building a period correct car, your choices are limited to Ford production boxes, and there are any number of reputable companies capable of rebuilding your existing steering gear. While the steering will never be rack-and-pinion crisp, and the turning radius will be larger than your modern car, original steering boxes can serve you well if completely reconditioned. Other things to consider when using vintage steering boxes are the amount of weight on the front suspension and the size of tire you are asking that vintage box to turn. Since small, narrow front tires are a big part of the hot rod look, tread width might not be an issue, but that 392 Hemi and

Once again, the hot rod aftermarket comes to the rescue with reproduction early Ford and Chevrolet spindles. With these and a dropped axle, you are well on your way to mounting brakes on your hot rod.

Torqueflite combination may call for a stronger steering box than the original 1934.

The good news is kits are available to mount later steering boxes in vintage frames. These kits take the mystery out of steering swaps and save fabricating time. Once again, if you are building a vintage-style hot rod, I recommend going with a late-model, recalculating-ball-design steering box. The Vega steering box has become one of the mainstays of hot rodding today, and rather than go scrounging around for a 1971–1977 Vega box, simply order a new one from a company such as Borgeson.

The Vega was a compact car, so the Vega or GM 140 steering box should be used for cars under 3,000 pounds. If you're building a vehicle much over 2,500 pounds, it would pay to move up to the larger, stronger 525 manual steering box, and the bolt pattern is the same as the GM140 steering box. This is generally the steering box recommend for traditional hot rods from 1935 to 1948. Uni-steer offers brand-new GM 525 steering boxes, as does Borgeson Universal, Flaming River, and Speedway Motors, among others. As a matter of fact, the wide use of this box has spawned a plethora of variations in steering ratios, Pitman arms, and installation brackets for many frames. Consult your steering specialist when choosing the steering box and ratio for your car.

The late-1960s (1967–1970) Mustang steering box was very popular with street rodders of the early 1970s, and many hot rods of that era are still running this box today. If you find a hot rod with this steering gear in place, fear not, parts are available to rebuild the unit, and Flaming River even offers complete new units.

I would be remiss were I not to mention the venerable Corvair steering box. The 1960–1963 boxes were aluminum and polished up nicely. Generally, the steering shaft was reversed in the box, so it could be mounted atop the frame rail and connected to the drag link. Magazines of the day sang high praises for this little steering box, and the *Car Craft* T-bucket buildup series used just such a unit in the late 1960s. The later 1964–1969 Corvair boxes were

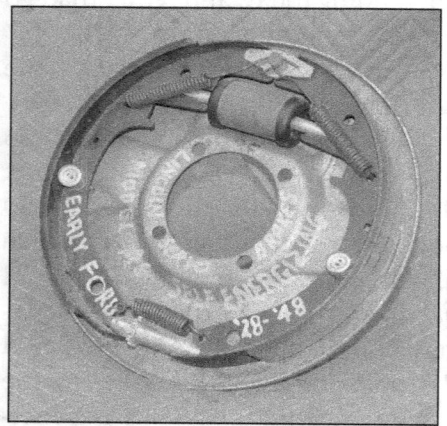

Upgrading to early Lincoln brakes is now very easy since they are available in reproduction form from companies like Honest Charley's Speed Shop. The larger Lincoln brakes are self-energizing, making brake shoe contact with the drum smoother, and fewer brake adjustments are required.

For a period correct hot rod of the 1960s and earlier, the single-reservoir master cylinder is correct. Always use new, rather than rebuilt, brake components whenever possible. Be certain to change the brake fluid annually to prevent corrosion. Chevrolet trucks of the early 1960s used a master cylinder that combined a hydraulic clutch with a single-reservoir master cylinder for the brakes. These were in widespread use on hot rods of the 1960s.

For a period correct hot rod of the 1960s and earlier, the single-reservoir master cylinder is correct. Always use new, rather than rebuilt, brake components whenever possible. Be certain to change the brake fluid annually to prevent corrosion. Chevrolet trucks of the early 1960s used a master cylinder that combined a hydraulic clutch with a single-reservoir master cylinder for the brakes. These were in widespread use on hot rods of the 1960s.

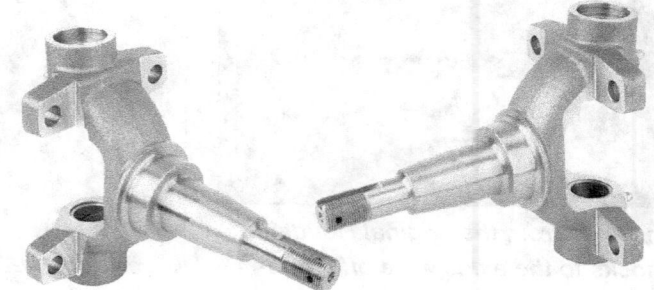

Reproduction 1954 Chevy spindles are available from Speedway Motors, but they are machined to accept disc-brake kits only. This is one way to save that early Chevy axle, but for more traditional rods, original spindles must be used with drum brakes.

cast iron and are stronger than the aluminum boxes.

Once again, today there is no need to search for an original Corvair box if you are updating a vintage T-Bucket, as Flaming River makes at least two different Corvair replacement boxes.

The final word on steering is to use new parts; be certain the design, fabricating and welding are all sound. Many vintage hot rods had questionable steering geometry, and there is no sense in restoring something that may be unsafe; rather, re-engineer the steering system with the correct vintage parts and proper geometry.

A 1933 Plymouth Reconstruction Project

Lewis McMillan takes his hot rodding seriously, not in a way that eliminates any of the fun mind you, but the man has an eye for the appropriate pieces and a healthy respect for vintage hot rods. His gorgeous black roadster is featured in Chapter 9, but like so many hot rodders, his garage is filled with multiple projects.

On the topic of finding a vintage hot rod, Lewis' story is a classic case of knowing old cars from your area. It actually begins with the fact that world-renowned artist and designer Bob Timberlake grew up in and around Lexington, North Carolina.

Early Ford steering boxes can be rebuilt and used in a hot rod, but for the most part the early design of these boxes provides a wide turning radius and more effort at the steering wheel. They were also designed for 4-inch-wide tires, so modern tires can stress the components.

The local area is known around the world as a major hub of the furniture manufacturing industry, and the McMillan family made their living producing fine veneers for the local industry. Like so many young men in the mid 1950s, Timberlake decided he wanted a hot rod. Blessed with a natural eye for design, he managed to take a 1933 Plymouth roadster

It seems most early hot rodders upgraded to the newer Ford products, and that works for steering too. Employing the F1 or F-100 steering boxes was a very popular way to build modern steering into a hot rod.

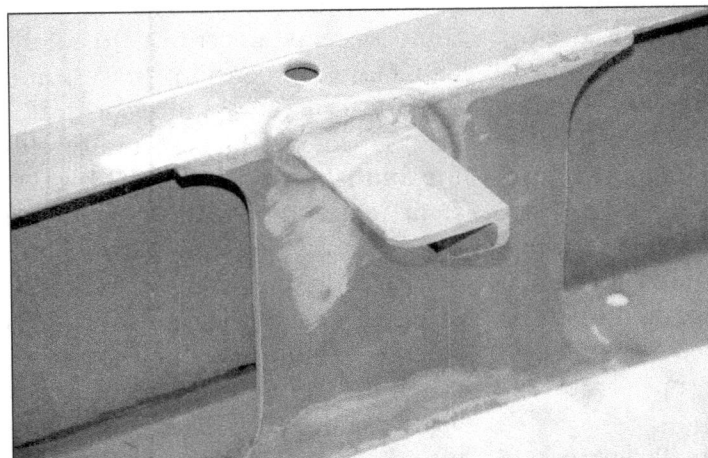

Brackets for traditional hot rods were generally basic, functional pieces such as this one. Angle, flat, and channel iron were the most common materials used, while round tubing and box tubing were exotic materials seen on race cars.

This original body bracket was obviously carved out of one piece of angle iron with a torch or hacksaw. The misaligned bolts and rough cut lines preserve the very spirit of this old hot rod.

and produce a hot rod that was classic in design, if not craftsmanship.

Like so many teenage boys, Timberlake knew what he wanted but had to rely on the skills of others to complete portions of the work. One such person's name is long forgotten, but he was "an old man who could weld." I might add the word barely to that sentence. Also, working on a limited budget meant ingenuity would be key, and so the old Plymouth body was channeled over the center section of the Plymouth frame. From roughly the firewall forward, a set of Model A frame rails were grafted in place. Anyone who has attempted to build a fenderless hot rod using a stock 1933 Plymouth frame understands the wisdom in this graft. Likewise, a new frame section was grafted to the rear of the 1933 Plymouth and then a Ford flathead V-8 and driveline was swapped into the place.

The roadster was finally painted white with bright red interior, and while it was a budget-built backyard hot rod, like virtually everything else Timberlake went on to design, this roadster had a great look that managed to embody the very spirit of a traditional hot rod. Lewis remembers seeing the car around the Lexington area, low-slung and stylish; it was the type of hot rod you didn't forget.

And so some 50 years later, while perusing the big swap meet in Charlotte, North Carolina, Lewis watched with a keen eye as a trailer went by with the remains of an old hot rod roadster. Using the instant referencing and recall all real hot rodders seem to possess, his brain did a scan and came up with this thought: "That sure looks like Bob Timberlake's old hot rod." Lewis followed the slow moving trailer down the aisle and when it finally was parked in the appropriate swap meet space, talk ensued. A deal was struck and sure enough, the Timberlake hot rod was coming back home to Lexington, North Carolina.

The roadster was put in storage for some time, but a couple years ago Lewis decided to get serious about bringing this old hot rod back. After a careful assessment of just exactly what he had purchased, he decided that a true restoration would not be the best route for this car. Building technique was crude at best, and trying to clean up the frame and associated welding would not produce the results he wanted. So the center of the frame was retained, and a new Model A front was grafted in place. The chassis was boxed this time and the welding is far superior to the original.

Great pains were taken to preserve the spirit of the car. For example, two long pieces of angle iron have been used as front body mounts. These mounts are not cut perfectly straight, and it was obvious the work had been done by hand with a hacksaw. Rather than true-up the original mounts or fabricate new ones, Lewis opted to leave them intact, to illustrate the fabricating tools available to the original builder.

Whenever possible original brackets were reused, and an intentional effort to keep things simple on the car gave this roadster a very cool look. Since safety and drivability are important, the upgraded chassis will serve the car well.

Work is progressing nicely on the old roadster, and with Lewis working at his usual meticulous pace the car should see the road sometime in 2011. Yes, it will be white and yes, it will have a classic red interior and a timeless flathead between the frame rails. It will embody the essence of hot rodding and carefree youth that the roadster did in the mid 1950s. It is a car worth saving and savoring.

In Summary

That takes care of the major systems associated with early hot rod chassis building. Remember, all of these systems are critical to safety, and faulty suspension, brakes, and steering can cause injury or death. For that reason, be certain all welding and fabrication is to the highest standards, and that the design of the suspension is fundamentally sound. Just because something was done 50 or 60 years ago does not mean it is correct or still structurally sound. Carefully examine all pieces of a vintage hot rod suspension before installing the parts and heading out on the open road. Using common sense, qualified craftsman, and proper parts helps ensure that you will be able to safely enjoy driving your hot rod.

At a glance you might mistake this for a Deuce roadster, but you'd be wrong. It is actually a 1933 Plymouth roadster with a filled decklid. Yes, it was a real roadster, not a coupe with the roof removed. Working out the crude bodywork has taken Lewis untold hours.

Ford Chassis Tips

Like it or not, Ford dominated the hot rod scene from the very beginning, a trend that continues today. Hot rodding can be divided into two groups: Fords and everything else. Even awards to Mopar, Chevrolet, and other makes often carry a Ford connection as the other brands compete for "Best Non-Ford" at many events. That, my friend, is called dominance.

While entire books can and have been written about building Ford hot rods and chassis, I felt it was important to include some good, vintage Ford tips. While most of these are off 1928–1932 frames, the concepts generally work on all vintage Ford and, yes, non-Ford hot rods. There is a look, a feel, and a connection to the past with a well-built vintage hot rod and much of that comes from the simple approach of the chassis. The '32 Ford frame is another project from Lewis McMillan's shop and yes, yet another original steel roadster body will be mounted to this chassis.

The other sources are varied, mostly just great hot rods with chassis features worth emulating. You might not use them all on your next project, but they are all worth keeping in mind for future hot rod projects.

Any discussion about early steering would not be complete without including the venerable Corvair steering box. These were used primarily in T-buckets and lightweight hot rods. Flaming River makes reproduction versions of the box today.

No doubt the most popular steering conversion today involves the Vega-style steering box and the larger 525 box. For safety and performance this is a good choice, but for the hard-core period correct hot rods these boxes are simply too new.

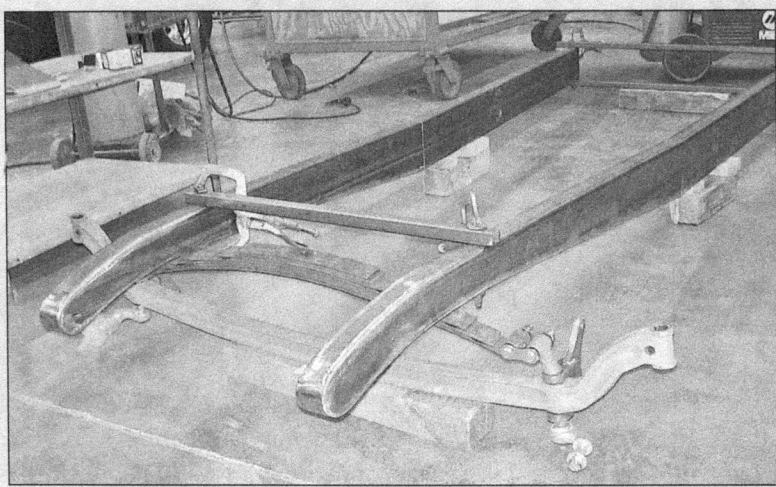

While it is fun to remember all the great hot rods of the early era, there were also some not-so-great hot rods. The key to building or refurbishing a vintage hot rod is to build it to the high level of the period, which means eliminating bad workmanship and replacing it with period correct pieces and workmanship.

CHAPTER 5

INTERIOR: REAL HOT RODS HAVE UPHOLSTERY

I have seen my fair share of really great hot rodders lose control of the project when it comes time to do the interior. Over the years many hot rodders learned how to weld, run machines (such as lathes and mills), rebuild motors, paint cars, and do extensive body modifications, but very few tackle the interior work on a hot rod. It must have something to do with sewing, but for whatever reasons, the interior is the single most common part of a hot rod to be contracted out. This chapter is not about how to do upholstery; any number of books deal with the mechanics of building and upholstering an interior. Instead, I will illustrate some dos and don'ts and provide information on how to use the right parts to achieve an interior that complements the rest of the car.

It's the Last Step

There are several common reasons that the interior of a car falls short of expectations in comparison to the rest of the car. For one thing, upholstery is generally the last step in the process. Often the owner ends up in the unenviable position of being very eager to finish the car and start driving, yet the budget is drained. He

In the 1950s and early 1960s, white interior was all the rage. It somehow spoke to the super-detailed, sanitary approach of building a hot rod. It also seems to magnify the intensity of paint colors. Today, it provides instant 1950 flavor. This is the old Tony LaMasa roadster, just as it appeared on the August 1960 cover of Hot Rod magazine with an occasional guest appearance on the Ozzie & Harriet Show.

INTERIOR: REAL HOT RODS HAVE UPHOLSTERY

Comfortable seating and race-inspired door panels give a performance feeling to this roadster. The 1950 steering wheel does a fine job of dating the interior.

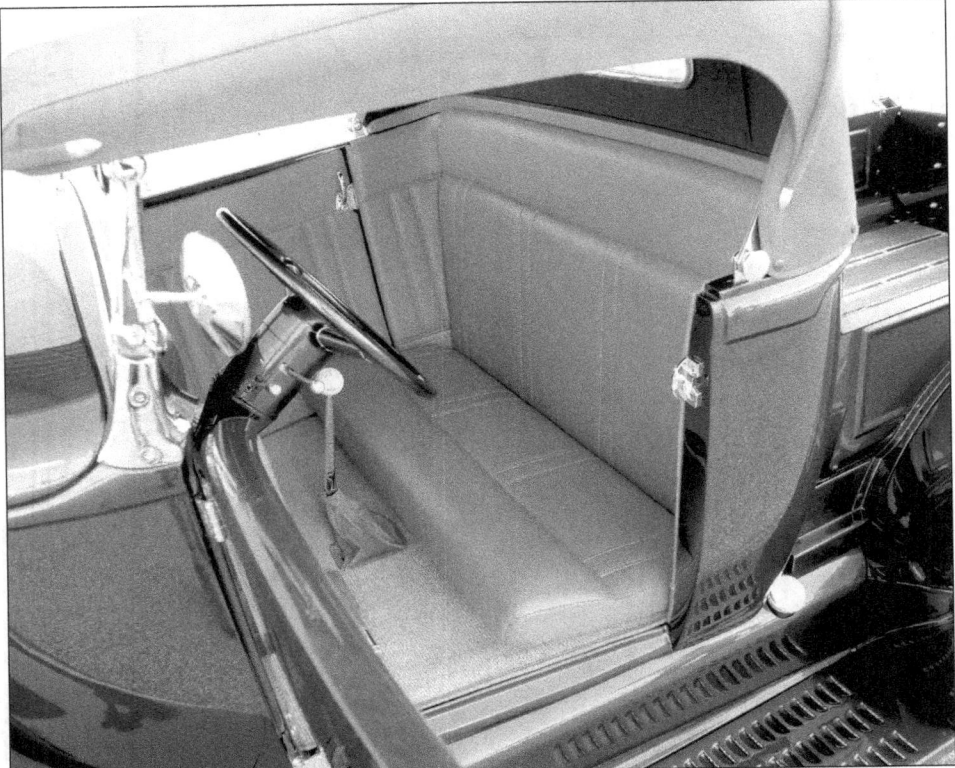

While tuck-and-roll or diamond-tufted interiors were common, often it is better to rely on a simple pattern and let the very-high-quality stitch work do the talking. Natural-color leathers always add vintage flavor.

or she is not able to afford the top-level products and craftsmanship on the inside of the car, so short cuts are taken.

When you don't plan your interior from the beginning of the project, your upholstery man is going to be very disappointed because he finds you have not considered how to attach things like headliners, wind lacing, and other upholstery panels. If you would like to save a few hundred dollars (at least) on your next upholstery job try doing this: Have your upholstery person come over and check out your car, and ask him what he needs in what areas before you begin the project. It will save you time and money in the end, plus you will have a better job too.

Another reason stems from the fact that very few hot rodders plan their interior from the start of the project. Rather, they address the interior after the car is painted, the floor boards have been repaired, the transmission tunnel has been built, and the steering column and box have been mounted. This situation brings several problems, one of which is the ergonomics of the car can end up being terrible—nothing is worse than being uncomfortable behind the wheel of a great-looking car.

I have a friend who has built several real nice hot rods over the years and drives them everywhere. The first step in his building process is to mount the seat and locate the steering column and pedals in the car. Many hours are spent carefully positioning these key elements because he learned early on if you are not comfortable in the car, you will not use the car. With the seating position established he knows exactly how much he can chop the top and still see out. This can be accomplished by simply taping across the windshield the desired amount of the top chop. If you can see out comfortably, it is a reasonable chop. If you can't, it may be one wicked car but reserved for short drives.

Fitting the Driver to the Car

Establishing a good seating position in a car is fairly simple. The steering wheel should be centered on your body, and while sitting comfortably your arms should have a relaxed break at the elbow. If you reach forward with your arms extended your wrists should rest atop the steering wheel. With your hands at 10 and 2 o'clock on the steering wheel, your arms should be comfortable, not reaching up to the wheel, nor hanging down to grip the wheel.

Be certain there is ample room between the steering wheel and the top of your thighs, so you can easily get in and out of the car. Once you have achieved the proper seating position, you will also have an uninterrupted view out the front, side, and rear windows. Now is the time to consider vision for the side view and rear view mirrors too.

Many traditional hot rods are channeled down over the frame. When you channel a car, special care must be taken to provide reasonable pedal leverage and even room for the pedals. If you are simply considering channeling a car, it pays to test the effects on the cabin before cutting the floor. Remember, channeling is effectively raising the floor in the car.

As the body is lowered over the frame, the floor rises. To simulate cabin changes caused by channeling, try raising the floor before you make that first cut. If you are going

While aluminum bomber seats and interior panels are all the rage in old-style hot rods, this type interior was reserved for all-out race cars in the 1950s. Your basic hot rod generally had a padded seat with at least worn upholstery in place.

Traditional hot rod interiors trend toward simplicity. A stock seat with a custom tuck-and-roll upholstery was considered top shelf in the early days. This roadster exemplifies a great hot rod interior.

When it comes to pure tradition, nothing works better than white Naugahyde with piping to match the body color of the car. Also noteworthy and era correct are the chrome-plated pieces on the seat frame.

The minimalist approach to upholstery works well in this track-T. Wool is stretched over the inner panels of the body providing a clean look and maximizing the interior space. Even the doorskins are upholstered on the inside, providing some storage. A large center-mounted dial is the focal point of the engine-turned dashboard.

to channel the car four inches, a few simple pieces of 2 x 4-inch lumber and a piece of plywood provide a good mock-up. It doesn't have to fit perfectly; just build a platform that allows you to mount the seat and extend to the firewall. Four inches might not sound like much, but when you take that much out of the vertical height of the cabin, a lot of things begin to happen.

First, you might notice that the steering column is no longer comfortable and suddenly your legs are pointing straight ahead, rather than forward and down as in a normal seating position. Leg room between the steering wheel and your legs is compromised, and while a smaller-diameter steering wheel will give you some of that room back, it also will demand more strength to turn the wheels.

You will also notice that pedal pressure is now much more difficult to achieve because, rather than using your natural weight to push down on the pedals, you are seated very low and find yourself pushing almost straight forward, meaning you must produce all the pressure with muscle rather than weight. Slightly longer pedal arms will provide a mechanical advantage if there is room for them, and generally in a channeled car hanging pedals are preferred over pedals protruding through the floor. Remember, pedals that pivot under the floor rotate down toward the floor, whereas pedal that are hung from above tend to be pushed straight forward with a slight upward radius.

Finally, check to be certain your leg is very comfortable when it is resting on the gas pedal. Your foot will remain on that pedal for many more hours than any other pedal, so it is paramount that this pedal is located perfectly to eliminate leg strain or cramps. If possible, the gas pedal and the brake pedal should be on the same plane, or the brake pedal just a bit lower than the gas pedal. This will minimize the time it takes to move from gas to brakes, and this time is important in emergency stopping. The thing to avoid is a low gas pedal and a high brake pedal, as the driver must then lift his foot off the gas pedal and up to find and meet the brake pedal. Not only is this fatiguing, it is also time consuming.

Finally, allow ample room between your pedals. Be certain you cannot snag your foot on the bottom side of the brake pedal, and be certain your foot will not contact the brake pedal when depressing the clutch. Nothing ruins a speed-shift quite like hitting the brake pedal when you were planning on hitting the clutch pedal.

In the minor, yet still worth consideration department, if you plan to use a floor-mounted dimmer switch (and all vintage hot rodders should), be certain it is located in an easy-to-find, intuitive position, so switching from high to low beams can be done quickly and easily.

If you consider ergonomics early enough in the project, then moving items, such as steering columns and brake pedals, can be done without much trouble. If you discover late in the project that these things are uncomfortable, chances are you will talk yourself into living with the discomfort, rather than relocating a steering column or, worse yet, a steering box. It takes a real man to put grinder to finished paint in the name of comfort, but in the end, it may be the best decision.

Sitting in this red and black 1939 pickup is like entering a time capsule. Everything is spot-on period perfect from the rubber floor mats to the upholstery.

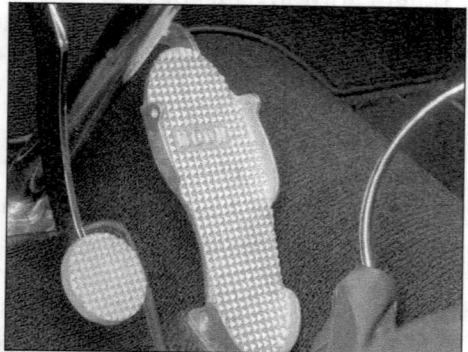

Feet of all sorts were big for gas pedals, and companies such as Moon, Eelco, and CalCustom offered foot-shaped pedals. This Moon pedal was designed for drag racing, and that lip on the brake pedal side could cause a little bit of foot interference when moving from gas to brake.

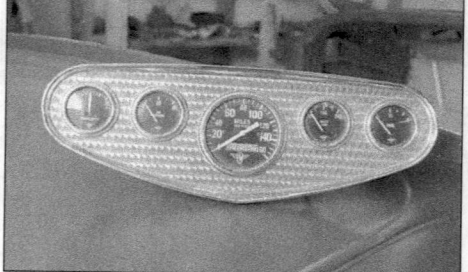

Friend and serious hot rodder Lewis McMillan took this gorgeous gauge cluster off his shelf. It comes complete with a story: It seems the fellow who owned these gauges sold his Deuce in 1956, but part of the price negotiation included not selling the gauges. They remained in that man's possession until Lewis rescued them several years ago.

If there was any doubt to the date of these gauges it was confirmed when the stamped date code of 1952 was found on the back side of the housing. The housing also bore a very nice Stewart-Warner script stamped in the cups.

INTERIOR: REAL HOT RODS HAVE UPHOLSTERY

Mounting Gauges and Switches

After you have achieved the proper seating position, it is time to locate items such as gauges and switches. Early Fords located the instrument clusters in the center of the dashboard until 1933, when they moved them in front of the steering wheel. If you are working within the confines of a gauge cluster in a 1932-or-earlier Ford, there is a good chance you have to glance to the right to check the gauges. Of course, the dashboard can be filled with the gauges arranged in order of importance. Generally, the speedometer and tachometer are located in the clear field of vision area, as they are the most often viewed gauges. Oil

The 1950 Ford gauge cluster is a great example of using what would have been modern equipment in the 1950s to properly date your car. Gauges such as this are relatively inexpensive and can be refinished by companies like Palo Alto Speedometer service.

In the 1950s, gauge manufacturers also produced some great-looking clusters to hold the gauges. Likewise, many of the more expensive cars, such as Auburn, had great-looking gauge clusters. Today, many are reproduced and there were also a lot of similar gauge cluster manufactured for pleasure boats of the 1950, like Chris Craft.

Some things leave no room for improvement, and the 1933 Ford dashboard is one of those items. When Ford finally moved the gauges in front of the steering wheel, it was done in high style. Oval gauges on either side of the large gold speedometer blend perfectly with the engine-turned dash insert and wonder woodgraining.

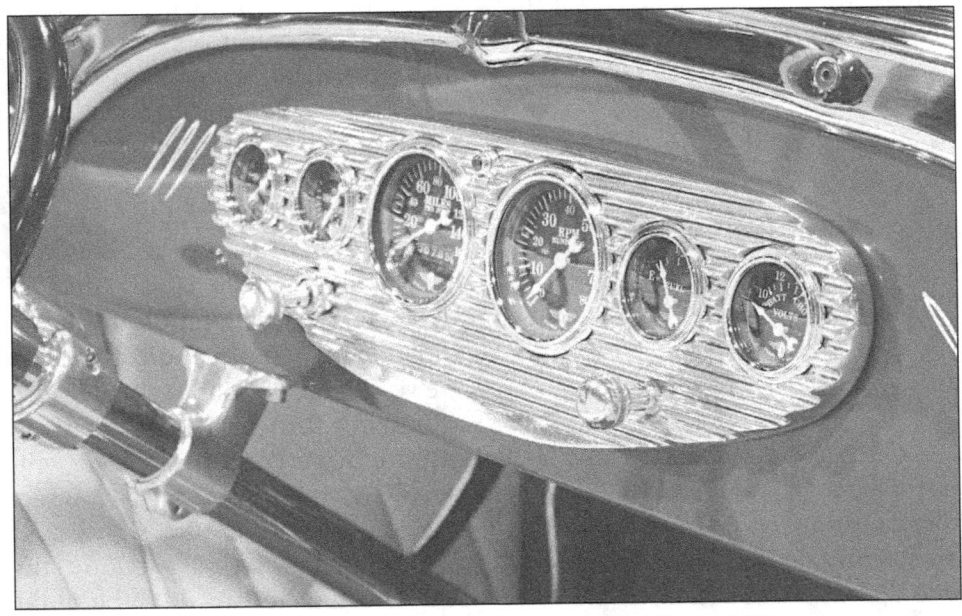

This a modern take on vintage instrumentation. The Stewart-Warner gauges carry the same style pointers and early Stewart Warner winged emblems under curved glass, but they are the smaller 2¼-inch gauges with 3¹¹⁄₁₆-inch speedometer and tach. It is a great looking set.

HOW TO BUILD PERIOD CORRECT HOT RODS

CHAPTER 5

Anything that says Police Special is going to look good in your dashboard. These gauges were manufactured for early police cars, and there seems to be quite a few of them around. The superior condition of this gauge explains the $200 price tag.

These large 2⅝-inch Stewart-Warner gauges have the coveted crescent moon pointers, meaning they were manufactured for industrial and some military uses. The name Stewart-Warner cannot be seen on the face, although if you look down behind the bezel you will see Stewart-Warner in block letters. The back side of the housings also bear the SW logo. These are postwar gauges, manufactured from 1946 until 1960. Fuel-level gauges command the highest priced due to rarity.

pressure, water temperature, and volts are generally arranged in that order followed by the gas gauge and other gauges, such as vacuum or oil temperature.

Once again placement is everything. Personally, I would never use a four-spoke steering wheel because I frequently monitor gauges; for that reason I prefer a three-spoke wheel with a clear view to my gauge cluster. Of course, the traditional Bell-style steering wheel is one very good looking piece, so if you prefer that style wheel remember to space your gauges appropriately.

Beyond location you must also consider the size of the gauges. Several modern gauge companies are making four- and five-in-one gauges with very small gauges surrounding a larger speedometer, generally all under one glass. These smaller gauges can be very difficult to read for aging eyes, particularly at night.

Speaking of aging eyes, the final items I try to keep in my field of vision are turn signal indicator lights and the high beam indicator light. We've all been behind someone with a blinking turn signal for 20 miles. Although modern cars have self-canceling turn signals, if you are using an early-style turn signal conversion, such as a signal-stat unit, the self-canceling feature may be gone. In that case, it is up to the driver to turn off the turn signal—a good reason to mount the indicator light up high in the field of vision.

The final consideration for interior planning revolves around creature comforts, such as heat, A/C, and stereo. These items can be used as accent pieces if they are vintage, such as hanging underdash heaters and vintage radios. However, modern pieces, such as high-tech speakers and even A/C controls and outlets, have little place in a truly vintage hot rod, so they should be installed discreetly with an eye toward making them blend in. Mounting such controls behind the factory dashboard speaker grille or in the glove box is a good idea to preserve the vintage flavor of your interior.

Carpeting

Let's start at the bottom and work up. While carpet color selection cannot be made unless you know the rest of the interior material colors, you can look for two basic styles of carpet. For the most part, early Fords form 1928 to 1941 used wire-loop, square-weave carpet. This same design is available today in synthetic fibers, but for a real early look, wool

It is the gauge that illuminated thousands of hot rod dashboards across the country. The combination of a Stewart-Warner gauges and a Sun tach was a winning combination then as well as today. This Sun tach is being reproduced today by SunPro gauges.

INTERIOR: REAL HOT RODS HAVE UPHOLSTERY

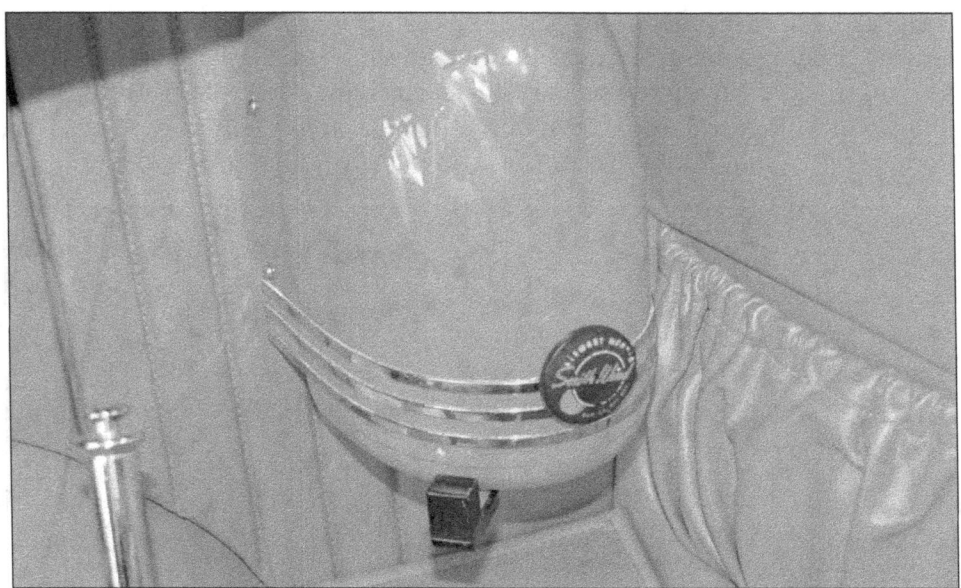

Few things can provide traditional flavor better than an early under-dash heater. This is an early Stewart-Warner Southwind heater that originally burned raw gasoline to provide heat. Surprisingly, most of them didn't blow up, and by 1948 SW had sold over three million of these units. They were used in military aircraft, on buses and as pre-heaters for big diesel motors. Today, this one serves as a glove box, but under-dash units with a hot water heater core still work great today and can easily be refurbished.

ally hosing out a 1967 Chevy work truck I once owned when mud would gather on the floor.

Seats

There were really only two choices in seating—bucket seats or bench seat. For the most part, bucket seats were found in sports cars, foreign cars, and adapted to the cockpit of a hot rod. The bench seat was by far the more popular of the two choices because of the ease of installation, and the fact that your favorite girl could sit right next to you, not necessarily in that order.

Vintage-flavor hot rods of today often employ aluminum race seats fabricated to simulate aircraft bomber seats, hence the term bomber seats. They look very cool, and while you might not think it, they are quite comfortable if constructed properly. However, such seats were reserved for race cars, and finding them in a street-driven hot rod in the 1950s was virtually unheard of, but today they are the choice of the new, old school builders.

is the way to go, and the good news is you can buy reproduction early Ford carpet from several sources, such as Lebaron-Bonney.

While the loop type was the most common carpet used, some custom installations used the wool-cut pile that was also used in automobiles from the 1930s to the 1950s. This gives the look of a very short, plush-style carpet, which is definitely a more expensive look than the loop carpet. By the 1960s, loop carpet was found in most U.S. cars but was made of nylon rather than wool, making it a great choice for open cars that may get wet on occasion. Some base-model cars did not have carpet at all, rather a textured rubber mat covered the floor, and virtually all trucks employed rubber mats. This treatment was sometimes seen in more performance oriented hot rods of the past and is gaining popularity today for a minimalist look. Rubber mats in trucks were standard fare even into the 1960s, and I can remember liter-

There is no denying the hot rod race car flavor of aluminum bucket seats. Speedway Motors and others sell reproduction bomber seats that are roughly modeled after seats from World War II bomber aircraft.

HOW TO BUILD PERIOD CORRECT HOT RODS

Upholstery

The option of using the original mohair interior fabric of the 1930s is seen out there, but even early hot rodders changed the upholstery fabric, as it was generally worn and tattered after five or ten years of use. The material of choice was vinyl, often referred to by the brand name of Naugahyde, or leather. The Tijuana interior is the stuff of legend, and for many southern California hot rodders the relatively short trip to Mexico netted them a tuck-and-roll or rolled-and-pleated interior for much less money. While good craftsmanship could be found, the materials used varied greatly—from horsehair to newspaper to pad seats and door panels made of cardboard. Often the quality of the leather and even the thread was less than desirable, but the price was right and some of the better TJ tuck-and-roll jobs lasted for many years. Today padding, thread, and most door panels are made of synthetic materials that are designed to resist moisture and compress and rebound at given rates.

Most traditional hot rod interiors used either leather or vinyl and the seat patterns would generally be either rolled-and-pleated, diamond-tufted, or a simple plain seat with stitching similar to the factory-original pattern. The rolled-and-pleated interior could be divided into three distinct groups: the 2-inch sewed pleat, the 4-inch sewed pleat, or the 2-inch pressed-pleat. The decision for a 2- or 4-inch pleat is largely a personal choice. For me, the 2-inch pleat always has more hot rod flavor than the wider version. The pressed pleat is vinyl fabric that has the 2-inch pleats heat pressed into place. This greatly reduced labor costs due to the lack of sewing time, and many hot rods used this material. As a matter of fact, using press pleats often adds more "real hot rod flavor" than a fine sewed version because many people view the seat and smile as they remember either having just such a seat or admiring them in the 1950s and 1960s. The material is still available today.

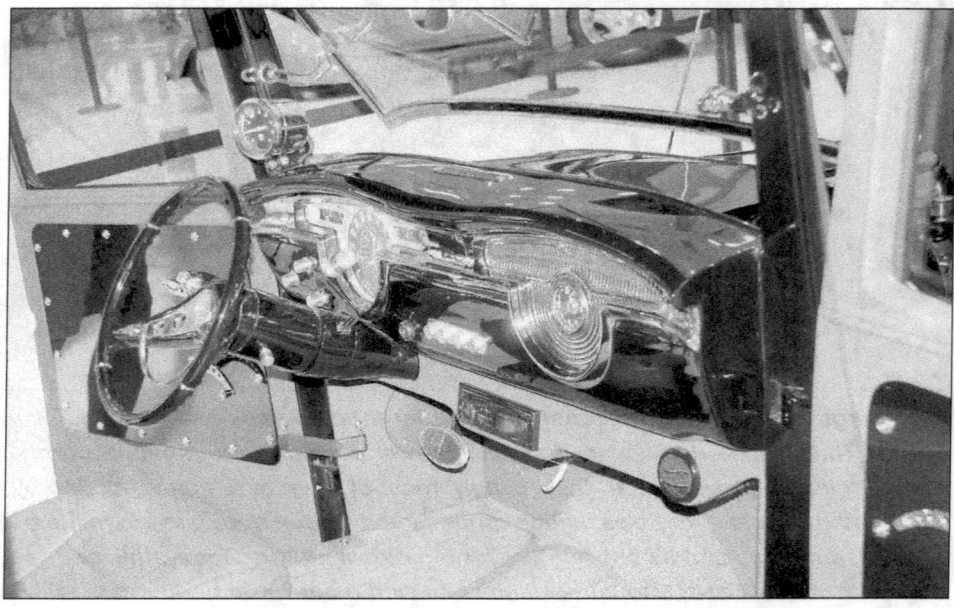

Bob Reed's Deuce Tudor has a dashboard from a 1957 Buick, and most of the center portion was removed to fit, but the great-looking dashboard grilles provide a vintage, art-deco look to his hot rod.

The 1959 Chevrolet dashboard is another very popular unit for dash swapping. Once again, this would have been modern equipment if you were building a vintage hot rod in 1962. The modular design of the dashboard makes modifications easy. These dashboards are also available in fiberglass reproduction form.

INTERIOR: REAL HOT RODS HAVE UPHOLSTERY

Inside this 1937 Chevy gasser is a stock dashboard that has an engine-turned, stainless steel insert holding two gauges. A red metal-flake Cal Custom steering wheel and matching shifter ball complete the interior appointments.

Once very much in vogue, the wood rimmed steering wheel has fallen from grace lately, but if you were to fiberglass the wood until it was smooth and then paint half the wheel to match your car, you might be on the way to starting your own trend.

No doubt the most radical of all rolled-and-pleated interiors was the candy-stripe interior. Generally white and a color closely matching the paint color were alternated in the pleats. The effect takes you right back to the 1950s and early 1960s, but like so many trendy styles, it is easy to grow weary of the look, so maybe a simple black or white rolled-and-pleated interior is a safer bet.

The diamond-tufted interior has been around since the day of the horse-drawn carriage, and there are two different ways to achieve the pattern. One is to stitch the diamonds in place, while the older method involves folding the material, so no stitching is used, and buttons hold everything in place. I had a diamond-tufted interior in my first hot rod along with a diamond-tufted roof insert. The roof insert was folded while the interior was stitched, and like all good hot rodders do, I knew how many buttons were in my interior—in excess of 500.

Fabric interiors were not as common as leather and vinyl, while crushed velvet, velour, and mohair were used on some cars. Most of the early rods steered clear of such fabrics, if for no other reason than these fabrics stain.

Door panels were generally matched to the seats in both material and pattern, and things like power windows were generally not used because many early power window units were hydraulic. These hydraulic units were quite heavy and no self-respecting hot rodder would dare add weight to his car under the guise of convenience. It is my belief that *real* hot rods simply do not have power windows, or for that matter air conditioning.

HOW TO BUILD PERIOD CORRECT HOT RODS

CHAPTER 5

The 1940 dashboard was considered modern because it was not just a flat face, consequently it was cut down and adapted to many different hot rods. Reproduction steel dashboards are available today from Bob Drake Reproductions.

Dashboard

You are going to be facing this thing the entire time you're driving, so making it pleasant to look at as well as functional makes good sense. Vintage hot rods often employed the stock dashboard with a replacement gauge cluster. In the early years of hot rodding, Stewart-Warner ruled the planet when it came time to selecting instruments for your dashboard. Many early hot rods simply updated the dashboard with a gauge cluster from a later model car, and units like a 1950s Ford had a neat-looking speedometer surrounded by four other gauges.

By the 1960s, the hot setup was to run Stewart-Warner gauges and a Sun tach. Sun Instruments made individual oil, water temp, volts, amps, and fuel level gauges too, but for some reason every hot rodder I knew wanted a Sun tach and Stewart-Warner gauges.

Often the stock gauge cluster on a car was supplemented with the instrumentation of a set of three

No doubt the best selling hot rod steering wheel ever produced was the Cal Custom, three-spoke, nine-hole steering wheel. They came in colors from white to red metalflake and everything in between, and will forever look proper in almost any hot rod.

Ford produced banjo wheels in the mid 1930s, as did other automakers. Their intrinsic good looks are as elegant today as they were 80 years ago. An aftermarket horn button carries the famous V-8 logo to complete the picture.

HOW TO BUILD PERIOD CORRECT HOT RODS

INTERIOR: REAL HOT RODS HAVE UPHOLSTERY

The 1940 Ford steering wheel is simple, yet detailed, and it is a great choice for hot rods capturing the early look. While the stock 1940 steering wheel was rather large, today you can find any number of companies reproducing this wheel in more modern diameters.

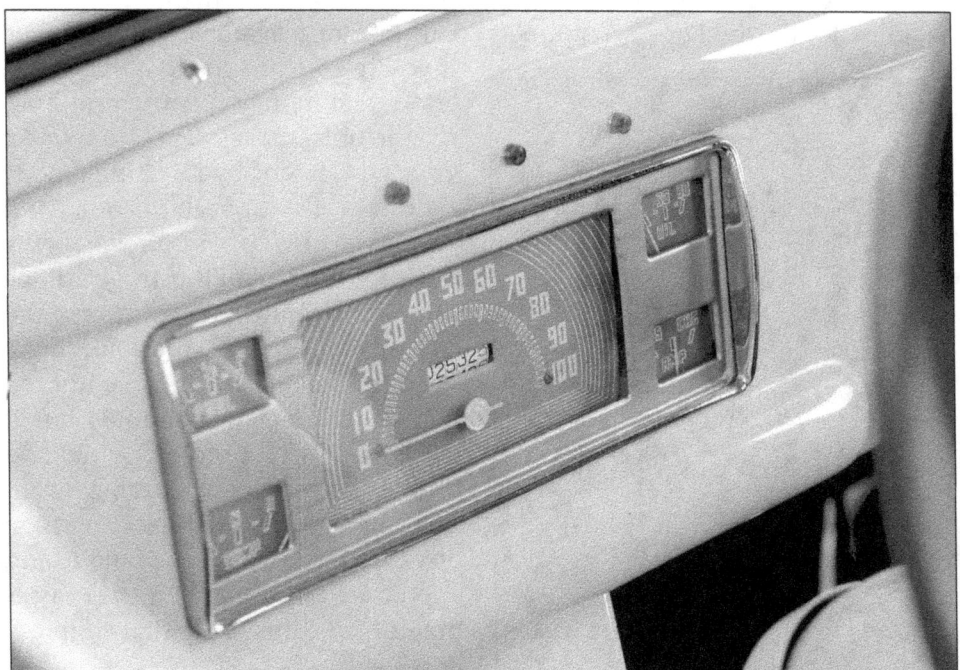

Doing less is often doing more, and in this case a 1940 Ford pickup truck has opted for stock instrumentation. The utter simplicity of it all is appealing, and the vintage graphics are similar to those found on home radios of that era. They just look like a dial face should.

or four aftermarket gauges located under the dash in a separate panel. The tachometer was generally located on the dashboard or attached to the steering column. Few memories are clearer in my mind than cruising at night with the glow of a Sun tach on the dashboard.

Swapping dashboards was popular with hot rodders too, and that continues to this day. It seems the 1940 Ford dashboard found its way into many traditional hot rods ranging from Model A Fords to 1939 Fords. Since these early dashboards could be unbolted, it was easy to remove the dash and then modify it to fit your hot rod.

Dash knobs and shifter knobs are great ways to personalize a hot rod and Plexiglas knobs in bright colors were popular along with 8-balls, pistons, beer tappers, and large molded dice, among others. All of these accessories are available today along with a wide range of custom door handles and interior trim.

In Summary

When planning your interior, keep the appropriate time period in mind, and whenever possible, keep it simple. Be certain to convey to your upholstery man exactly what you want, and stop by often to check on progress. That way, if the upholstery shop has decided to put sculpted arm rests with dreaded tweed inserts on your doors, you can stop things before it is too late.

Like most things on traditional hot rods, the axiom, "When in doubt, leave it out" will serve you well. You can always add a bit of vintage flavor or a small accessory later, but if you start off with too much it will always be too much.

CHAPTER 6

BODY AND MODS: SELECTING THE RIGHT SHEET METAL FOR AN ERA

Even the period perfect chassis, wheel and tire combination, and motor selection combined cannot outweigh the single most important element in building a period correct hot rod—the body. While body modifications are all-important, before you can modify an old car body you must first own one.

The choice for a proper body for a vintage hot rod is generally limited to Fords. Yes, Chevrolet, Plymouth, and Dodge cars felt the hot rodders touch too, but in numbers vastly smaller than Fords. In the Ford ranks, almost any body style works with the exception of the four-door sedans. Oh sure, there was the occasional four-door hot rod that was noteworthy back in the day, and it can be done again today. However, if you're going to spend all the time, effort, and money constructing a hot rod, it only makes sense to protect your investment by selecting a body style that also appeals to other hot rodders. There is the lure of being different, and building truly unique cars, but it almost always comes at a cost. You may think that building a 1930 Essex coupe into a great hot rod will be different and unique, but it will probably cost more to build and bring substantially less money when the time comes to sell the car. If you do it right, the car will be unique and appreciated by some, but the masses prefer Fords. It is really that simple.

Body-Style Choices

So the question is, which body style is right for you? It is best to first

Royce Fewell of Findlay, Ohio, built this timeless Deuce in 1991. The car relies on a chopped Carson-style top and the soft blue pearl paint to make vintage statement. This example proves when it comes to old hot rods and body modifications, often less is best.

define exactly what it is you plan on doing with this hot rod. Is the car going to be a local cruiser, with use generally restricted to a 200-mile radius of your home? If so, that channeled roadster might be just the answer.

Do you plan on making long journeys with your better half? Suddenly, trunk space and comfort may become an issue, so maybe that 1940 coupe is the best hot rod for you.

Or maybe that roadster shouldn't be channeled after all.

Maybe you would like to go for the trifecta of hot rodding—show, go, and race. In that case, you build a hot rod for the occasional pass down the drag strip, but good enough to stand tall in a show and reliable and tame enough to drive great distances. If this is your dream, things like quick-change rears, healthy motors, and an expanded budget are in order.

Let's look at some of the popular body styles and discuss why you might want to own each one.

Roadsters and Phaetons

Simply put, the roadster is the quintessential hot rod, and frankly, nothing beats a roadster on those perfect top down days. By definition, a roadster has no side windows and a folding or removable top. This makes a lot of the steel body Deuce replicas actually convertibles since they sport roll-up windows.

If you live almost anywhere but California, those perfect top-down days may add up to about nine per year, and you'll be working or out of town for six of them. For that reason, roadsters tend to be very popular

If you want to make a real vintage hot rod statement, locate a set of super-rare and equally as expensive Kinmont disc brakes. These are considered to be the ultimate vintage brake setup by many hot rodders, but the price will keep all but the most dedicated builder from using them.

For East Coast hot rod flavor, it is just hard to beat a deeply channeled coupe with a stock-height top. This Model A is period perfect with a sectioned '32 grille shell mounted in front of the crossmember.

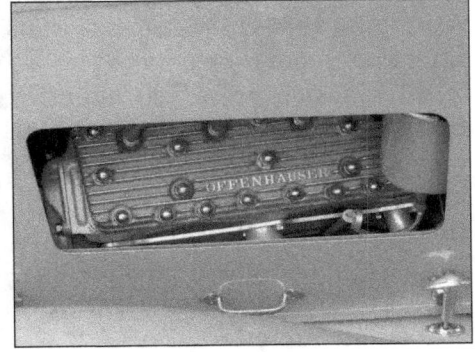

While the body remains original, the only sheet metal work involved is these windows cut in smooth hood sides to expose the full-house flathead. It is a reflection on a time when hot rods were all about what was under the hood.

where the weather is moderate. But having said that, for the adventurous person who loves to experience the elements, the hot rod roadster is the way to go. Nothing elevates your mood faster than a ride in a topless roadster, and nothing seems to draw a larger crowd than a great roadster. When it comes time to sell, there seem to be plenty of people longing for the experience. That's the good news.

On the downside, be realistic and consider seasonal limitations in the area you live. Maine is a great place to live, but if you're a roadster owner your season is seriously limited—possibly a hot rod coupe would make more sense. But, then again, making sense out of great hot rods is something I could never manage.

Ford produced its last roadster in 1937. The newer the car, the more protection from the elements. The infamous T-bucket leaves you completely exposed as you almost sit *on* it, not in it. As the bodies become larger, you are able sit down deeper in the car, providing more protection from the wind. So, the Model A is better than a T, the Deuce beats an A, and the 1934–1937 Ford roadsters offer even more protection.

If roadsters were the mainstay of hot rodding in California, the coupe was the hot rod of choice almost everywhere else. Once again the weather was the deciding factor. Early hot rods were often daily drivers for their young owners, so shelter became important. This fact was not lost on new-car buyers either, and I would be willing to bet there was a big difference in the number of roadsters and phaetons sold in Coon Rapids, Minnesota, versus Newport Beach, California, from 1928 to 1937.

Coupes

Coupes were the real vintage hot rods in many parts of the country, and they served hot rodders well as they were small, light, and compact. Those very attributes made them unreasonable when hot rodders were family men, but now the kids are

The roadster body style is the quintessential hot rod, and when you do a radical top chop and lay the windshield back, it gets just plain nasty. Dave Thomas introduced this roadster in 2003.

Seldom seen in hot rodding circles today, the phaeton, or tub, was a popular hot rod in the 1960s, although never to the extent of the roadsters. This 1927 Model T tub carries plenty of vintage style thanks to the red wire wheels, four-cylinder motor, and matching interior.

BODY AND MODS: SELECTING THE RIGHT SHEET METAL FOR AN ERA

There is a lot to like about this roadster, from the molded rear fenders to the patina purple paint and well-done deeper purple scallops. The gas tank resides behind the seat and fills through the quarter panel. Bob Metz of Shelbyville, Indiana, built the car in 1959 for Ruel Dunbar of Akron, Ohio. The car was shown extensively from 1960 to 1963 on the ISCA tour, and then put in the garage for 40 years before being purchased in 2003. Today, the car is 99.9 percent original, as built from the paint to the tires! Only the carpet has been changed in the car, making this a true time capsule.

In the 1950s, it was not uncommon to leave the '32 Ford three-window coupe in stock form with just a dropped axle, wide whitewalls, and your choice of hubcaps. Once again a fine example of less is more.

gone and the coupe seems to be back in favor as young and old alike long for that real hot rod flavor.

The Model T coupe is enjoying a resurgence of sorts and is the most affordable coupe out there, followed by the Model A coupe. Both of these cars are crude by design when compared to the V-8 Fords of 1932 to 1948. For that reason, many hot rodders gravitate toward the later model cars, and the two most iconic hot rod coupes on the planet are the 1932 Ford and the 1940 Ford—and maybe not in that order. While postwar coupes seldom have the aggressive hot rod nature of an earlier car, they provide the combination of the classic coupe profile with more room, longer wheelbase, and generally better ride quality than the early cars. For the long-haul driver, a 1941–1948 coupe from Ford, Chevrolet, or Dodge and Plymouth makes a great car.

Today, the Model A Ford is extremely popular, and the sheer numbers produced dictate that they are affordable. Coupes make a lot of sense; they provide shelter without losing any of the hot rod attitude. The versatility of the Model A is another attribute; it looks great in stock form rolling on a set of Kelsey-Hayes wire wheels, or sporting an aggressive 6-inch top chop and 4-inch channeling. Fenders or no fenders, these little coupes make great hot rods and the interchangeability of parts among all four years allows you to build a Model A with a combination of body parts from 1928 to 1931.

Sedans and Victorias

I wasn't sure where to place the Victoria since Chevrolet called a similar body style a five-passenger coupe. But if you are looking for a hot rod with a back seat you're talking sedans and Victorias. Once again, it seems the 1928–1940 sedans are most popular for vintage-style hot rods.

It may be a bit more difficult to build a sinister sedan, but with the right focus you can have seating for four and a true traditional hot rod all wrapped in one. The vintage hot rod sedans tend to be 1926–1934 models, then the fat attack cars ranging from 1935–1938, followed by the 1939 and 1940 sedans that would be considered iconic hot rod sedans again. It took some time for hot rodders to warm up to the 1935–1938 sedans, and for that reason, they were not as common as the earlier sedans in hot rod circles. The Fordor sedan is even less likely to be a hot rod, although once again, with the right treatment it can be done.

Personally, when it comes to back seat hot rods, I would prefer anything called a Victoria. Next on my list would be the 1928–1929 Model A and the 1932–1934 Ford sedans.

Sedan Deliveries

The sedan delivery is a light-duty commercial vehicle, and it is a bit of an orphan. The car people claim it is a truck while the truck people claim it is a car. Call it what you like, these little haulers have been popular with hot rodders since the day they were made. With just two seats up front, and sometimes just one, these little trucks were the perfect race car support vehicle, surf wagon, or business vehicle.

The interior storage makes these cars perfect for long hauls, and it is easy to put a traditional hot rod look on one of these vehicles. Some people prefer to put seats in the back, but I suggest this is a pretty boring way to travel—with a limited view you may as well be sitting in a 55-gallon drum. For that reason, I consider the sedan delivery a two-passenger vehicle with room for tools, tires for racing, pop-up tents, and coolers for rod running. Limited sight when driving is another pitfall of the sedan delivery due to the lack of side quarter windows.

Body Modifications

Assuming you have chosen the body style most suitable for your needs, the next question is, What modifications should you perform on the car?

It appears that most of the really great hot rods rely on simplicity to

The 1928–1929 Model A Ford coupe is enjoying a resurgence, and one look at a well-proportioned hot rod, like this one, explains the sudden popularity. Chopped, channeled, or full fendered, the Model A is a very versatile hot rod.

The Tudor sedan provides plenty of hot rod flavor with room for the kids or cargo on the back seat. While Fordor sedans were seldom seen in hot rodding, they too can make great hot rods for group travel.

make a statement, in stark contrast to the modern-era method of doing micro-surgery to every square inch of the car. While there is no denying that many of our modern hot rods are grand creations, the fact remains it only takes a few well-executed modifications to build a timeless hot rod. Go beyond that, and history may not be as kind.

Common modifications in the traditional arena are chopping the top and channeling the body over the frame, followed by the much less common modification of sectioning the body. And there are many other, less dramatic modifications you might want to consider.

Top chopping is the act (art if done correctly) of removing area through the windshield and side glass of a hot rod, thereby lowering the roof, generally performed in a range from 1 to 6 inches. The lower the roof, the more aggressive the profile and the more difficult to see where you are going.

Channeling refers to removing the floor from the body of the car and lowering it over the frame.

Choosing the right body style for your needs is a big decision. The sedan delivery has long been a staple of hot rodding. While they offer great hauling ability, remember they are two-seat vehicles with limited vision. Some sedan deliveries only had a driver's seat to allow for longer cargo.

This is a great comparison of altered profiles, the coupe in the foreground is channeled but not chopped, while the coupe in the background has been chopped and channeled. The difference in profiles is striking.

This generally requires new body mounts to be fabricated, although some early hot rods actually had the body welded to the frame during the channeling process. Channeling can range anywhere from 1 inch to 10 inches, and once again, it provides a lower profile. Remember, every inch of channeling is an inch less leg room, head room, and steering wheel room.

Sectioning a body is no doubt the most daunting of these three body modifications. This involves literally cutting the car in half on the horizontal plane, lowering the top half back down on the lower half and welding it all back together. Panel fit, alignment, and proportions are critical, and if a section job is not perfectly planned, the car can end up looking just plain awkward.

In the rare occasion that you chop, channel, and section your hot rod, be certain to plan seating, steering, and pedals well in advance.

Much as with roadsters and coupes, there seems to be a bit of a geographical divide on these modifications. Top chopping seemed to be more popular on the West Coast, while channeling seemed more prevalent on the East Coast. Of course, both modifications were found on hot rods everywhere, but for some reason East Coast hot rods were often channeled and not chopped, while West Coast cars that were channeled were also generally chopped. I can think of no real reason for this other than possibly Mother Nature helped to channel East Coast cars by devouring the floor boards with rust. Sectioning the body was not particularly common anywhere, as this is a major undertaking. I dare say 50 percent of the cars sectioned ended up in a salvage yard somewhere, in two sections.

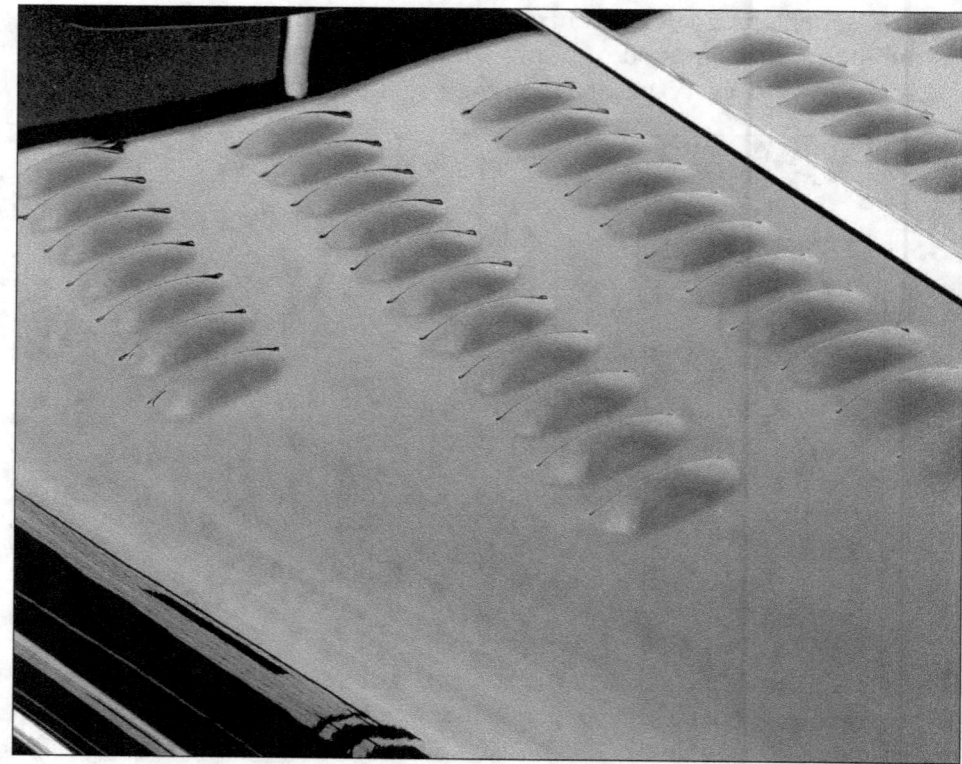

Louvers are all cool, but if you are building an early-style hot rod, look for a louver press with these early-style rounded louvers. It's a subtle difference, but they date a car perfectly.

The rear deck lid is filled with louvers too, and the 1950 Pontiac taillights are a natural. Other noteworthy items include the 1937 Ford trunk handle, the simple hanging license plate and the whitewalls turned in is simply a great touch.

BODY AND MODS: SELECTING THE RIGHT SHEET METAL FOR AN ERA

Selecting taillights and other accessories from a production car go a long way to placing your car in the proper era. Late 1940s/early 1950s Plymouth taillights work well on this 1933 Plymouth hot rod.

Bobbed fenders are fenders that have been shortened. It was common practice to bend 1/4- or 3/8-inch rod to contour the fenders. Dick Roy built this vintage hot rod in 1956 in Ontario, Canada. The car needs refurbishing today, but the fine craftsmanship can be seen in the rusted fender.

Whatever the reasons, if you are building a traditional East Coast car, consider channeling the car and leaving the top stock height. It might not be quite as wicked looking as a chopped and channeled car, but it will fit an era perfectly. When I built my first hot rod in 1969, I channeled a Model A coupe body over the frame about 5 inches in the front and 4 in the rear. The top was not chopped.

Other modifications, like hidden hinges, were seldom seen, although one of the most famous hot rods of the early era, the Joe Nitto roadster, had hidden hinges. A more common modification was flared door hinges, where the stationary portion of the hinge had a fairing built to streamline the air; this was no doubt part of early aerodynamics. Generally peaked and shaved grille shells, louvered panels, three-piece hoods, and rolled rear pans were the most common modifications. Lighting was also generally kept clean and simple with the 1939 Ford teardrop taillight and the 1950 Pontiac round lights being two of the most popular examples.

Vintage hot rods should include windshield frames for cars 1939 and older, and while suicide doors were all the rage for the past 15 years, it is a modification that takes a lot of work and often makes getting in and out of a car awkward. Plus, you only know the doors are reversed when they are open so you reap little benefit for all the work. Finally, Ford tried it for a couple years and went back to conventional doors, which should tell you something.

Fender Choices

With 1934 or older cars, the other big decision is to choose between a fenderless hot rod and a full-fendered version. What do you prefer? For the most part, race cars of the 1940s and 1950s ran fenderless, and since many street-going hot rods wanted to look like race cars, they too decided fenders were not required equipment. However, when reviewing magazines of the era and noting some of the finer hot rods, it was a pretty even split between fenderless hot rods and their full-fendered counterparts.

Fenderless Hot Rods

Today, it seems most builders of vintage-flavor hot rods are going the fenderless route. This makes sense for a couple of reasons. First, it is a lot less work and less expense to build a car sans fenders and running boards. And dare I say, there is even more chassis work involved in a full-fendered car, for while a Highboy-style hot rod can tolerate several different wheel and tire combinations, when building a full-fendered hot rod, the wheel and tire must perfectly fill those fenders or the whole car is lost. The other advantage of building a fenderless car is there is no mistaking this creation of yours as anything but a hot rod—even the unknowing realize it is a hot rod.

In some states, it is still illegal to drive a car with no fenders on the street. This has long been the case and hot rodders who want the fenderless look mount cycle fenders on their cars. These fenders are just as the name implies, fenders that resemble those on a motorcycle. Often, these fenders were made from the steel ring that once surrounded the spare tire on cars, such as on a 1936 Ford. Cut the ring in half and you had enough material for two fenders, complete with a pleasing stamped reveal in the middle of the fender.

Cycle fenders could be a styling statement or a method of complying with state fender laws. Many states require fenders, so this fender style provides the hot rod with a fenderless look but the protection of fenders. Simple tubular mounts hold the fender to the backing plate; the fender turns with the wheel providing constant coverage. This is the front of the Dick Roy Deuce Coupe.

While Highboy roadsters are all the rage today, one look at the vintage Woodard/East/Moeller Deuce roadster should be enough to convince you that full-fendered Deuce roadsters make great vintage hot rods. The roadster was originally built in the mid 1950s.

Full-Fendered Hot Rods

The pluses for a full-fendered car come from a strictly esthetic standpoint. Done right, they are simply stunning hot rods and the sight of a curvaceous fender flowing over a wide whitewall tire is enough to make many hot rodders opt for fenders. Some people insist full-fendered hot rods are easier to keep clean, but having owned and driven both versions, I found the full-fendered car more difficult to keep clean since you had to reach under fenders and running boards to clean suspension components, the lower engine area, and the inside of wheels and tires.

Details like fender welting add character to the car, and many 1950s cars had chrome fender welting. This look is not for everyone because it quickly dates a car. Today, color-matched fender welting is available from numerous sources, such as Juliano's Interior Products.

For those considering building a traditional hot rod today, it would pay to seriously consider going with the full-fendered approach, as you won't be lost in a sea of similar styled Highboy hot rods. It is also my personal belief that all Victorias should have fenders.

Reproduction Bodies

The fiberglass reproduction body was one of the most important players in the rebirth of traditional hot rodding in the 1970s. Companies like Wescott's in Boring, Oregon, build high-quality products that make a great foundation for building a hot rod.

In the past 15 years, the reproduction steel body has become a reality and many hot rodders regard these as real steel hot rods. Well, sorry, it is still a reproduction body, and the only thing making it a bit more authentic is the faithful use of the materials used to construct the reproduction body. This gives hot rodders a choice: Find an original body, which is still the best way to build a hot rod, or use a reproduction body, and in that case the material used is irrelevant.

If you decide to use a reproduction body in the construction of a vintage-flavor hot rod, you will find that using an exact replica of the car works best. Stretched, bigger doors, and wider bodies are the stuff of modern street rods, and frankly, when these dimensions are changed, the entire look of the car is just a bit different.

A great combination is running a full-fendered car with a chopped top. George Lange's 1933 Ford is a beautiful example of a 1960s-style hot rod with unpolished American Mags.

In the world of reproduction bodies, you can now find fiberglass bodies and steel bodies, both are considered reproduction cars. At a glance you probably think this truck is steel, but in fact a faded blue paint scheme covers a complete fiberglass body.

CHAPTER 7

CHOOSING THE RIGHT PAINT, PATTERN, TEXTURE AND FINISH

There are many exciting, pivotal moments in building a hot rod—getting the suspension under the chassis and being able to roll it out into the driveway for the first time is one, lowering the motor and transmission into the frame is another, and of course the first time that hot rod motor fires to life is a major milestone in the building process. For me, none of those can compare to the day you finally lay down a perfect paint job on your hot rod.

When it comes to building vintage hot rods, color selection is a bit more complicated because both colors and paints have changed over the years. It was common practice in the 1950s and 1960s to build a hot rod, and as rust was repaired and the body was modified, primer was applied to the affected areas. Primer on a filled grille shell, deck lid, or louvered hood was simply a sign that this hot rod was a work in progress. It was also common to paint the firewall either white, black, or the forecasted body color.

Often a hot rod would be seen for a couple years with telltale primer spots, and in some cases when the spots began to connect the entire car was put in primer. While the sight of a full-primer hot rod was not uncommon, I remember far fewer of them than the aforementioned primer spot or primer panel cars.

My own primered hot rod was an example, and for the six months that it remained in primer everyone asked, "So, what color are you going to paint the car?" As it turns out, yellow was the answer, but this story serves to illustrate the point that primer was never considered a final

Traditional hot rods seem to respond best to utter simplicity. This 1940 Ford sedan is a fine example of an early hot rod in a period correct red. Note that the red is more muted than the modern brilliant reds seen on new cars today. Judging by the finish, I would guess this is red lacquer.

CHOOSING THE RIGHT PAINT, PATTERN, TEXTURE AND FINISH

Early flames and scallops were done by hot rodders in their backyard, not by a talented artist or graphic designer. That means many early scallops and flames were very basic and often not symmetrical. This is a great example of early scallops as you might have seen them in the early 1950s.

Of course, not all hot rods were painted; some were driven in primer while the owner performed work or saved money toward the paint job. This rare 1935 Ford roadster has the weathered look of real primer, and the white firewall is a perfect touch.

finish by early hot rodders. I never met a hot rodder with primer on his car that didn't have a color in his mind for the car. The fact that the only primer available at the time was lacquer primer made finished paint even more important.

Lacquer primer does not seal the surface and, over time, moisture works its way through the primer and the body begins to rust under and through the primer. Lacquer primer also had a tendency to chalk up after being exposed to the elements; there is nothing particularly good looking about faded primer with rust spots showing through. Finally, primer was available in three colors for hot rods: black, gray, and red oxide. I don't remember ever seeing tinted primers until the 1980s.

Today's epoxy-based primers have the ability to completely seal the metal from the elements. This makes it viable to use primer as a final finish. Other hot rodders prefer to use actual topcoat paint with a flattening agent in the paint to dull the

A more modern approach to the primer look is to put flattening agent in black urethane to gain protection from the weather in the process. It doesn't really look like lacquer primer, but the effect is close enough for many rodders. Paint companies are now selling a flat-black urethane pre-mixed for the primer look.

HOW TO BUILD PERIOD CORRECT HOT RODS

CHAPTER 7

While primer came in three basic colors—red oxide, light gray, and black—today a flattening agent is used to produce vibrant colors in suede finish. It is an attractive look, but not accurate for a true vintage hot rod.

Modern primers and paints are far superior to the products available to hot rodders in the early days. They cost a lot more, but the results last much longer than the old lacquer-based products.

finish. This provides a matte finish that never really looks quite like primer, but rather like flattened urethane paint. This is the same treatment used on the interior panels on modern cars and while a suede finish in colors is an interesting approach to modern hot rods it has nothing to do with true vintage hot rodding. Primer was chosen to support the final topcoat color. Light and bright colors were generally sprayed over light gray primer, dark colors were sprayed over black primer, and red primer was used generally as a base for colors in the red family.

Choosing the Proper Finish

A case can be made for finding a hot rod with faded paint and adding primer spots to the car for that true vintage look. Of course, it really should be lacquer primer for the authentic look, so it may pay to spray the bare metal area with a two-part epoxy primer first, then spray the lacquer primer over the same area for effect. This look would be very authentic, and much like in the days of early hot rodding, it is a great way to get your car on the road and complete the rest of the work as you drive.

The second choice is to use primer on the entire car. Many modern interpretations of the traditional hot rod seem to include primer as the final finish. Having driven both full-primer and primer-spotted cars, I can tell you one thing for certain: Keeping a primered car clean is one of the most difficult chores in all of hot rodding. Bug juice bakes into the surface and leaves white stains, sap refuses to be lifted, and if the car is out in a rain shower followed by bright sunshine, be prepared for all kinds of spotting and streaking. There is a reason cars were painted with slippery, smooth topcoats and not primer. The

This 1940 coupe is not covered in lacquer primer, but it has one of the best faux primer paint jobs I've seen. A word to the wise, keeping a flat finish clean can be a big job, as everything seems to bond to the surface.

CHOOSING THE RIGHT PAINT, PATTERN, TEXTURE AND FINISH

What we have here is the time-tested, never-grows-old, always-looks-great black paint on a hot rod. Color can be introduced on the wheels, dashboard, and under the hood.

actual task of keeping the car clean is enough to dissuade me from ever running a car in primer as a final finish. I also hold this much to be true: Every hot rodder dreamed of owning a car with a brilliant finish, a strong motor, and a nice interior. They might never have met those goals, but that was the dream, so when I build a hot rod today I am living the same dream, and finished paint is high on my list.

Assuming that a true final finish is part of your plan, the next decision is what color and what type of paint to use on that vintage hot rod. First of all, if you simply can't decide what color to put on the car, there is one color that is always correct on any hot rod, and that color is black, but I'm getting ahead of myself.

Lacquer Paints

Lacquer paint captures the authentic finish of period correct hot rods. These paints were widely used from the mid 1920s to the 1960s. While lacquer is currently available, it is illegal in certain areas of the country due to environmental considerations. Lacquer paint is inexpensive and is one of easiest types of paint to work with. The home car builder can easily spray it on, touch it up, and buff it out. In most cases, it delivers a brilliant high-gloss finish, but this paint is also somewhat fragile. It is not as resilient as other paints against ultraviolet radiation and common automotive chemicals.

And remember, there is no such thing as a safe paint to spray, so always use proper safety equipment, including the best respirator you can buy.

Nitrocellulose Lacquer

In the early years of hot rodding, lacquer was the paint of choice, and the very early cars were painted with nitrocellulose lacquer. The old basic enamel was also available, but because of the slow drying time it was not a good choice unless a booth and baking were available, whereas fast-drying lacquer could be painted in a home garage or even in the driveway. This paint was first developed in the 1920s by DuPont, and the fast drying time was a big plus for assembly-line cars. You may think that automobile manufacturers didn't consider drying time in the 1920s, but you would be wrong. The reason Henry Ford chose black as the standard color for his Model T Ford was the simple fact that it dried faster than any other color, which kept the production line moving, and no, not all Model T Fords were painted black, but I digress.

The nitrocellulose lacquer was popular with hot rodders too, since most shops didn't have anything resembling today's modern downdraft spray booths. The quick drying time allowed the hot rodder and customizer to lay down multiple coats, repair minor problems like dirt, runs, and orange peel between coats, and then buff it to a fine finish. Some people still insist that black nitrocellulose lacquer is the blackest black, but that is a heated debate.

One downside to nitrocellulose lacquer is it has a tendency to yellow with age. Hot rodders and customizers often painted the base color, then water sanded that base with 400-grit sandpaper and followed it by as many as 20 coats of clear lacquer. The results were a deep gloss

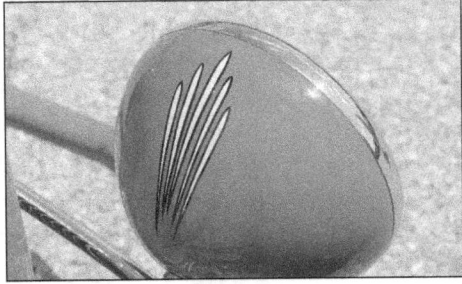

Pinstriping is one of the oldest methods of dressing up a car. Dating back to the days of carriages, this art form is found on many vintage hot rods. Teardrops such as these are simple and effective.

CHAPTER 7

Early scallops often resembled half-moons, and today it is a very effective way to give early flavor to your hot rod. This Deuce Cabriolet also incorporates the early Ford V-8 emblem emblazoned on the side of the hood. My hat is off to the person who taped and painted that logo over those louvers.

and added protection, but the clear had a mild amber tint to it and could cause slight changes to the color as it was applied. Making that effect even worse was the fact the lacquer continued to yellow with age and even a dark color took on a certain amber hue over time. The only cure was a repaint.

Another common problem with nitrocellulose lacquer is cracking, a paint flaw commonly known as crow's feet. This paint defect occurs as the lacquer shrinks and splits into three distinct cracks forming a pattern similar to a bird's footprint, hence the term crow's feet. This is often caused by excessive layers of paint, typical of early custom paint jobs with multiple coats of clear. Conversely, nitrocellulose lacquer can be quite resilient too, and many an old hot rod paint job has been brought back to life with a gentle color sanding and multiple hand polishings.

Lacquer has a vintage look to it, so if you are building a car that predates 1954 or so, nitrocellulose lacquer is the only correct paint. It is still available today from specialty paint outlets and the clear and black lacquer is often used as a woodworking finish as well. Solvents, brake fluid, and thinners quickly soften and damage this paint, so take care to protect the finish. Nitrocellulose lacquer has a hard look to it and requires more maintenance than modern paints. Routine polishing and waxing will keep that gorgeous lacquer luster alive for many, many years, and what better way to spend an afternoon than waxing a great-looking hot rod.

Acrylic Lacquer

There were enamels on the scene since the 1930s too, but generally the higher quality hot rods were still getting that wonderful hand-rubbed lacquer finish. Acrylic lacquer was developed to eliminate some of the shortcomings of the earlier lacquers, and General Motors used it as its paint of choice from the 1950s through the 1960s. As with earlier lacquers, the ease of application, fast drying, and ability to buff the paint to a high luster made the paint popular with hot rodders. The added bonus was that the new acrylic lacquer clear topcoat was gin clear, giving custom paint jobs the desired depth with nary a hint of yellow. This crystal-clear paint

This 1933 Ford roadster carries a graphic paint scheme reminiscent of very early race cars. The white wire wheels and covered headlights and grille shell add to the effect. Basic colors like white and non-metallic burgundy are era correct.

to enhance the drying process and obtain the best results. Most often, enamel paints require more touch up and finishing work than other types of paint. Some enamel paints come in a two-stage system with a clear topcoat, while others are offered as a single-stage system with no clear coat.

Alkyd Enamel

While top-level cars were enjoying hand-rubbed lacquer, a lot of lesser cars were finding joy in a good baked enamel job. My first car was done in just that manner. I did most of the body prep, shaved the hood and deck lid, and then a local body shop painted the car a nice black and white two-tone paint job with baked enamel. They replaced both rocker panels, fixed a few door dings, and painted the car for $85. The year was 1964 and I remember that black enamel being as dark as a modern BMW. It was durable, and since it required no sanding, buffing, or polishing, the car was ready to go the next day. It looked great and lasted for many years. I remember the shop owner telling me to wash the car with just cold water and gently wipe it dry for two weeks if I wanted a really good finish. It seemed to work and orange peel was at a minimum, a testimony to the painter's skill. Of course I also waxed the car at least once a month.

As I mentioned earlier, if you didn't have a spray booth and a way to heat the car, it was very difficult to deliver a clean enamel job. Mixing and spraying the old alkyd enamel was critical, as it was easy to go too dry and produce low luster and orange-peel finish, or go too wet and produce the dreaded run. But, if the right shop applied the paint in a good bake booth, the finish could be darn presentable.

There were several interesting products available for applying a glass-like enamel job. I actually owned a heated spray cup at one time. It looked like a regular spray gun cup, but there was a heating element in the bottom. Mix up your enamel, and plug in the cup until it was hot, then spray away. Of course, since it took more than one cup to cover a car, a fellow should really have two cups, one on the gun, the other one cooking. I remember using it once on a frame I was painting, and I must say the old enamel did flow out nicely. Of course, with 20/20 hindsight the concept of heating flammable paint is not the brightest thing I've ever done and sadly not the dumbest either. Here's the new rule: *Never* heat any flammable liquid, paint or otherwise.

These enamels are still available today, but there is little need to use them because the newer acrylic enamels are superior in every way and produce a similar "enamel look" paint. The enamel paint has a thick look to it compared to lacquer. This paint has been in use since the 1930s, and it is an authentic finish for any vintage hot rod. It tends to

Hot rods and brilliant colors go hand in hand. Here, bright orange is accented with black pinstriping and a small black scallop on the grille shell. This is very typical of a Northern California–style hot rod. The pinstriping carries a heavy Tommy "The Greek" style. Tommy "The Greek" Hrones was one of the best stripers of all times.

When transparent candy colors came along, blending colors in flames became easier. This is an interesting photo because the car in the foreground is wearing a nice set of candy apple flames, while the 1940 in the background has solid-pigment paint properly blended.

produce the best effects when spraying solid, non-metallic colors, but the finish is soft compared to lacquers.

Protection is required while painting, including a good respirator and covering everything because basic enamel will stick to wheel bearing grease . . . well, maybe not that bad, but it will attach itself to everything in the shop, so cover up before spraying. While lacquer overspray turns to dust, enamel overspray is like a fine mist of honey. Most solvents, thinners, and brake fluids damage dried paint, so care must be taken with the final finish.

Acrylic Enamel

Much like lacquer, enamel took a quantum leap when it became acrylic based. This material can be allowed to air dry and with that comes the same dirt contamination problems as using alkyd enamel. However, with the addition of a urethane catalyst hardener (sometimes referred to as converted enamel) and the proper drying speed reducer, acrylic enamel is a good choice for the home paint job. It should be pointed out that using the hardener changes the chemistry of the paint—it is much more toxic than air-dried enamel, so all safety precautions must be taken when spraying catalyzed acrylic enamel.

Acrylic enamel can be sanded and buffed to a flawless finish, so small particles and imperfections can be removed via this process. The final finish is somewhat softer than lacquer and more flexible. It is extremely durable and can produce a proper look for a vintage hot rod. The finish has a slight bit more of that modern wet look than lacquer, but the additional durability of acrylic enamel makes it the number-one choice of many hot rodders. The paint is widely available today, and DuPont Centari and PPG Delstar are both good choices for painting your next hot rod. These paints can handle metallics better than alkyd enamel because of the faster flash time, but acrylic enamel still seems best in non-metallic colors, but then I generally prefer non-metallic colors on hot rods.

Acrylic enamel is a great single-stage paint that is simple to mix and easy to apply, and it produces great results. It is also more affordable than the more modern two-stage urethane paints. Acrylic enamel is available in virtually any color you can imagine.

Urethane Paints

The final class of paint is urethane paint, used on modern cars. Often referred to as two-stage paint or basecoat/clearcoat paint, most of the modern urethane paints involve a basecoat that dries in a flat finish followed by a clearcoat that provides the final shine. These paints offer terrific brilliance, depth, and a wet-look shine that requires next to no maintenance for years. They are resistant to solvents, acid rain, and the elements. Pearls, candy apple, sparkling metallics, and metal-flake paint can all be applied with the basecoat/clearcoat technology. And laying down a perfect candy apple paint using modern urethane paints is simple compared to achieving the same uniform color and depth using acrylic lacquers.

That's the good news; now for the bad news. First, this modern paint is very dangerous, toxic to the point that it should only be sprayed wearing a full coverage suit and using an outside air source. Also, the paint should only be applied in a modern down-draft spray booth. More bad news: The paint is very expensive. Finally, modern basecoat/clearcoat paints simply don't belong on true

Non-metallic colors have more depth than their metallic counterparts and make repair simple. The brilliant blue on this Model A coupe is brighter than most pigments of the 1950s, but with all those fuelie stacks and a Moon tank the coupe has plenty of vintage flavor.

vintage hot rods; the finish is just too good for a 1950s- or 1960s-style car.

Of course, if you are building a vintage-flavor hot rod, by all means use the modern two- or even three-stage urethane paint available today. The perfect finish and durability make it worthwhile, but if you are considering a color with flattener in it for your vintage-flavor hot rod, I suggest you look at lacquer or acrylic enamel—it will be a more authentic look.

At the end of the day, most hot rodders had a dream, a vision of how that chopped and channeled coupe would look in 1950 Oldsmobile Ivy Green metallic or 1957 Caddy Amethyst. Maybe your tastes go more toward one of the great non-metallic colors, such as basic black, Hugger Orange, Chrome Yellow, or a great vintage red. In the area of red, you must be a little careful because reds in the 1950 and 1960s were not as brilliant as modern paint colors. Take a red off a modern VW Jetta or any number of new cars, and it will be simply too bright for a vintage car. Now if you're going for vintage flavor, fine, lay down that retina-scorching red and enjoy the finish. If you are bound to true vintage colors, pick a red from the 1950s and 1960s for accuracy.

Custom Urethane Paints

While most early hot rodders were thrilled just to have their cars painted in a color chosen from a paint chart or a new car dealer showroom, the trend toward custom-mixed paint on the high-end rods really started to take off by the late 1950s and early 1960s. Throughout the 1960s and 1970s, Cadillac produced a great range of heavy metallic paints under its Fire-Frost paint colors, and hot rodding was leaving the non-metallic world behind and experimenting with metallic paints. Of course, if some is good, more is better, so metal flake was born—huge pieces of sparkling metal imbedded in paint under many, many coats of clear.

These were difficult finishes to apply. Improperly applied, candy could produce cars with no two panels the same color, or worse yet stripes displaying the spray gun fan pattern could be seen. Transparent paints were tricky; some would look good in the bright sunlight, but under a street light you could see the spray pattern stripes. Metal flake was also difficult to master, keeping the pattern of the metallic even was all important and keeping the flakes in suspension was important too. At one time I had a spray cup with a small air-driven agitator in the bottom of the cup that continually mixed the metallic in the cup. Of course, the same result can be had by gently swirling the cup after each pass, and some painters dropped a couple marbles or even clean nuts and bolts in the spray cup to help agitate the mix and prevent the metallic from settling out during the swirling action.

After mixing the flake with clear and applying it to the car, you will notice some of the flake is standing on edge, protruding from the clear that delivered the flake to the body. Some painters gently sand the flake with 800-grit, but personally I found one very clean human hand, rubbing over the entire surface nets a more uniform finish than sandpaper. Sanding flake has the potential of leaving streaks and scratches, but as with all custom-painting techniques, what works for one painter may not work for another.

The problem with pearls was keeping the spray consistent. The temptation with lacquer pearl is to lay it down like a good topcoat, when in fact you must paint it on the dry side, yet not too dry. If you laid pearl down too wet, the pearl would sink into the paint and you had unwanted blotching in the paint, if it was put on too dry the pearl would seem to stand up in the finish and provide an odd pattern in the pearl. Pearl paint is a three-step process: base color, pearl, and then a topcoat of clear. Today's modern paints can reduce this to a two-step process with colored-pearl basecoats and a simple topcoat of clear.

Today most of those problems are cured. Frankly, if you are planning on doing candy apple, metal flake, or pearl on your vintage hot rod, the modern two- or three-stage urethane paint is the way to go. Laying down a basecoat followed by a clearcoat will produce candy apple paint that is not only perfect, but it can actually be spot sprayed and blended in, if necessary. I drove a candy apple Aztec Gold sedan delivery for many miles. I repainted the rear fenders and even spotted in the lower rocker panels like any basecoat/clearcoat product. The product was from House of Kolor, and it worked great.

Vintage candy apple paint was applied as three-step paint: a gold metallic, silver metallic, or white pearl base followed by the transparent color of your choice, and then topped with clear. Open a can of vintage candy apple lacquer, and you could see all the way to the bottom of the can, thus the transparent and mile-deep look of the paint. But the commercial candy paints of the day used dyes rather than true pigments to tint the clear, and unfortunately those dyes did not hold up to sunlight as well as pigments, so fading could become an issue. This may not be as much of a problem today with the UV-rated clears.

Today, many candy apple finishes can be completed in two stages with just the basecoat and the topcoat, while others use a three-stage approach. I can assure you of one thing: Painting pearls and candies with the modern urethane system is easier and will net superior results in uniform finish, durability, and luster.

The Metalflake Company was one of the very first custom paint mixers in the country. Since it still has a lot of the same colors available, this is a good source for true vintage candy colors. Rather than mix complete paints, they provide color concentrates that are compatible with paints ranging from acrylic lacquer to modern urethane. The Metalflake Corporation still has all the special-effect finishes we remember from the 1960s—Metal Flake, Glowble, Vreeble, Eerie-Dress, Spindrift, Star Pearl, Microglow, Flip Flop pearl, and Mirra—even the names sound vintage. While the term metal flake is still used, the glitter is actually made of solvent-resistant polyesters. There are several suppliers of flake, pearl, and candy paints online, which makes it possible to mix your own custom colors and finishes.

Of course, I would be remiss were I not to mention Jon Kosmoski and his House of Kolor line of paints. Kosmoski made a name for himself mixing and spraying some of the finest custom paint jobs in the country—candies, pearls, flakes, and more. Although he no longer owns the company Jon is still a big part of the custom paint world, and the products he founded are second to none.

Special Effects

Over the years, many different special effects have been used on hot rods, ranging from something as conservative as pinstriping to wild flame jobs, panel painting, and lace work. All of these effects have a proper time and place. Flames seem to be appropriate for virtually any vintage hot rod, and scallops seem to fit in anywhere flames would be appropriate. When painting either flames or scallops, do your homework and study the shape, size, and colors used for the period of your car. Bear in mind that before the advent of transparent paints, the blending of flames was sometimes little more than stripes of color or translucent paints fogged over each other in a misty blend.

Likewise, the shape of flames has evolved over the years from quite primitive looking flames to more flowing flames. Flames on hot rods were used as a graphic expression of fire and speed, and while there are any numbers of theories on how the paint scheme came to be, it seems reasonable to believe that engine fires spewing flames through the side louvers of a hood were involved. However, the flame paint pattern that has come to be the very badge of hot rodding and an icon of speed were not designed to look like real fire, rather it was a graphic that signified fire and

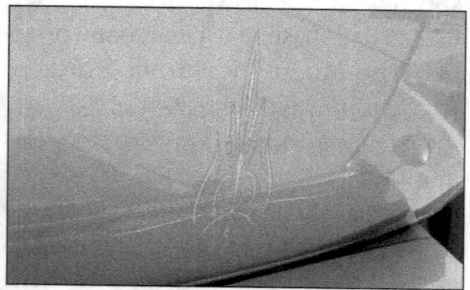

Later pinstriping began to use two, three, four, or more colors in the design and lines tended to flow more with fewer sharp points. The lines also became finer as time passed. This two-color design is very effective and tasteful. Restraint is a big part of effective pinstriping.

Flame paint is the quintessential hot rod graphic. Early flames used solid colors and blending the colors involved thinning the colors and slightly misting one color over the other. The blends were only as good as the person behind the spray gun. Note there is a slight fog of white around the headlights and grille.

CHOOSING THE RIGHT PAINT, PATTERN, TEXTURE AND FINISH

This coupe has flames that closely resemble a burst of fire coming out of the hood louvers. It has been said the early flame jobs were inspired by a blown motor shooting real flames out of the louvers in similar fashion.

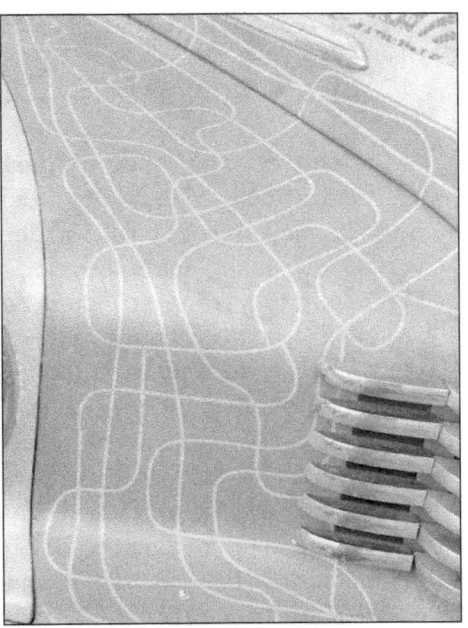

Endless line is just what the name implies. After laying down a base coat of white, then pearl, and a single coat of clear, the fineline tape is laid down in a pattern with no beginning and no end. Then candy blue paint is sprayed over the taped panel. After the tape is removed you have a blue panel with white lines. Easy enough; the hard part is making a pleasing pattern with the lines.

speed. For that reason the super realism flames done by modern artists today have no place on a true vintage hot rod. I am not debating the talent involved in painting realistic fire, rather pointing out that traditional flame graphics are a very different treatment.

Later treatments such as panel painting, endless line, lace, spatter, and airbrush effects should be reserved for cars from the mid 1960s forward. Many of these special effects lasted but a few short years. Things like lace paint were out of style by the time the paint dried, and yet if a conservative bit of lace paintwork is done on a custom-style hot rod, it immediately transports you back to the 1960s.

Panel painting and most paint effects of the 1960s and 1970s reflected the wild psychedelic culture of the time. Like most things from that time period, it had very little staying power. It was true pop-culture stuff, but today, those brave enough to apply some panel paint, scrolls, and cobwebbing will draw a crowd and date your car firmly in the 1960s.

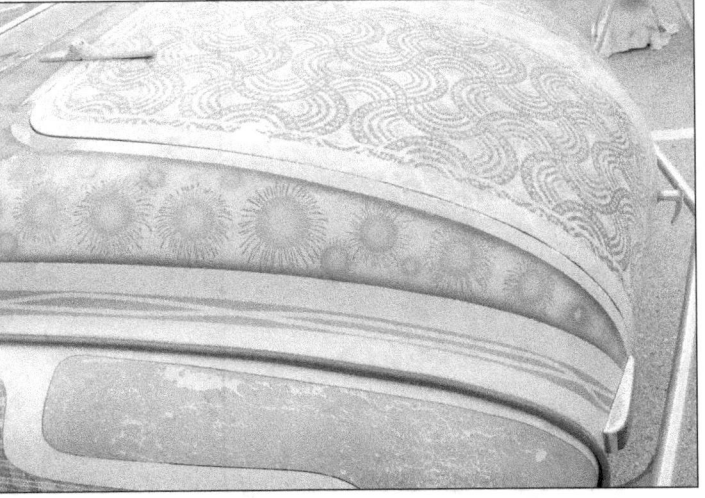

Water spots were done with an airbrush, blowing a drop of candy paint until it is spread out like these. Endless line and some very strange lace paintwork cover the deck lid of this gasser.

HOW TO BUILD PERIOD CORRECT HOT RODS

When Not to Use Paint

The perfect complement to great paint is great chrome. Vintage hot rods and their owners enjoyed great paint and chrome plating on everything from the suspension to bumpers and interior moldings. While there are times when painting a formerly chrome-plated part makes sense (although frankly I can't think of one right now) generally speaking, if the piece was chrome plated from the factory, painting it is a mistake. Send it to the plating shop and have it chrome plated again. The whole monochromatic idea—paint the bumpers, door handles, outside mirrors one color—was a product of the 1980s and 1990s and the look lasted about as long as tweed upholstery. You can mix chrome plating, zinc plating, and anodizing for very effective contrasting finishes to your paint choice, and contrast in finishes is very important for a successful hot rod.

If you are reviving a monochromatic hot rod with tweed interior, all is not lost. After cutting the tweed off the seats and headliner, the tweed works well as wrapping material for the painted parts being sent to the chrome shop.

If ever there was a chrome reliant hot rod it is the venerable T-bucket. These little iconic roadsters are just not complete without a substantial amount of chrome plating. After the paint it approach of the 1990s, hot rodders are now returning to traditional chrome plating to give their hot rods a vintage look. Of course this means you must have a chrome plating budget built into the building plan. This T-bucket is done right with complete chrome front suspension, ample chrome on the motor, a chrome or polished firewall and chrome plating on the rear suspension too.

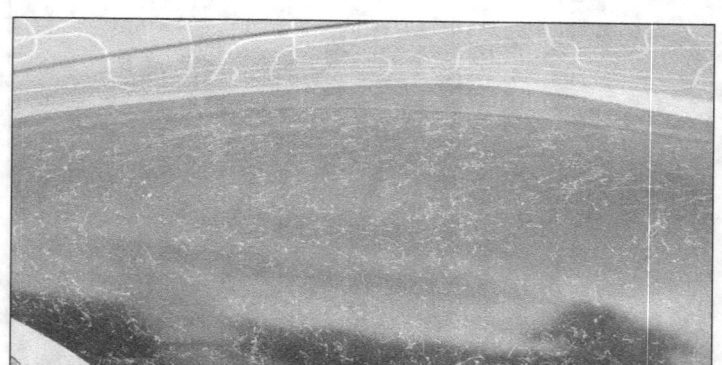

Cobwebs are another custom painting trick. This one must have been discovered by accident because it is as simple as not putting enough thinner in the paint, turning up the pressure, and letting the cobwebs fly. Air pressure, paint viscosity, and distance from the panel vary the pattern.

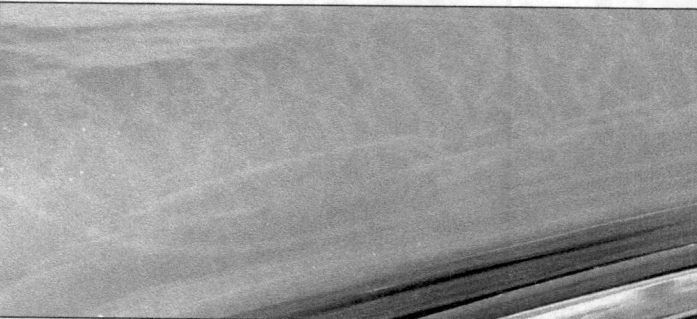

Lace doesn't always have to be wild. This subtle approach is lace under candy. The effect can be achieved by laying the lace down for the first couple of coats of candy apple. Then remove the lace and put one or two more coats of candy color over the entire panel, followed by clear. In the end you have buried the lace in the color.

Panel paint and spatter paint fit into this same era, and once again, while special-effects paint is not particularly popular today, it was a very big part of hot rodding in the 1960s and 1970s. If that is your target date, do not be afraid to use some of these treatments.

One final word on custom treatments: Sometime in the late 1970s, airbrush artists discovered the van, or maybe van owners discovered airbrush artists. Welcome to the age of the mural and yes, some hot rodders opted to have a picture painted on their car. When it comes to putting a mural on a hot rod, there is one simple rule that always applies: Don't do it.

Picking the Final Finish

As mentioned at the beginning of this chapter, picking the paint scheme and color for your hot rod is a serious task, one that dictates the overall success of your build. Choose your colors wisely and be certain the color and finish chosen match the overall theme of the car. Screaming Hawaiian Sunset Pearl might not be the right choice for that deeply channeled, flathead-powered Model A roadster. Remember that the best hot rods often are the simplest—clean by design and easy on the eyes. These cars tend to hold their appeal forever.

Pearls, candies, and metal flake are all appropriate for late 1950s and forward, while flames, scallops, and pinstriping are appropriate on virtually any vintage hot rod. I see a fair amount of candy and pearl paint; it takes a real man to step up to the outrageous effect of heavy metal flake. It was considered by many to be too gaudy when it was introduced, and those feelings remain today. But, with the right color, and the proper mood and accessories on the entire car, few things draw a crowd quite like a good flake job on a hot rod.

Choosing the finish may depend on the planned use of the car, and while there is no denying the durability and flexibility of modern urethane paints, there is still something about lacquer. It produces a finish that has a good depth and a rock-hard look. Modern urethanes have a plastic, wet look. Of course, that flawless lacquer finish requires much more attention than modern paints, so if you don't enjoy waxing a car, pick something other than lacquer. The acrylic enamel lies somewhere in between, and for my own hot rods, it is my favorite. It gives the added durability of enamel but still has a vintage look when color sanded and buffed.

The choice is yours—primer, flat, non-metallic, metallic, or custom finish. Regardless of your choice, one thing is certain: Few days are more rewarding in the process of hot rod building than the day you pull the masking tape and paper off your freshly painted hot rod.

Fading paint was popular in the 1960s too. Once again, with the advent of candy apple paint, blending became an exercise in overlapping transparent paints to make transitional colors. Practice your blends on a practice panel to be sure you like all the transitional colors, then paint the car.

This is a take-off on scallops that would be appropriate for a late-1960s-style car. Modern design and great blending make for a good look.

CHAPTER 7

Few people actually have the guts to mix up some metal-flake paint and put a good flake job on their hot rod. While the sparkle can be overwhelming to some, there are few things that can provide more personality to a car than a good flake job like this one.

This Plymouth coupe is dripping with nostalgia. From the mild metal-flake paint to the flames that remind me of the flames that came on model car kits of the 1960s, this coupe has the look. A painted-on pair of aces is another vintage touch. Hot rodders seem to have a fascination with gambling, with aces and deuces going wild.

Laying down a perfect purple pearl paint job like this would have required a very talented painter in the 1960s. Today, modern basecoat/clearcoat technology puts pearl within reach of many painters. The cost of custom paint is expensive, but the results offset it.

CHAPTER 8

Vintage Car Gallery

There still remains an intangible factor in hot rodding that is difficult to define by simply listing parts and pieces. One of the great unsolved mysteries of hot rodding is how some cars have "all the right stuff" yet still do not have "the look," while another car captures the spirit of hot rodding with or without the proper parts.

The difference is often just a matter of minor adjustments—a color that is slightly too bright, or too subdued, the wrong tire size, or just the wrong wheels and tires on a hot rod. But it goes beyond that, it takes a seasoned eye to recognize the good, the bad, and the ugly in the hot rod world. And it takes a real rodder to do something about it. Few things are more difficult than removing a piece from a car that you paid a ton of money for, but if the piece is wrong it simply must be removed. I know of more than one hot rodder who just couldn't bring themselves to replace wheels that were too wide, or air breathers that were too tall because they had too much invested in them. As a result the car suffered.

So while I have discussed many of the proper parts needed to build a vintage hot rod, there is still no better way to learn about a great hot rod than to look at a lot of them, and when you find that iconic car don't just look at the car, study it. Take notes on the relationship between the fenders and wheels, the exterior and interior color, and even the diameter of the steering wheel. Look at it long and hard because capturing the look can be an elusive art. Even great craftsmanship cannot make up for poor taste. An ugly car with flawless workmanship is still an ugly car.

With that in mind, I thought it would be appropriate to present a gallery of hot rods that do a great job of representing the vintage hot rod movement. Some of the cars are 1950s cars that have survived the years and become true time capsules, while others are cars that have been built within the past 10 or 15 years but carry the classic charisma that only a great vintage hot rod can muster. Most are Fords, because most were Fords, and that will continue

Lewis McMillan originally purchased this '32 Ford as a body only at the L.A. Roadster Show. Thirty years later, he mated the body to an original frame and in the process discovered the car has a real hot rod heritage. The car was originally hot rodded in the 1940s by Arvel Youngblood.

HOW TO BUILD PERIOD CORRECT HOT RODS

for as long as vintage hot rods are on the roads. It does not mean you can't build a great vintage hot rod from other stock, but be forewarned, it is more difficult. I hope you can garner some ideas from these cars that will give your own hot rod project that perfect look.

Reviving the Youngblood Roadster

Lewis McMillan builds hot rods with a true reverence for the early days of hot rodding. To say Lewis is a traditionalist is to say Harley Earl liked to draw cars. When Lewis builds a hot rod, it is based on a conglomeration of parts gathered over a lifetime of collecting. Things like Ford script, tie rod ends, vintage gauges, rare tapered-leaf springs from 1918, and earlier Model T Fords are purchased when found, and then set aside for whatever project is deserving of such rare vintage parts. While Lewis has a bone-stock Deuce phaeton in his garage, he also has owned a very nice, chopped three-window for 40-plus years, and there is another roadster body or two lurking in his warehouse of hot rod goodies.

Lewis purchased this Deuce roadster body at the L.A. Roadster Show swap meet in 1978, and had it shipped back to his home in Lexington, North Carolina. The body was in excellent condition and it sat in storage for the next 24 years while other projects were completed. The never-ending process of searching for and purchasing parts continued, and Lewis was always hunting parts from Hershey, Pennsylvania, to the L.A. Roadster show. The plan was to build a very correct, early postwar hot rod that would typify a high-quality roadster from 1944–1954.

Of course, this build started with an original 1932 frame. Lewis boxed the rails to the firewall up front and also added boxing plates to the rear kick-up area of the chassis. A 1927 Model T rear crossmember was installed in the frame to provide clearance for the early Culver City Halibrand quick-change center section that is sandwiched between 1940 Ford axle tubes. Lincoln drum brakes and tube shocks complete the rear suspension.

Following the torque tube forward, we find a 1940 Ford transmission connected to a 1946 Mercury engine. The motor has been bored .060, and the Howard M-14 is a wicked grind that leaves no doubt that this is hot rod motor. Offenhauser heads top the motor, and a pair of Stromberg 97s breath through a genuine Thickstun air breather.

Under the motor a vintage Okie Adams dropped axle and a Hollywood Frame and Axle tapered-leaf spring from the 1940s provide suspension and stance. Lincoln drum brakes are used up front too, and the stock 1932 Ford steering box

Lewis McMillan had built the motor and chassis for the car before discovering the provenance of the car, but happily the 1946 Mercury flathead was period perfect for the car. All accessories on the motor are originals, not reproduction items. The Howard cam gives the flathead a distinctive growl, and note that all wiring and plumbing use period materials.

Up front an Okie Adams dropped and filled axle combines with a rare Hollywood Frame and Axle tapered-leaf spring from the 1940s. Lewis lives for such finite detail in his hot rods, and the end result is apparent.

has been filled with 1934 Ford gears, which provides an improved steering ratio of 15:1, while the '32 box was 13:1. A set of early tube shocks with the appropriate flared dust tubes are mounted to the front with modified F-1 truck brackets.

Of course, while the chassis was being built, Lewis was also working on finding parts and doing bodywork. While on his annual sojourn at the L.A. Roadster Show swap meet in 1973, he purchased a vintage windshield of unknown origin. The windshield was typical of many postwar custom-built windshields. However, after getting it home, the piece proved to be too rough to use, so Buster Henderson fabricated a new windshield using the original as a pattern.

Until this point, Lewis was simply building a truly period perfect hot rod of his own vision, using parts he had located over a 30-year period, but all of that was about to change. The day he decided to start working on the roadster doors became a pivotal moment in this car's build. The doors were solid and the first step was to get any debris out of the inner door panel.

When Lewis turned the driverside door upside down and shook it, years of dust and cobwebs came out of the door, along with an old matchbook, a Regal Pale Beer can/bottle opener, and a 1944 nickel. At first glance, these were just interesting bits from a car with a past. Regal Pale Beer was brewed in San Francisco, so finding a can/bottle opener from that brewer in a California body was not big news. The 1944 nickel was not worn, so it had obviously been in the door since the 1940s. The match book was a generic Shell Oil matchbook, with no street address to identify where it came from; but wait, there on the inside of the matchbook, in pencil and barely visible was a name: Arvel Youngblood.

Because of Lewis McMillan's deep-rooted interest in anything having to do with old hot rods and hot rodders, the research began almost immediately. Who was this Arvel Youngblood? Well, as it turns out, Youngblood was like a lot of young men returning from the war; he found a Deuce roadster and resumed hot rodding. Before the war, he had raced a Model A roadster, but now he had a Deuce, and it would be raced on the dry lakes. Further research, with help from Don Montgomery and his great books and archives, provided photos of the car on the lake bed. This Deuce roadster was no longer just a vintage hot rod assemblage; it was now the resurrection of the Youngblood roadster, a car with true provenance.

From the rear, this roadster just shouts vintage hot rod. From the early Halibrand quick-change rear peeking out from under the gas tank to the genuine Ford 1939 taillights the car is picture perfect. Even the deck lid handle is NOS. Once again, notice how the headlights fit perfectly between the wheel and the grille shell, a detail worth emulating.

An early Culver City Halibrand quick-change rear end is suspended by a 1918 or earlier Model T tapered-leaf spring. Tube aircraft shocks have been chrome plated; the rear brakes are early Lincoln units.

As fate would have it, the chassis work and engine selection were fine for the Youngblood roadster, and since it was run as a Highboy, Lewis McMillan's vision of a great roadster was very similar to Arvel Youngblood's thoughts. The only variation was the windshield; the Youngblood roadster ran a stock-style windshield in the 1940s, but Lewis opted to keep the vintage windshield that had been painstakingly replicated for the roadster.

After the body was perfectly prepared for paint, RM black urethane paint was sprayed, one of the few concessions to modern materials. The original '32 Ford hood tops are joined by Rootlieb smooth hood sides and a genuine Ford Deuce grille shell carries an NOS '32 Ford radiator emblem and cap. In front of the grille Lewis fabricated a vintage-style headlight bar and mounted a set of headlights from a 1943 Seagraves fire truck. The 1939 Ford taillights are just that, Ford taillights, not reproductions. Virtually every piece on this car was built by Ford.

Turning his attention to the inside of the roadster, Lewis used an original-style '32 Ford seat and had Ray Hester stitch up the wide rolled-and-pleated design. Everything was strictly traditional, and the Deuce dash holds a genuine 1932 Auburn dash insert filled with rare 2⅝-inch Stewart-Warner gauges. The 1940 steering column and wheel fit the time period perfectly, and even the dashboard controls are vintage, with a 1946 Chevy truck choke cable.

An unexpected bonus for Lewis occurred when he told a fellow hot rodder in California that he had the Youngblood roadster and that he would love to find one of the original SCTA dash plaques. The holes were in the dashboard, so Lewis knew a plaque had once graced the dash. Obviously it had been removed sometime in the past. But since the roadster was raced often there must be others out there somewhere. It seems Youngblood went through a divorce in the 1950s, and some of his things remained with his former wife. When she passed away, several original dash plaques became available and one was located and purchased for Lewis. It is the crowning touch to the entire car.

The interior is based on a stock seat with very traditional oxblood leather done in wide rolls and pleats. This is a very early roadster body, built sometime before November 31, 1931, so it has the wide upholstery flange. The body also carries an R code indicating it was assembled in the Richmond, California, plant.

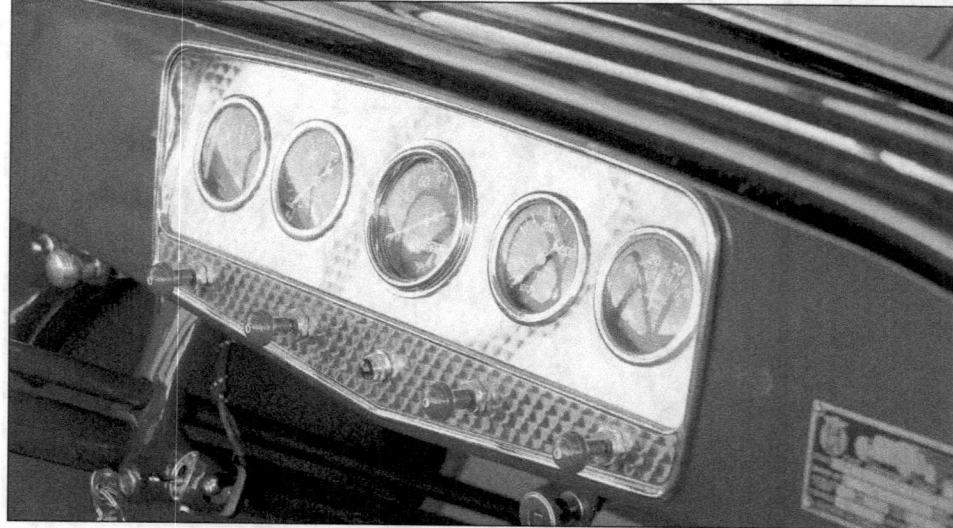

That is a genuine 1932 Auburn dash insert filled with 2⅝-inch Stewart-Warner gauges. Lewis mentioned that finding the fuel gauge was one of the more difficult pieces to locate. The dashboard is a study in vintage hot rodding.

After discovering this was the Arvel Youngblood roadster, Lewis asked a hot rod friend in California to keep an eye out for an original timing plaque. It took some time, but eventually one of the original El Mirage dry lake dash plaques was found in mint condition. It is the crowning touch to the car. The car was classified as a Merc Rdstr Class B, and on June 6, 1948, it ran 96.56 mph.

Even the deck lid handle is an original '32 Ford piece. Fresh out of a genuine Ford box this piece was more than 70 years old before it was ever installed on a car.

The interesting thing about the Youngblood/McMillan roadster is that both owners had a similar vision for the car. Even if Lewis had never found out about Youngblood, the car would look eerily similar today. What happened to the car during the 30 years between 1948 and 1978 remains a mystery, but judging by the lack of modifications, missing parts, or butchery it would appear the car may have been in storage for many of those years. Lewis also managed to build the car to an extremely high standard, and yet it does not have the feeling of an over-restored or over-built car. The roadster still feels true to the post–World War II time period.

Today Lewis enjoys the fruits of his labor and his friendships with many hot rodders who helped locate rare parts and information about the car. But to truly appreciate this roadster, you must see and hear it in action. The high-compression flathead produces an aggressive growl, and the car is suitable for around-town cruising or taking to the open road. The car has a certain grace about it at speed that is difficult to describe. But ultimately, it is the spirit of the car that shines through—a car that accurately takes you back to a time when young men returning from a war built great hot rods with no way of knowing their efforts would be so appreciated 70 years later. For those hot rodders looking to capture that spirit, there is no finer template to follow than this one.

The Class of '59

Being a genuine nice guy always reaps huge benefits; call it karma, the golden rule, or the old saying, "What comes around, goes around," but good things often happen to good guys. When you combine being a genuinely nice guy with old cars, there are few stories to top this one.

Mike Goodman is one of those nice guys who always seems to have time to help, listen, or laugh as the case may be. The fact that he has been an avid hot rodder his whole life and has a garage full of flathead-powered hot rods no doubt contributed to his current vocation at Honest Charley's Speed Shop in Chattanooga, Tennessee.

Now Mike has four Deuces filling his garage, a great three-window coupe hot rod, a future project that consists of a rough roadster body and frame and a pair of five-window coupes that oddly enough are both painted '32 Ford Medium Maroon with black fenders. The only discerning feature on the Model B coupe is that the body molding is painted black. But it is not only what is in Mike's garage that is of interest, but also how this particular coupe came to rest there. This is a rare case where a barn car finds a new owner, rather than a new owner finding a barn car.

The day started like so many other days at major hot rod events; Mike Goodman and his team were busy setting up the display booth for Honest Charley's Speed Shop. Just because they were working hard doesn't mean they weren't having fun talking with other hot rodders and vendors alike. And so it was that Archie Hinton of Belpre, Ohio, approached Mike with a simple question, "Would you be interested in buying an old hot rod?" Now Mike Goodman has been around hot rods long enough to know the answer to that question is always "yes," and this is how Mike related the rest of the story to me:

Mike responded, "Well, I might be. What kind of old hot rod do you have?" to which Hinton replied, "a 1932 Ford coupe." Of course, this really piqued Mike's interest, and the discussion went further, with important facts like, "Built in 1959, flathead motor, and yes, Archie Hinton and fellow Shifters Car Club members were the original builders of the car." The discussion ended with

Archie Hinton saying, "I'm firm on my price so don't try to negotiate." Mike assured him if the car was as described he would be very interested in buying the car.

The following week Mike Goodman was standing in Archie Hinton's garage looking at a perfect time capsule from 1959. The deal was made, and the car was hauled home to Tennessee. Before he left with the car, Mike had one last question for Archie, "Of all the people in that vendor building, why did you decide to offer this great old hot rod to me?" Archie explained it this way, "Well, you sure seemed to know a lot of people. You seemed to know a lot about old hot rods, and most importantly, you seemed like you really enjoy hot rodding. I wanted my car to go to someone who would enjoy the car, and you seemed like a good candidate." So it really does pay to be an all-around good guy who enjoys life.

Once the Deuce was back in Mike's garage, he set about making the old hot rod roadworthy again. The first step was to take inventory of exactly what makes this a great hot rod. Probably the best thing about the whole car is it is such a prime example of an average hot rod from the 1950s. This was no magazine cover car, it wasn't laden with expensive body modifications or expensive chrome plating and exotic upholstery, and it holds no track records. Rather it was a well-built budget hot rod that was assembled in 1959 by a high school student and fellow club members.

Modifications to the original '32 Ford were minimal. The Medium Maroon and black paint was applied in 1960, and the only body modifications were a filled roof and a filled cowl vent. Lighting front and rear remained stock, so this was a pretty conservative hot rod. The real work was in the chassis with a 1956 F-100 steering box replacing the original '32 box. Archie had swapped in a 1936 Ford 21-stud, 221-ci flathead mated to the original transmission.

Mike Goodman had the good fortune of having a hot rod find him; this particular coupe is a great example of a home-built hot rod from the late 1950s. The car was last painted in 1960. New tan steelies and Coker bias-ply tires replaced the aged rubber on the car.

Mike made the decision to leave the car as a time capsule. All work on the car was directed toward making it very roadworthy. Oddly enough, when Mike bought the car, it had mechanical brakes on the front with hydraulic brakes on the rear.

So what is a fellow to do with a car that has remained completely untouched since 1960? The options are always the same: You can leave the car exactly as it is today with a well-faded lacquer paint job, and let it be an obvious time capsule. Or, you can restore it to the glory of 1960 with a fresh lacquer paint job, saving the original interior and adding some fresh details to the motor and chassis, all the while being very careful not to over restore it. The last and, in my opinion, the least desirable choice would be to change the car and modify it to the new owner's tastes.

Mike told it to me this way, "Hey, this car has been a hot rod just like this since 1959, and I wasn't about to change the basic spirit of the car in any way." Good call there, and he went on to explain that all the work done on the car would be directed toward making it a safe and reliable driver. To that end, Mike set about doing a gentle upgrade on the Deuce.

The tired 1936 flathead motor was removed and replaced with a 10-year-newer version of Henry's V-8. The 1946 motor was built to famed Beachboy's song *Little Deuce Coupe* standards as, "She's ported and relieved and she's stroked and bored." A Mercury crankshaft gave the motor the famous 4-inch stroke while the bore was a conservative 3⅜ inches. Grant cast rings moved in the fresh cylinders while the cam had been reground to Isky 400jr specifications. Up top an early Offenhauser 3x2 intake rested between a set of Offenhauser finned-aluminum heads. A trio of Stromberg 97s fed the flattie, and the Mallory points-style distributor provided a better spark thanks to the MSD 6A ignition box that was discreetly hidden from view. Red's headers exited the spent gases through a set of Smithy's glass-pack mufflers.

The 1946 flathead motor was then mated to a fresh 1939 Ford Toploader transmission that had been filled with Lincoln Zephyr gears and a double-detent shifter. This transmission was plenty strong for the flathead motor, and that power was passed back to the original '32 Ford rear end. No doubt the weak link in the driveline was the rear axles, but then Mike has never been one for hard launches so the axle is doing just fine thank you.

Even in 1959, the approach to the brake system was unique; something I had never heard of before. The front brakes were left mechanical, while the rear brakes were hydraulic with the master cylinder for the rear brakes activated via a balance bar system, not unlike some systems seen on race cars today. Mike opted for new reproduction 1939 Lincoln-style drum brakes up front. These are self-energizing brakes with large brakes pads. They simply stop better than the Ford units and have the bonus of being all new. On the rear, the 1940 Ford brakes were brought up to new standards. A new 1940 Ford master cylinder and all new brake lines completed the safety orientated brake rebuild on the car.

It is interesting to note that this car still runs the original Deuce front axle. It has not been dropped, and likewise, the common practice of upgrading to tubular shocks was not done, rather the Houdaille shocks are still in service. Mike added new dog-bone links and spring shackles during the refurbishing of the car.

When Mike purchased the car it had a hopped-up, but tired, 1936 Ford flathead under the hood. He built a fresh 1946 flathead and swapped it in place. One concession to modern equipment comes in the form of the new Walker radiator and fan combination, but the car is designed to be driven.

Sometime in this coupe's past, the rear axle was painted bright red, then black. Today it is pure patina, and tube shocks were added along with new shackles to freshen the rear suspension and make the car a better driver.

The cowl vent had been filled on the coupe, but Mike opened the vent back up to allow fresh air into the cockpit. This is the only thing he changed on the body, and red oxide primer makes it look as if it were done 30 years ago.

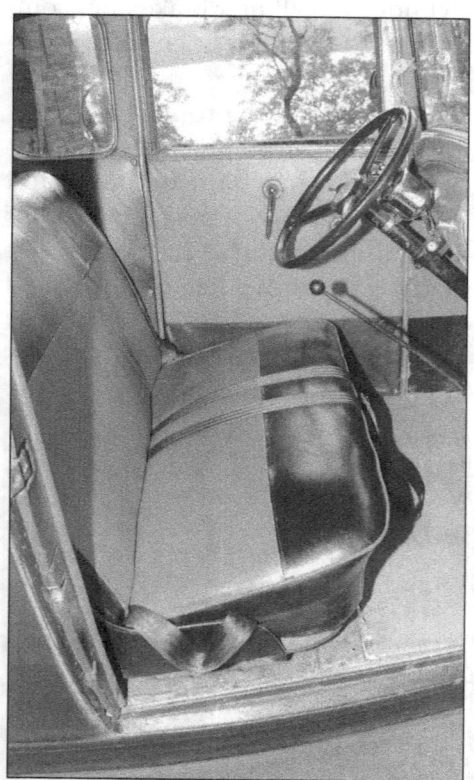

The interior was done in the late 1950s, and since this was a budget car, the simple red and black pattern includes no pleats or other upholstery. Rather, this interior may have been stitched at home or by a local trim shop. New seat belts are a smart addition.

The original mechanical brake rods were left on the car, and while many people have no idea what they are, those in the know look just a little longer to see if hydraulic brakes are present. Rolling stock for the Deuce comes in the form of new steel wheels that measure 16x4½ inches up front and 16x6 inches on the rear. The Coker bias-belted tires are 5½x16 inches up front with 7.00x16 inches on the rear.

The original fuel tank had typical rust-related problems, so a new OEM-type gas tank from Vintique was installed. New tailpipes were routed around the stock gas tank, and the exhaust was done in mild steel tubing to keep it period perfect.

After a thorough cleaning of the body, Mike decided to leave it in the original 1960 lacquer finish, complete with small rust blisters showing here and there. The only change he made to the body was opening up the cowl vent. Anyone who drives a hot rod with no A/C will tell you a filled cowl vent is a mistake. A little red-oxide primer around the newly opened vent completed all the exterior paint work on the car.

Next, attention turned to the inside of the car. The original dash has a well-worn woodgrain finish, and the stock gauge cluster has been replaced with a cluster filled with Classic Instrument gauges with a custom Honest Charley Speed Shop face. Simple toggle switches are period perfect, and all the wiring in the car was replaced with a modern wiring harness from American Autowire. By using the American Autowire Hwy 15 harness, the look of early braid and lacquer wire is preserved, but with modern wire under the accurate appearing, brightly colored cloth wire covers. This provides the safety of modern wiring and the great looks of vintage braid.

The only other nod to reliability and convenience is a Powermaster alternator and a new Walker radiator and electric fan. These upgrades were made because Mike drives this car, and not just around town, either.

After resting in an Ohio garage for many years, the Deuce five now sees frequent use. Mike Goodman has driven this vintage hot rod from Chattanooga to Las Vegas and back twice! Here the coupe takes to the open road while competing in the Coker Tire Challenge. (Photo Courtesy Tommy Lee Byrd)

Wayne Pugh has managed to build a hot rod that looks as if it has been around for decades, when actually it was just assembled over the past few years. A great combination of vintage parts and reproduction parts makes this hot rod work. The unchopped sedan rides atop a modified original Model A frame.

The rear spring is from a 1940 Ford and the 9-inch Ford housing carries drum brakes. A single Model A taillight is centered on the rear of the car while dirt tracker tires wrap around 16-inch 1935 Ford wire wheels.

The car was driven on the Driven Dirty tour that is the brainchild of Ken Fenical of Posies fame. In 2009, the coupe made the round trip haul from Chattanooga, Tennessee, to the SEMA Show in Las Vegas with nary a problem along the way. While this is a whole lot longer trip than Archie Hinton ever planned in 1959, it clearly illustrates that with quality parts and workmanship, these old hot rods can be reliable fun cars to own and drive. They need not be garage queens or relegated to local cruise nights. Since very little has been changed on this car since 1959, it offers a crystal clear view of what backyard hot rodding was like in the 1950s.

A+ for Flavor

If there is one consistent message found throughout this book, it is that the key to a great vintage hot rod is simplicity. But here's the tricky part: It may be simple, but it is not easy. Building a really great vintage hot rod takes on an almost reverse focus, one that has the builder looking at what is not needed as much as what is needed to complete the car. Wayne Pugh built the 1928 Model A Tudor Sedan shown here, and during the build he did a masterful job of sticking to the basics and using this basic hot rod theory: If the part doesn't help the car go, stop, or steer, it is optional. By adhering to this plan the car is so pure at times it almost looks like parts are missing.

Wayne began the project in 2004 when he purchased a solid 1928 Ford Tudor sedan body and doors from the swap meet at the NSRA Street Rod Nationals in Louisville, Kentucky. The body was hauled home to Georgia where it was mated to an original

Model A frame. Sure, he could have purchased a reproduction Model A frame for less than $1,000, but part of appreciating vintage hot rodding is by building not just the proper style, but by using the old methods. Those methods included boxing the frame and Z-ing the frame 2 inches in the rear. Under that rear kick-up, a modern 9-inch Ford rear axle housing was located using 1940 Ford wishbones and a genuine 1940 Ford rear spring. A Panhard rod was fabricated to help locate the frame over the suspension. Up front a Super Bell dropped I-beam axle carries a set of Mustang disc brakes. A Vega-style steering box was mounted to the stock Model A frame to complete the suspension.

Of course, many of these parts are modern, but with the proper packaging, the vintage flavor is strong enough to make these components fade into the overall picture. The Pete and Jake's hairpin radius rods, 1940 Ford wishbones, and a Model A body riding on top of the frame are all proper pieces of the vintage hot rod puzzle.

One quick glance under the hood might lead you to believe this is just another crate motor engine bay, but nothing could be further from the truth. This hot rod is powered by a genuine 1965 Corvette motor that displaces 327 ci. From the double-hump heads to the oil pan, this is all pure vintage Corvette. An Engle cam and rockers add performance, and Venolia pistons were used in conjunction with the stock rods and crankshaft, while an Edelbrock intake and carburetor provide fuel to the Vette motor was added by the owner with help from Mark Bernath and machine work by Bailey.

Although the chassis was finished in gloss black with bright red suspension, when it came time to bring the old body back to life, Wayne opted for a fairly rare color in the ranks of vintage hot rodding. Silver paint was not a common sight, but with the red accents and the 1935 Ford wire wheels the car has a great look. The color is 2005 Ford Silver. Doug Ivie performed the bodywork, and Winston's Custom Painting did the final finish. Those bright red wire wheels are wrapped with Coker Ribbed 5.00x16s up front and Coker Uniroyal 235/85-16s on the rear.

Body modifications were limited to a filled roof using a late-model station wagon ribbed roof and deeper rear wheel wells. A Rootlieb hood with stock-style louvers makes the connection from the Model A cowl to the '32 Ford grille shell, and the stock Model A gas tank is still in service. Lighting front and rear includes a set of original Guide headlights found at a swap meet, and a single Model A taillight mounted in the center of the body.

Inside the sedan a 1940 Ford dashboard has been adapted to the Model A, and a set of VW Bug bucket seats continues the vintage theme. A Stewart-Warner three-gauge panel hangs below the dash, and a 1940 Ford steering column and wheel match the dashboard. Rubber matting on the floor finishes the look, and although there is a stereo, it has been hidden from view. The partial black-and-white interior gives the

Up front Firestone tires combine with 1935 Ford wires for a classic, old hot rod look. The heavily fluted sidewalls of these tires add character to the tires. The hubcaps are '32 Ford and the absence of any beauty ring contributes to the clean and simple look.

Red suspension provides contrast to the silver body and black frame. Hairpin radius rods are very traditional, and note the tie-rod end used to attach it to the frame. Rootlieb built the hood that makes the transition from Model A cowl to Deuce grille shell.

Sure, you could put Corvette valve covers on a crate motor, but what makes Wayne's motor so cool is that it is actually a Corvette motor that once powered a 1965 Corvette. Much like the rest of the car, simplicity is the key to success under the hood.

The 1940 Ford dashboard was cut down before fitting it to the Model A body. Wayne is still using the original Model A gas tank, so the dashboard was carefully mounted in front of the tank. The steering wheel and column is also 1940 Ford.

sedan a vintage work-in-progress look. Wayne may eventually get around to finishing the interior, but for now he is having too much fun driving the sedan. Just two years after being rescued from the swap meet at the Street Rod Nationals this sedan returned to that same venue as a completed hot rod.

Dream 1940

Derrell Dudley has a 1940 coupe that could easily have been built in 1965, but beyond that the coupe is one of those hot rods that simply demands attention. You cannot walk past it. Maybe it's the half-dozen Holley 94 carbs and polished stacks, or it could be the Pagan Gold firewall. But when you combine those assets with a great hot rod rake, a flat finish, and whitewalls, you have a coupe worth remembering.

Now it wasn't always this way; as a matter of fact, after lusting for a 1940 coupe for more than 25 years, Derrell purchased this car as a finished street rod in the mid 1990s, an era I often refer to as nineteen-ninety tweed. Yes, exterior graphics and tweed are two of the most conspicuous ways to date a car, and this 1940 was wearing both of them. While it is too early to tell how history will treat tweed, it is difficult to believe that in 20 years hot rodders will be looking for pink-and-turquoise tweed. One thing was certain by 2008, it was time for a change. Derrell decided the car should appear to be a mid-1960s hot rod; no parts past 1968 were used on the car, save the Mustang II suspension and brakes.

The chassis with the Mustang II-style front suspension with dropped spindles and cut coils provide a definitive hot rod rake. Out back the stock frame is C'd to clear the 9-inch Ford

Looking at the Derrell Dudley 1940 coupe you might be thinking this hot rod has been around since the 1960s. Well, this coupe is actually a veteran of the tweed-and-pastel era, and only recently has Derrell taken the coupe back in time. The look is spot-on 1962.

HOW TO BUILD PERIOD CORRECT HOT RODS

rear. After 10 years of hard running, Derrell decided that a new 350-ci 290-hp crate motor would be the basis of power, but in keeping with the early theme, multiple carbs seemed to be almost mandatory. A call to Charlie Price at Vintage Speed in Vero Beach, Florida, netted just what the coupe needed: six Holley 94s resting atop an Offenhauser intake. The finned Edelbrock valve covers now have a flat-machined surface in the middle where long-time artist Bob Dale painted two 1950s-style pin-up girls. Block hugger headers would violate the 1968 cutoff date so a set of Corvette exhaust manifolds were used along with a mechanical seven-blade fan that spins inside a Vintage Air shroud.

Speaking of Vintage Air, remember the idea was for this car to look like a mid-1960s hot rod, not necessarily act like one. Texas is a state where A/C is not considered an option, so a compressor was mounted down low and out of sight on the engine, and the cold air exits through the stock radio speaker grille and several hidden outlets under the dash. Brackets were designed for the Denso alternator down low and out of sight too.

Externally the coupe remains nearly stock, with a shaved deck lid and the addition of a 1941 Ford front bumper being the only modifications. Original lighting remains front and rear, and the final finish on the car is Hot Rod Black from the Hot Hues palette, while the firewall, engine and dashboard were all treated to a Pagan Gold finish. The paint scheme is a salute to the days when many hot rodders painted the firewall and interior pieces the color that they one day dreamed the entire car would be.

With the abundance of white firewalls on the scene today, this Pagan Gold firewall and motor is a refreshing change that still has a great vintage look. The rolled-and-pleated Naugahyde carb cover is pure 1960s style.

The heart of any hot rod is the motor, and since Derrell had all intentions of running his coupe without a hood he wanted a great-looking motor. To that end, no less than six carbs top the small-block Chevy motor. Custom-painted pin-up girls adorn the aluminum valve covers bolted to the vintage double-hump heads.

Inside the car, more Pagan Gold was sprayed on the 1940 dash, while gold-and-white upholstery dates the car perfectly. The wood Grant steering wheel is seldom seen in hot rods today, but was a very popular wheel in the 1960s.

Any real hot rod 1940 coupe must have a great stance, and this one nailed the look. While the front is low, it is not the ultra-low seen today, rather the rear has been lifted to provide more rake, and that is exactly how it was done in the 1960s. Drop it in the front, raise it in the rear.

On the inside, the dilemma between bench and buckets was resolved with a traditional bench seat of unknown origin. After several samples were sewn, Derrell decided on gold-and-white pearl vinyl in a traditional rolled-and-pleated design. The effects are stunning, but don't overlook the appropriate details, such as the chrome garnish moldings, the Limeworks steering column, and the NOS Grant wood steering wheel.

With the coupe nearing completion, it was time for the all-important final details. Period correct chrome reverse rims were ordered from Wheel Vintique with cone lug nuts and center caps. The BFG Silvertown whitewalls are from Coker Tire.

And so after a couple of years Derrell finally had the 1940 of his dreams. For the most part the car was also built in a vintage manner, at home with help from friends and family. Guys like Chris Brummer, Boo Dale, and his son Jay Dudley worked long hours in Derrell's home garage, and of course, his wife Susan was a major supporter of the project.

T-Time

In the hot rodding world the Model T had pretty much gone the way of typewriter, but today the Model T coupes and sedans are enjoying a renaissance of sorts. Let's face it, if you chop the top 6 inches, channel the car 4 inches, and Z the frame front and rear you have lowered the overall profile by more than a foot and in the process uncovered a very distinctive hot rod profile. Now none of this was lost on Paul Duval, a hot rodder residing in Hendersonville, North Carolina.

Paul purchased the car as a running, but rough, hot rod. The plan was to simply clean things up a bit, remove some of the clutter, such as the side-mounted spare tires, and simply enjoy the car in all its patina glory. Ah, but the best laid plans of street rodders often go awry, and when it was suggested the top was a bit too tall, there was but one cure. The roof was cut 6 inches in the front and 4 inches in the rear. This great hot rod roof-rake amplified the attitude of the coupe and, of course, attention then turned to the fact that maybe, just maybe, this car was way too cool to be left in an unfinished state. The good news is you can take the body off the frame on a fenderless car in no time.

And so the Model T coupe underwent a complete rebuild with attention to detail and attitude dealt with in equal portions. While Henry Ford preferred to paint his cars black because black paint dried faster than the other colors, this coupe was painted black because it was simply the right color for a hot rod. (It should be noted that prior to 1913, and by the end of the Model T production, the Model T was in fact available in several other colors including green, gray, and red.)

The coupe rests on an interesting frame, the center section is original Model T with a box tubing front, and the rear clip was added by Custom Works by Michael in Bostic, North Carolina. The hot rod chassis blends the 2x4 box tubing that is Z'd front and rear with the stock center section in such a way that it appears to be all box tubing. Up front a Pete and Jake's dropped and drilled axle holds Wilwood disc brakes and receives

The Model T had all but disappeared from the hot rodding scene for the past 15 years, but lately it is making a comeback, and with hot rod coupes like this one, it is little wonder. The heavily chopped top and traditional appointments on this car make it a hot rod with true vintage flavor.

A finned-aluminum panel holds Classic Instruments inside the coupe. Once again, new parts with the right attitude.

The 1953 Mercury flathead still has a factory-spec bore and the famous 4-inch stroke. The Offy heads have been painted red with polished fins, while a staircase effect trio of Stromberg 97s top off the hot rod mill. Stainless mesh covering on the radiator hoses is the only distraction from the vintage flavor. Note the front portion of the chassis has been Z'd to lower the profile.

Details like preserving the brass identification tag atop the headlights is always a good way to let people know these are true early parts. Guide has been making lights and lenses for a long, long, time.

directions from a Unisteer rack-and-pinion steering system, while a traditional transverse spring and tube shocks smooth out the highway. These concessions to modern motoring may distract slightly from the vintage style of the car, but they make up for it in drivability and safety.

Out back a Ford 8-inch rear holds 3:53 final gears and is located via a contemporary four-bar arrangement with coil-over shocks providing adjustable ride height suspension. Rolling stock for the coupe comes in the form of Wheelsmith 16-inch wire wheels fitted with Coker Firestone bias-ply whitewall tires that are size 6.00x16-inch front and 7.50x16-inch rear. Spinning those big 7½-inch rears is a task handled by a nicely warmed over flathead. By 1953, the Mercury flathead V-8 was displacing 255 ci and producing 125 hp; 1953 would be the last year of the venerable flathead engine.

The engine was in such good condition that it still displaces the original 255 ci. Paul had Bridges Auto Parts handle the machining of the internal parts. The stock rods, pistons, and crankshaft are now balanced and an Isky 3/4 cam lifts the valves in the block. The water pumps are from Speedway Motors, and the engine is topped off with a set of finned-aluminum heads from Offenhauser. An Offenhauser intake holds a trio of Stromberg 94s, while Speedway Motors supplied the ignition. A set of Sanderson headers completes the high-performance street flathead. A Tremec five-speed transmission is coupled to the flatmotor with an Honest Charley bellhousing. This combination allows the little coupe to motor on effortlessly at highway speeds.

What is refreshing about this coupe is the restraint used in the overall build. The stock door handles and hinges are still in place, and while the firewall has been smoothed it remains body color. One subtle change that often goes unnoticed is the abbreviated sun visor. When the panels were laser straight, the Dupont Chroma Premier black paint was laid down by John Smith. Mark Peters gave the body and chassis that final touch of detail with some of the finest pinstriping you'll find anywhere.

Inside the coupe is pure 1950 with a black-and-white checker pattern. James Auto Upholstery in Fletcher, North Carolina, installed the marine-grade leather and Bentley cut-pile carpet. The steering column is from Lime Works combined with a genuine 1927 Model T steering wheel, and Stewart-Warner gauges in a finned-aluminum panel monitor the flat motor.

And so what Paul and Krishna Duval had envisioned as a basic beater in vintage patina has become a fully detailed traditional hot rod. The car represents the hottest trend

Building an early traditional hot rod out of anything but a Ford is not easy, but Larry Shoaf has managed to take a 1927 Chrysler roadster and build a hot rod that looks as if it came right off the pages of a 1952 magazine.

To say the body was rough when Larry discovered it buried in vines alongside an old garage would be an understatement. Rust repair and panel replacement were a big part of the project.

in street rods today—the skillful blending of old-time attitude with modern hot rod parts for reliability and drivability.

The Shoaf Roadster

I have mentioned several times that most traditional hot rods are Ford based, but for those bold enough, great hot rods can be built based on virtually any car, and often the rarity of the car adds real interest to the finished product. Larry Shoaf built just such a hot rod, and while this car may look as if it were taken right off the pages of a 1956 *Rod & Custom*, nothing could be further from the truth. Actually Shoaf discovered the remains of a 1927 Chrysler Roadster collapsing in the woods behind a local garage within the past 10 years. It was a glimmer off a stainless steel headlight that caught his attention one winter day, and further exploration exposed not one, but two Chrysler roadsters.

And when I say remains I mean just that. Two decent cowl sections, doors, and quarter panels that were heavily rusted to the beltline of the door, but the rare parts were there. It was a real steel roadster and luckily for this Chrysler product, it had been discovered by one of the few men who could fabricate the needed panels and make the roadster whole again. It took the remaining parts of both cars to make one body, with one extra cowl remaining.

After laying out rusted panels on the floor of the shop in something that resembled an archeological ruins site, the pieces were roughly assembled with Cleco fasteners and bolts to establish what the wheel base should be on the car since there was no chassis with either body.

Larry then set about building his own frame, starting with 2x6-inch box tubing, then cutting pie-shaped wedges from the firewall forward to form a tapered frame rail similar to most early rails. The 6-inch-wide tubing allowed room for a sculptured line on the bottom of the frame, much like a 1934 Ford frame. Speaking of 1934 Ford, a vintage MorDrop 1934 Ford axle is located up front with 1948 Ford drum brakes. This authentic-looking frame was then filled with a custom-formed K-member. Being a believer in Chrysler power for Chrysler cars, Larry removed a 318 from a 1970 Dodge van and rebuilt it in his home garage. Topping the motor is the famed Mopar Six-Pack, three 2-barrel carbs. The entire setup was purchased from the local Dodge dealer under the Mopar

The neat, no-frills approach to the 318 Dodge motor works well. The color matches the scallops on the wheels of the car and provides a nice contrast to the blue paint. In true hot rod fashion, Larry rebuilt the motor himself, and it has a pretty healthy cam.

In the final analysis, the roadster is pretty true to the rendering and the early-style split windshield and roll bar give the roadster a very early 1950s style. The color is called PPG Navy Blue. Larry sprayed the car with basecoat/clearcoat urethane.

Parts program and was surprisingly affordable.

Out back Larry narrowed the 9-inch Ford rear to fit the roadster and used a set of coil-over shocks and a home-made four-bar for suspension. The coil-over shocks are the one concession to modern hot rodding on the car. When it was completed the chassis looked like a factory frame. It's difficult to believe it all began with just two pieces of box tubing.

While the chassis is impressive, the body on this roadster is what really makes it a standout. Even in 1927, Chrysler was a luxury brand, and to that end the roadster had a golf bag door on the passenger side of the car, in front of the rear wheels—open the door, slide in your golf bag, and head off to the country club. Larry was tempted to keep the door as a curiosity, but due to the advanced rust in the lower corners and his belief that it would distract from the hot rod attitude of the car the door was eliminated during fabrication of the new body panels from the beltline down. He did the same thing for the doors and went almost as high on the cowl. So from the beltline down this roadster is all-new metal.

Out back Larry did a masterful job building a rear view that could have been built in 1954. He began by removing the rather strange double-panel deck lid from the Chrysler and forming his own one-piece deck lid. The rear pan was then fitted with a recessed license plate opening and a pair of recessed 1951 Hudson taillights. A rolled rear pan was fabricated with exhaust ports that really lend a vintage feel to the rear treatment. The crowning touch was a hand-formed rear nerf bar.

The front of the body received a smoothed cowl in preparation for the owner-built, all-aluminum windshield frame that even has attachments for a top. Larry also hand-formed the hood and grille shell, including a gorgeous opening for the three air breathers. The three-piece hood was also designed so the roadster can run without the side panels. The grille shell was modified with a recess for the 1927 Chrysler emblem, and aluminum grille bars complete the front of the car. The headlights are a set of BLC lights found at a swap meet.

After untold hours of fabrication, panel fit, and finishing, Larry sprayed the PPG Navy Blue paint on the roadster. Larry's son Mike Shoaf penned the original illustration, which included cream scallops, but Larry was so pleased with the simple blue look that he decided to forego the scallops for now.

Inside the car a custom seat was fabricated, and Ray Hester worked his magic in leather. The dashboard is filled with vintage Stewart-Warner gauges, and Larry opted to scratch-wire the car himself. The attention to detail, fit, and finish would have made this car an instant show winner in the 1950s and 1960s.

So what makes the Shoaf roadster work as a timeless vintage hot rod? Once again, simplicity comes into play, along with a keen eye for traditional appointments. Things like the single-hoop roll bar, the nerf bar, rolled rear pan, and the odd but effective Hudson taillights all give the feeling of a vintage hot rod. The breathers protruding through the hood are reminiscent of early race cars, and the hot rod rake and steel artillery wheels complete the period perfect feeling.

Resisting the temptation to use any kind of a Ford grille shell also gives the car an early feeling. The fact that this roadster was entirely built by Larry Shoaf is both a display of his considerable talents and also explains why he builds hot rods by day at his Rodcrafter's Shop in Welcome, North Carolina. This roadster

Bob Van Horn's coupe has a colorful past—the hot rod that was stolen in the night in the 1960s and didn't return to the street for more than 40 years. The car remains almost exactly as it was in 1965, but it now wears a new color.

is a perfect example (both literally and figuratively) of a vintage-flavor hot rod roadster.

'40 Found

The great disappearing act happened back in the 1950s, and it still happens today. Every hot rodder has a story about a car that has simply gone missing. But if hot rods never went missing, we would never have the great tales of hot rods found, and stories such as this one.

Just exactly when this 1940 Ford coupe was converted into a hot rod is unclear, but what is known is Bill Kincheloe bought this car in the early 1960s, and it was decent hot rod at that time. Like most hot rodders, Bill had a vision of his own for the car so he removed most of the suspension and sent it off for chrome plating. A hot 327 was installed under the hood and a fresh paint job in the then-popular Surfer Yellow made the coupe a real standout. The paint work and custom tricks, such as shaving the door handles, were done by none other than famed customizer Gene Winfield. The complete yellow lacquer paint job cost $225 in 1965, and the total tab for all of his custom work came to $419.30.

By the time Bill finished the 1940 coupe, he had a car that was fast and detailed enough to be a show car too. Bill used the car during his stint in the Air Force but awoke one morning to every hot rodder's worse nightmare: The 1940 was gone, stolen out of his driveway during the night.

Police eventually recovered the car, but it was minus the engine, transmission, and seat. Discouraged with the condition of his once pristine hot rod, Bill parked the coupe in a garage where it sat for 18 years. Eventually, he realized he wasn't going to put the car back on the street, so he sold it to an old Air Force buddy who had always admired the car. That fellow was certain he would put the car back on the street some day. But the coupe spent yet another 18 years languishing in a garage until the current owner, Bob Van Horn, purchased the car in 2002.

Now Bob Van Horn is no stranger to hot rodding either. As a matter of fact, he was living in California in the early 1960s and owned three 1940 Fords during his stay there. When he purchased the coupe the documentation and Winfield

You might be able to emulate the look of the 1960s, but you will never be able to have a master craftsman like Gene Winfield paint your entire car for $225. The modifications made to the car were clean, simple improvements.

invoices helped him trace the history on the car. The old hot rod was rock solid, the Surfer Yellow paint had faded and checked over the 40 years but the car was in such good condition that Bob scrapped any thoughts of changing it; rather, he decided to bring the car back to its early 1960s glory, with the only major change being the color.

The chassis and suspension were in remarkable condition, and even the 1960s chrome plating was salvaged on the suspension. After weeks of careful cleaning and polishing, the 2½-inch dropped axle and 1940 Ford backing plates were sparkling chrome again. The coupe had remained without an engine for some 40 years, and since it last had a 327 under the hood, Bob thought it would be fitting to install another 327 and 1940 Ford transmission in the car. An Offenhauser adapter plate makes the transition from Chevy motor to early Ford transmission. The rear spring, shackles, and shocks were also chrome plated in 1965, so those pieces were also restored.

This is what the 1940 coupe looked like when it rolled out of the California garage after being stored for 36 years. Surfer Yellow paint by Gene Winfield had faded a bit, but the 1941 Studebaker taillights, shaved deck lid, and white running boards all remain intact today.

When the car was stolen in the mid 1960s, thieves removed the motor, transmission, and seat from the car. Bob Van Horn installed a period correct 327 under the hood and dressed it to the time period, complete with a generator.

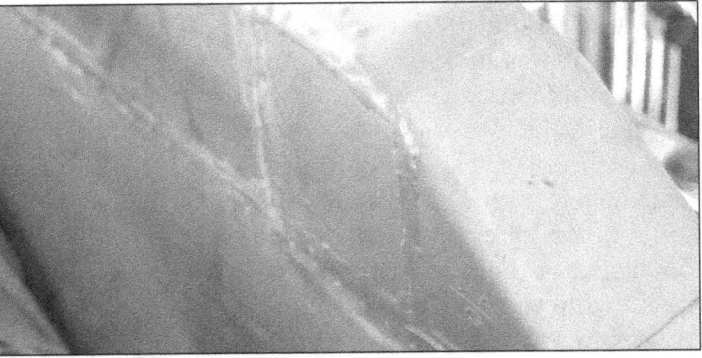

The original 1940 radiator is still in service. Because the flathead motors used two hoses top and bottom, it was common practice to solder a patch over the flathead hose outlets and position a new single port in the middle. To duplicate that vintage look today, you could take a new Walker radiator and simply solder two pieces of brass to the upper and lower tanks (no need to make holes of course). Then paint the radiator, and presto—you have a radiator that looks like a modified original. Details like this really date a car.

When it came time to restore the body, Bob couldn't think of any additional modifications that would improve the coupe, so he set about stripping the car to bare metal and repainting the car Lokar Burgundy. Things such as new bumpers, chrome fender welting, and those vintage white running boards from the 1960s keep the car strictly traditional. The 1941 Studebaker taillights carry blue dots and the shaved deck lid has simple but effective pinstriping.

On the inside the traditional approach continues. Since the original seat had been "removed" in 1966, a replacement seat was located. Jeff's Custom Upholstery in Merritt Island, Florida, stitched up a rolled-and-pleated interior that was era correct, right down to the white headliner and burgundy piping. The 1955 Ford steering column was left intact, and Bob rewired the entire car. Tracing the steering column to 1955 might indicate that this car was originally a hot rod in the late 1950s. The dashboard had been tastefully modified, so it was left just the way it was in 1965, right down to the Sun tach.

The only trace of Surfer Yellow paint left on the car is found on the rims, where a set of full-spun aluminum Moon discs cover all but the outer ring of the rim. Diamond Back radial whitewalls are about the only concession to modern parts on the entire car, but since Bob drives his hot rods, these tires were a logical choice.

And so, almost 40 years to the day, this once-stolen coupe was returned to the street. The craftsmanship and style of the 1960s remain intact, and Bob Van Horn has done a fine job of preserving another great American hot rod.

The 1941 Studebaker taillights are both rare and beautiful, and seem to fit the contour of the 1940 Ford fender better than the Ford taillights. Chrome fender welting is a nod to the 1960s when chrome was an important part of hot rodding.

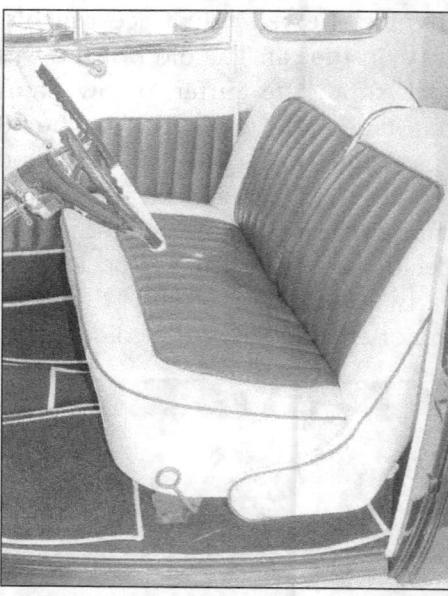

After finding a replacement seat, a 1960s-style white and burgundy Naugahyde was stitched in the traditional rolled-and-pleated pattern. By running a white header panel on the seat, the interior appears to be white when looking from outside the car. Burgundy piping on white panels completes the look.

Today, the coupe still has a great 1960s look with the non-metallic Lokar Burgundy paint. The white running boards are more apparent when contrasting with the darker color. Great pains were taken to save and restore the white rubber boards.

CHAPTER 9

Cool Old Parts

If there is one common thread woven through every story in this book, it is the fact that each car owner is a parts hound—a real hunter, a person who faithfully attends major swap meets, peruses ads in print and online, and generally maintains a network of traditional hot rodders. It is through these sources and constantly learning about vintage parts that they manage to gather all the good stuff to build great hot rods. We all know them, and for some reason when I enter one of these garages, I am always astounded at what they have amassed over the years; not just stuff, but the good stuff—the right stuff.

There is a tendency to write it off as, "he's so lucky, he always finds great parts," and I do believe to some extent that some people have a gift that makes vintage hot rods and parts pass before them.

I have one friend in particular, Troy Byrd, who always seems to be at the right place at the right time. Go to a swap meet with him and while he's looking at an old front engine dragster he notices that as the owner is unloading the trailer a genuine magnesium American wheel is being used to hold the door open. A quick query about the wheel leads to a purchase at an astoundingly low price.

But for every example like that one there are hours of walking hot, dusty, cold, muddy isles of swap meets, stopping to go through boxes, and look inside cars for sale for hidden treasure. Parts hunting is a lot like fishing; you seldom hear the stories of days of searching to come up empty, rather you hear the tales of the great finds. So when you are thinking how lucky these folks are, remember you could be just as lucky if you put in the time to go looking for parts.

Although searching for random parts can be both fun and profitable if you have a project under way or are collecting parts for a project, a list of desired items is extremely helpful. Begin your research at home and take a notebook with you to help you remember that you need—the dual-quad intake with square ports, or even better, a part number for the piece. Nothing is more frustrating than coming home with a really nice Olds intake only to find out it doesn't fit your Olds motor.

It also pays to travel. Many parts are regional. Let's face it, if you are hoping to find a rare Detroit Racing Equipment intake manifold for your Caddy engine, there are probably more of them in the Midwest than on the West Coast. By targeting that area, you are more likely to find what you are looking for, just as there are probably more Morbec wheels in Texas than there are in New York because the wheels were manufactured in Texas. So you would be more likely to find a set of them at the famed Pate Swap Meet than you would at Hershey.

Of course, small local swap meets often net fewer treasures, but when you do find them, they are often at bargain prices. The big swap meets are filled with people who make a living selling old car parts, so they are up at first light scavenging better deals on hard-to-find parts.

The big vintage car swap meets, such as Hershey, Carlisle, Pate, L.A. Roadster Show, Turkey Rod Run, or the Ty-Rods fall swap meet in Connecticut, are great places to find parts, but don't forget other less-traveled venues. Local wooden boat

HOW TO BUILD PERIOD CORRECT HOT RODS 129

shows often have a small swap meet. They can prove to be great places to find vintage gauges, dash inserts, and special performance parts for marine applications that will make your motor unique. Parts, such as dual side-draft carburetors for Y-block Fords, are just one example of somewhat exotic looking parts that would work on a vintage hot rod.

Likewise, if racing is big in your area, there is often a racers' swap meet at the end of the season. I used to regularly attend one in Charlotte, North Carolina, at the Metroliner Fairgrounds, and it was amazing what would turn up there—everything from quick-change rears to Halibrand wheels and all types of performance parts.

Now I'm sure many of you may be thinking that eBay offers a huge range of parts. While it is a great resource, along with many other online sites, here is a news flash: Oftentimes a fellow who has been hanging on to a set of 16x10-inch magnesium Halibrand wheels for more than 50 years does not have a digital camera nor possibly even an Internet connection. However, he does know about the Ty-Rods Swap meet in Connecticut, and you'll find parts and people just like him at virtually every swap meet in the country. Plus, it's a whole lot more fun to talk face to face with a vendor, negotiate a price, swap a couple lies, put the piece in an old red wagon, and head back to the truck with your new purchase. It is my fervent belief that clicking a mouse and watching the auction ticking to a close will never surpass this experience.

Of course, not every part on a vintage hot rod is an old part. Things such as weather stripping, wiring, seat frames, and accessories are best purchased new. Many years ago reproduction parts had a reputation for substandard quality, but today the reproduction companies supply fine quality parts that fit and work like new. Of course, it still pays to do your homework and get referrals on where to find quality parts, but for the most part the major suppliers are producing really nice pieces.

From complete bodies to reproduction taillights, building a vintage-flavored hot rod has never been easier. Some reproduction pieces are even an improvement on the original. I searched long and hard to find a set of NOS 1950 Pontiac taillights for my roadster and they were perfect. The plastic lenses were a nice uniform red with no sun fading or cracking. Today, the reproduction Pontiac lights come with glass lenses and a better bulb socket.

Of course, many hot rodders opt to use a reproduction body and frame to build their hot rod, and it matters little if it is a steel body or a fiberglass body. One word of advice though: It is generally best to purchase all of the big pieces from one shop. The body and chassis will be matched, the brakes will be compatible with the rest of the car, and so on. Not all hot rod parts work well on every reproduction chassis, so once again, shop wisely and talk to people who have built a car like the one you intend to build. Ensuring the compatibility of aftermarket parts goes a long way toward making your hot rod building experience a good one.

Should you be wondering about the accuracy of parts? One of the easiest methods to ensure you are putting era correct parts on your car is to simply buy a stack of old magazines from the time period. Check both the ads and the cars featured in the magazines. *Rod & Custom*, *Honk*, *Rodding and Restyling*, and *Hot Rod* are invaluable research tools. During the process of researching this book I have

Dick Lewis built this Deuce roadster in the early 1990s, but everything on the car was produced prior to 1960. From the blown flathead to the early Halibrand quick-change, this coupe is period perfect. As for those aluminum early-Ford-style rims, they are a set of super-rare aluminum wheels that where original equipment on vintage Chicago Streamlite camper trailers, and yes, early Ford hubcaps pop right on them.

gathered photos and great vintage parts along with ads and photos from days past illustrating what parts were available and in some cases what the parts cost when they were new. This is both entertaining and informative, and you will certainly find some parts that are period perfect for your own project. You might also find some parts that you never knew existed, and you can add them to your swap meet and internet search list.

One thing is certain: Parts are fun to hunt for, and great to find. And when you assemble the right collection of parts, the hot rod you build will be greater than the sum of its parts. Enjoy the hunt, and enjoy the build.

Vintage license plate toppers are very cool, and when you can find scarce ones from your region they are even better. Dick Lewis is a member of the Vagabonds car club.

Recently Speedway Motors began reproducing the famous metal-flake steering wheel that was so popular in the 1960s.

Marketing pieces, such as this B.F. Goodrich badge, were big in the 1950s and 1960s. Today they add just the right touch to your vintage hot rod.

Jerry Sentz has a great example of an East Coast hot rod. The chopped and channeled Model A coupe sports a honeycomb grille in a Deuce shell with robin's egg blue paint. The white roof insert is also period correct.

CHAPTER 9

The 1947 Oldsmobile taillight is a great choice for hot rods; it provides ample rear lighting and a clean, simple look.

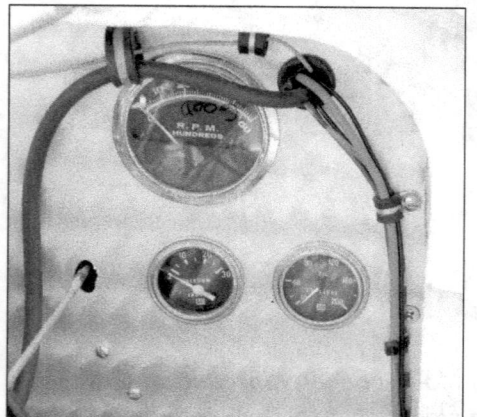

Vintage gauges in an engine-turned panel keep the traditional look going on the Kendall coupe. Such gauges were considered essential for track-side tuning.

This Mobile Oil Can makes a great catch can for the radiator. Using automotive containers seems like a natural, and a time period can be established using period pieces. Note the nice aluminum bracket too.

Pete Trumbauer rescued this old race car from behind the original racer's house. The Deuce three-window was raced from 1954 through 1961. Ed Burnham owned the car and Tony Volz drove it. In spite of the intrinsic value of a '32 Ford three-window, Pete has opted to leave the car in race trim.

Pete added a pair of 1939 Ford taillights to the roof and a license plate to make the car somewhat street legal. Again, it is in amazing condition for the punishment that it endured, and today it is a wonderful time capsule of East Coast stock car racing.

COOL OLD PARTS

With the appropriate amount of chopping and channeling, you can actually get a T-coupe profile lower than a Deuce coupe. Louvers, Pontiac taillights, and whitewall-wrapped Radir wheels are all appropriate.

Steve Sullivan has put together one of the best period perfect hot rods I have had the pleasure of viewing. From the red oxide primer to the Hemi motor, this roadster pickup just shouts 1958.

Simple homemade headers work well on this flathead. Using tapered torque tubes from something like a 1937 Ford was once popular; the Ford emblem tack welded on the headers is a nice touch; and white finish is the proper color for early headers.

HOW TO BUILD PERIOD CORRECT HOT RODS

CHAPTER 9

The quintessential hot rod coupe, this Deuce three-window employs wide whitewalls, Rader mags, and vintage-style headlights to accomplish the look of the 1960s. The soot on the door is from the open headers and provides a great graphic over red-oxide primer.

The patina was perfect on this roadster, but what really brought me in for a closer look was the set of super-rare Edmunds Hemi valve covers. This is a great roadster.

Running headers through a side panel often entails an unsightly seam running the full length of the hood side. On this Model A, just the lower rear corner remains stationary when the hood opens, eliminating the long seam.

Kill Stickers. Nothing would strike fear into the driver next to you at the light more than a window full of class winner stickers. Available in reproduction vinyl, the original water-base decals are best for true 1960s hot rods.

Chrome bullets come in all sizes and are still available today. This Deuce shell is filled with mesh with a bullet on each crossing point of the mesh. That's a lot of work, but also a lot of vintage flavor.

COOL OLD PARTS

You can only appreciate how much a 7-inch chop is after seeing a stock height Model T roof. This coupe takes on a very cool 1960s look with the stock height roofline.

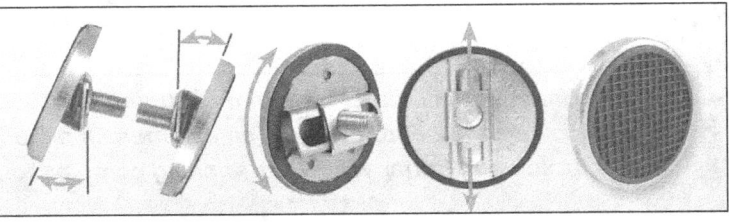

Pedal placement and angle are critical to driving comfort and safety. These Adjusta-Pedals from Bob Drake are one of the best problem-solving products I have seen in a very long time. This takes an early-style pedal pad and gives you almost infinite adjustment to angle and vertical and horizontal position.

Tim Stutely took on the challenge of converting a 1931 DeSoto into a traditional hot rod. At first glance, I thought it was a Model A with an odd hood treatment. The '32 Ford grille goes a long way toward fooling people.

The DeSoto hood sides are held in place with mechanical latches. The louver treatment makes the hood sides the highlight of the car. The hood sides are mated to a custom-fabricated one-piece hood top.

HOW TO BUILD PERIOD CORRECT HOT RODS

A generator is mandatory equipment for any accurate hot rod build prior to 1965. They look great when chrome plating is added. There are several suppliers of alternators that look like generators too.

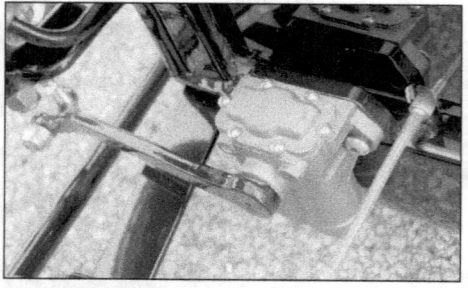

Lever-action shocks were standard fare on early Fords, and Armstrong shocks are oil-filled lever-action shocks that were very common on many sports cars of the 1950s and 1960s. You could soften or stiffen the ride by changing the weight of the oil. The aluminum body polishes up nicely too.

The 1952 Buick taillight has long been popular with hot rodders. They are still relatively easy to find today.

Barry McNeill did a fine job of capturing the 1950s look with his flathead-powered '32 Ford pickup. The commercial grille keeps it all truck, and the green and butter yellow is a winning combination.

This is one of my favorite photographs I have ever taken. Larry and his daughter Jennifer Judkins at speed in a '27 Ford roadster. It just seems to capture the very essence of hot rodding and explains in one single photo why you would want to build a hot rod. The photo was taken in the late 1980s.

Leather straps were common on race cars of the 1930s, and they are still available today. The spring in the center of the belt holds tension on the hood.

This Model A coupe has a no-nonsense look, with a nice blister for the Pitman arm, black wheels, and chopped top to give a pure hot rod look. The full-height Deuce shell has been channeled in front of the Model A crossmember.

This is real vintage stuff, and few people have the guts to go for it, but diamond-tufted metal-flake vinyl will date the inside of your hot rod like no other material on the planet. A matching metal-flake steering wheel completes this awesome interior.

CHAPTER 9

Beyond adding a performance image to your hot rod, open lake pipes just have a very cool sound. Not nearly as loud as open headers, they make exactly the right amount of noise.

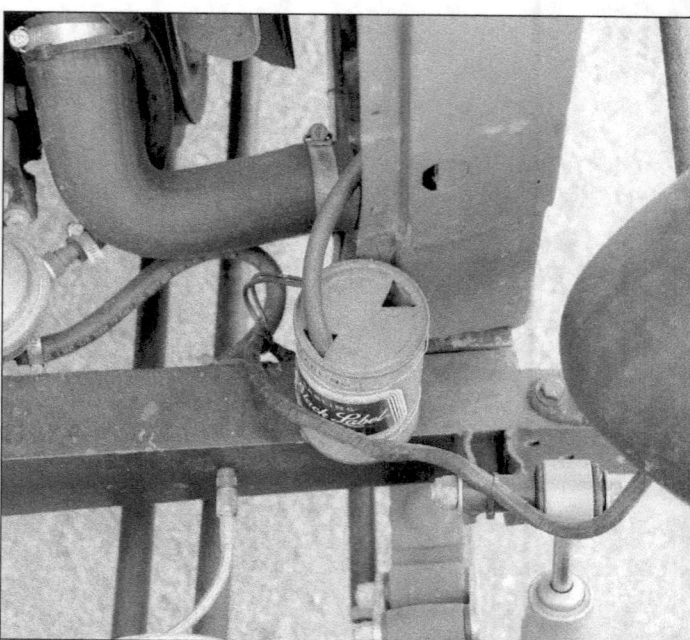

Beer cans have been used for overflow catch cans forever. If you are going for 1950s style, the can must be steel, and it must have the trademark church-key triangles punched in the top.

One drawback to driving a hot rod truck is the lack of dry storage. Few things are more appropriate than a military footlocker used as storage in the bed of a hot rod truck. Returning World War II vets used these items to store everything. The military still used footlockers in the 1960s, so there are plenty to be found.

This may be the best-looking backing plate I have ever seen. Vent holes around the perimeter have a stamped bevel while the cut-out reliefs have a stainless steel mesh inside them. Add red and black paint, and you have a picture-perfect backing plate.

COOL OLD PARTS

In the early 1960s Chevrolet trucks used a dual master cylinder with the right side providing brakes, and the left side providing a reservoir for the hydraulic clutch. Hot rodders were quick to latch onto this setup as a simple way to work a clutch.

Banjo steering wheels have always been popular with hot rodders, but what really caught my eye was the beautiful banjo-style steering column drop. What a great touch on a vintage interior.

The iconic East Coast hot rod consists of a coupe channeled the depth of the frame with a stock height top. This is a fine example of the breed. Note the recessed firewall to accommodate the late-model V-8.

CHAPTER 9

What I found interesting about this roadster pickup was the bolt-on aluminum brackets for attaching the radius rods. They have a built-in boss to accept the tapered attachment of a tie rod end.

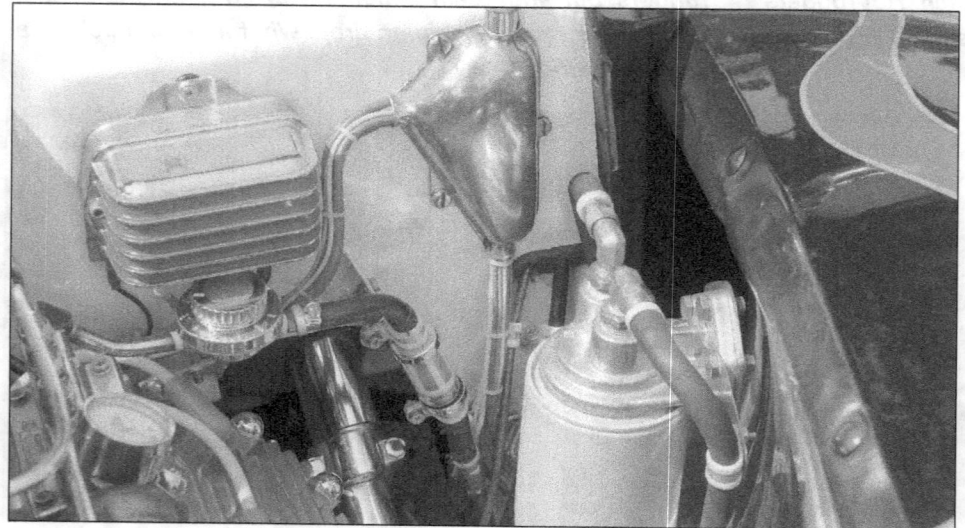

There is a lot going on in this photo, from the early Cal Custom finned voltage regulator cover to the chrome-plated wire loom cover—this white firewall is filled with proper equipment. The remote oil filter is another neat performance item.

Simple black faces with white numbers seem to work best on old hot rods. Those indicator lights are vintage too, but are still available. Jaguar used similar lights, so don't be afraid to peruse catalogs of vintage foreign cars.

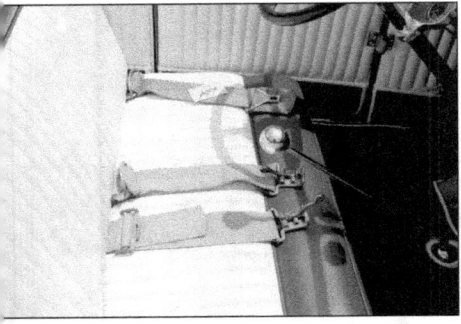

The best source for seat belts in the 1940s and early 1950s was the local army surplus store. Surplus military belts were found in many race cars and hot rods. Today, the reliability of the belts may come into question, but they sure look good.

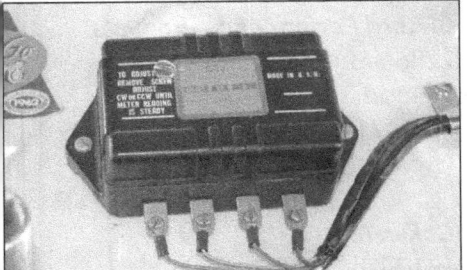

Until the mid 1960s, Sun tachometers used a sending unit that was mounted to the firewall. The batteries inside would often leak and ruin the units. Today, there are several companies that rebuild these sending units.

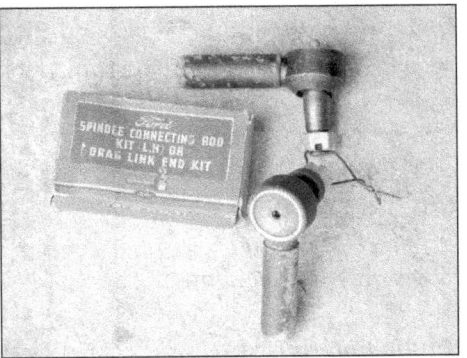

This is the kind of stuff you keep an eye out for at a swap meet. NOS tie rod ends for early Fords. Why is that important? Simple; they have a Ford script stamped in the face, which immediately dates the car.

Sure, that Halibrand rear caught my eye, but if you look above the buggy spring, you will notice the entire floor of this roadster is painted white. This vintage treatment adds a special touch to the entire car.

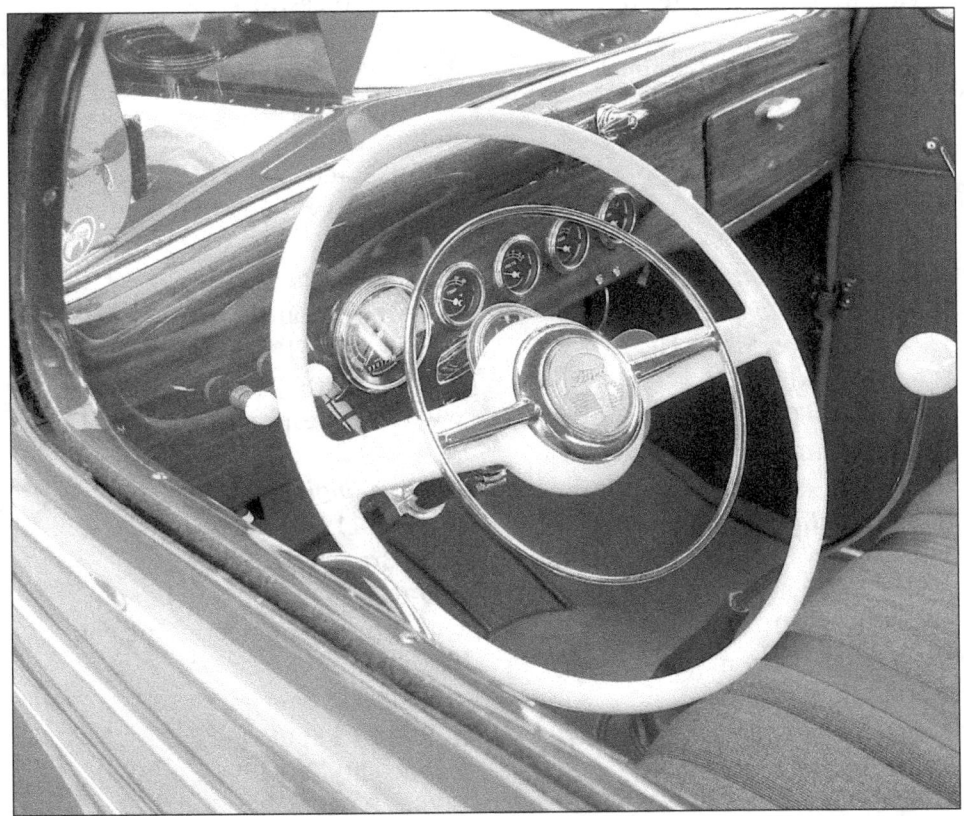

Sure, the early-style upholstery and woodgrain dashboard are all period correct, but the early 1950s Ford steering wheel in ivory dominates the whole interior. This gorgeous steering wheel is accented with matching dash knobs.

Source Guide

American Autowire
150 Heller Place #17W
Bellmawr, NJ 08031
800-482-9473
www.americanautowire.com

American Stamping Company
75 Downing Street, Suite A
Olive Branch, MS 38654
662-895-5300
www.ascrails.com

Bendtsen's Speed Gems Transmission Adapters
13603 Johnson Street NE
Ham Lake, MN 55304
763-767-4480
www.transmissionadapters.com

Bob Drake Reproductions
1819 NW Washington Boulevard
Grant Pass, OR 97526
800-221-FORD
www.bobdrake.com

Borgeson Steering
91 Technology Park Drive
Torrington CT, 06790
860-482-8283
www.borgeson.com

Brassworks
500 Linne Road - Unit I
Paso Robles, CA 93446
805-239-2501
www.thebrassworks.net

Brookville Roadsters
718 Albert Road
Brookville, Ohio 45309
937-833-4605
www.brookvilleroadster.com

Charlie Price's Vintage Speed
1916 63rd Court
Vero Beach, FL 32966
772-778-0809
www.vintagespeed.com

Chassis Engineering, Inc.
Box 70, 119 N 2nd St.
West Branch, IA 52358
319-643-2645
www.chassisengineeringinc.com

Classic Instruments
1299 M-75 South
Boyne City, MI 49712
800-575-0461
www.classicinstruments.com

Clifford Performance Products
22850 Sheffield Court
Wildomar, CA 92595
951-471-1161
www.cliffordperformance.net

Coker Tire
1317 Chestnut Street
Chattanooga, TN 37402
866-267-6827
www.cokertire.com

Cornhusker Rod & Custom
1987 Road 7300
Alexandria, NE 68303-9801
402-749-1932
www.cornhuskerrodandcustom.net

Cragar Classic Wheels
P.O. Box 558
Milford, IA 51351
909-947-1831
www.cragarwheel.com

Currie Enterprises
1480 North Tustin Avenue
Anaheim, CA 92807
714-528-6957
www.currieenterprises.com

SOURCE GUIDE

Dayton Wire Wheel
115 Compark Road
Dayton, OH 45459
937-438-0100
www.daytonwirewheels.com

Dennis Carpenter Reproductions
4140 Concord Parkway S
Concord, NC 28027
800-476-9653
www.dennis-carpenter.com

Diamond Back Classic Tires
4753 Highway 90
Conway, SC 29526
888-922-1642
www.dbtires.com

Engineered Components, Inc.
P.O. Box 841
Vernon, CT 06066
860-872-7046
www.ecihotrodbrakes.com

Egge Products
11707 Slauson
Santa Fe, CA 90670
866-988-3443
www.egge.com

The Glass House
446 W Arrow Highway #4
San Dimas, CA 91773
866-415-5982
www.theglasshouse1.com

Halibrand Performance
500 S Washington Avenue
Wellington, KS 67152-3042
620-326-2111
www.halibrand.com

Hilborn Injection
22892 Glenwood Drive
Aliso Viejo, CA 92656
949-360-0909
www.hilborninjection.com

H&H Flatheads Navarro Racing Equipment
4451 Ramsdell Avenue
La Crescenta, CA 91214
818-248-2371
www.navarroengineering.com

Honest Charley Speed Shop
1309 Chestnut Street
Chattanooga, TN 37402-4418
800-954-2600
www.honestcharley.com

Hot Heads Research & Racing
276 Walker's Hollow Trail
Lowgap, NC 27024
336-352-4866
www.hothemiheads.com

House of Kolor
210 Crosby Street
Picayune, Mississippi 39466
800-845-2500
www.houseofkolor.com

Hurst Racing Tires
P.O. Box 2818
Oregon City, OR 97045
503-656-1572
www.hurstracingtires.com

Joblot Automotive
P.O. Box 75
98-11 211th Street
Queens Village, NY 11429
718-468-8585
www.joblotauto.com

Johnson's Hot Rod Shop
2439 East Meighan Boulevard
Gadsden, AL 35903
256-492-5989
www.johnsonshotrodshop.com

LeBaron Bonney Company
6 Chestnut Street
Amesbury, MA 01913
978-388-3819
www.lebaronbonney.com

Limeworks Speedshop
7717 Greenleaf Avenue
Whittier, CA 906602
562-698-1227
www.limeworksspeedshop.com

Lobeck's Hot Rod Parts
560 Golden Oak Parkway
Cleveland, OH 44146
440-232-0210
www.lobeckshotrod.com

Lokar Performance Products
10924 Murdock Drive
Knoxville, TN 37932
877-469-7440
www.lokar.com

Mac's Antique Auto Parts
6150 Donner Road
Lockport, NY 14094
716-210-1340
www.macsautoparts.com

Mooneyes
10820 Norwalk Boulevard
Santa Fe Springs, CA 90670
562-944-6311
www.mooneyes.com

Motorcity Speed Equipment
2000 Winner Street
Walled Lake, MI
248-669-5810
www.motorcityspeedequipment.com

Newstalgia Wheel
1321 Stuart Street
Chattanooga, TN 37406
800-281-2819
www.newstalgiawheel.com

SOURCE GUIDE

O'Brien Truckers
29 A Young Road
Charlton, MA 01507
508-248-1555
www.obrientruckers.com

Pete and Jake's Hot Rod Parts
401 Legend Lane
Peculiar, MO 64078
800-334-7240
www.peteandjakes.com

Posies Rods and Customs
219 N. Duke Street
Hummelstown, PA 17036
717-566-3340
www.posiesrodsandcustoms.com

Radir Wheels
65 River Road
Montville NJ, 07045
866-334-3470
www.radirwheels.com

Reds Headers & Speed Equipment
31-410 Reserve Drive, Suite 4
Thousand Palms, CA 92276
760-343-2590
www.reds-headers.com

Rootlieb Hoods
815 Soderquist Road
Turlock, CA 95380
209-632-2203
www.rootlieb.com

Ron Francis Wiring
200 Keystone Road, Suite #1
Chester, PA 19013
800-292-1940
www.ronfrancis.com

So-Cal Speed Shop
1357 E. Grand Avenue
Pomona, CA 91766
909-469-6171
www.so-calspeedshop.com

Speedway Motors
340 Victory Lane
Lincoln, NE 68528
800-979-0122
www.speedwaymotors.com

Stainless Specialties
P.O. Box 5126
Cleveland, TN 37320
423-728-3300
www.stainless-specialties.com

Stewart Warner
P.O. Box 128
East Petersburg, PA 17601
717-581-1000
www.stewartwarner.com

Summit Racing
200 Southeast Avenue
Tallmadge, OH 44278
800-230-3030
www.summitracing.com

Tanks, Inc.
260 Welter Drive
at Hot Rod Lane
Monticello, IA 52310
877-596-3842
www.tanksinc.com

Team III Wheels
1965 West 140
San Leandro, CA 94577
510-895-8880
www.team3wheels.com

Walker Radiator
694 Marshall
Memphis TN, 38103
800-821-1970
www.walkerradiatorworks.com

The WheelSmith
221 S. Susan Street
Santa Ana, CA 92704
714-556-3861
www.thewheelsmith.net

Wheel Vintiques
5515 E Lamona Avenue
Fresno, Ca 93727
559-251-6957
www.wheelvintiques.com

Wilcap Co & Sharp Speed Equipment
P.O. Box 763
Pismo Beach, CA 93448
805-481-7639
www.wilcap.com

Winters Performance Products
1580 Trolley Road
York, PA 17408
717-764-9844
www.wintersperformance.com

www.ingramcontent.com/pod-product-compliance
Lightning Source LLC
Chambersburg PA
CBHW081451070526
44586CB00019B/2304